Finding a Way Home

Finding a Way Home

A Critical Assessment of Walter Mosley's Fiction

Edited by Owen E. Brady and Derek C. Maus

University Press of Mississippi
Jackson

www.upress.state.ms.us

The University Press of Mississippi is a member
of the Association of American University Presses.

First printing 2008
∞
Library of Congress Cataloging-in-Publication Data

Finding a way home : a critical assessment of Walter
Mosley's fiction / edited by Owen E. Brady and Derek
C. Maus.
    p. cm.
  Includes bibliographical references and index.
  ISBN 978-1-60473-088-3 (cloth : alk. paper) 1.
Mosley, Walter—Criticism and interpretation. 2.
African Americans in literature. 3. Home in literature.
4. African Americans—Race identity. I. Brady, Owen
Edward, 1946– II. Maus, Derek C.
  PS3563.O88456Z66 2008
  813'.54—dc22   2008007628

British Library Cataloging-in-Publication Data available

Contents

Contents

Acknowledgments

Projects like this one are always collaborations, and we would like to acknowledge a number of people who have helped us to focus critical attention on Walter Mosley's work. First, we would like to thank Walter Mosley himself for creating a body of work that provides nourishment for both the soul and the mind, in the process giving us all something worth talking about at greater length.

Next, we would like to thank each of the scholars who have contributed essays to this volume; their enthusiasm for the project, their critical dialogue with us, and their cooperation in meeting deadlines—often short ones—have made the work both enjoyable and fruitful. The fact that they did so while dealing with the usual stresses of contemporary academic life and in some cases sadly also while coping with the additional strain of personal loss makes us all the more grateful and honored to be collaborating with such a diverse and far-flung collection of individuals.

We would also like to thank the librarians at Clarkson University (in particular Barbara Osgood) and at SUNY Potsdam (in particular Jenica Rogers-Urbanek) for their assistance in acquiring primary and secondary texts that facilitated our work. Support and advice from faculty colleagues buoyed us through the process, and we owe special thanks to John Serio and Dan Bradburd at Clarkson, and to Steve Stannish at SUNY Potsdam. We would also like to thank our students, especially those with whom we read Mosley's work, for participating in discussions that served as laboratories for many of the ideas that found fuller expression in this volume.

Finally, Barbara Schofield Brady deserves recognition for her many discussions about Mosley that helped refine the concept of home as well as her eagle-eyed editorial help in checking sources and proofreading the manuscript. Likewise, Anastasia Osolin's support, both emotional and material, was invaluable in maintaining the focus and energy required to complete such a project.

Introduction

—OWEN E. BRADY AND DEREK C. MAUS

Home is one of the great themes and tropes of the African American literary tradition. Writers from Frederick Douglass to W. E. B. Du Bois to Walter Mosley have made clear their desire for a place to be somebody, a place to feel at home, respected, secure, and comfortable. Certainly any catalogue of those who prominently engage this theme in the post–World War II period alone include Richard Wright, Ralph Ellison, James Baldwin, and Toni Morrison.[1] Situating home exclusively in terms of its desirability tropes it as a normative ideal; however, the discourse in African American writing reveals home to be a more ambiguous term, a place of paradox, where home is experienced as *both* refuge and exile. Thus, for an African American writer to be at home in America means to feel the warmth of communal bonds but also to feel homeless, abandoned, isolated, and reviled by America. The power of this paradox resonates in *The Souls of Black Folk* (1903), as Du Bois reflects on the death of his firstborn son. Sitting in his own well-appointed and comfortable home—his "little coign of happiness" (509)—erected by his talent and energy, Du Bois echoes a common theme in the blues, talking about his son being better off dead than alive and reviled. Despite his near-despair at the death of his son and the future of all black children, Du Bois continues for his whole career to resist the oppressive forces then arrayed against even the Talented Tenth. He describes the gap between the promise of the American Dream and the racist reality of America in hope, not altogether hopeless, of renovating the American home. The irony in Du Bois's case is that his life ended in self-imposed exile in Ghana, a poignant reminder of the intractability of the problem, even in the face of fifty-plus years of diligent, hopeful effort. Thus, home is a *vexed* concept for African American writers who dwell in and on it, who attempt to frame its emotional dimensions, furnish it with cultural and historical detail, and populate it with fully human characters in various locales and times. It is in this great discourse of home—one whose inherent questions about meaning and construction implicate history, culture, community, and identity—that this volume situates Walter Mosley.

Home is a relational term. It locates us in time and space as well as within networks of values and human relationships. In the present, it is a term that defines the realities that both offer opportunities for self-making and propose the limits for that crucial process. Home also shapes identity—as in homeland or hometown—marking the individual with values and customs of a specific geographical place. But home generates a future, too. It is a goal in an ongoing process of human self-definition that can be designated as "homemaking," the quest to find or to create out of whatever resources available, a space to exist securely, safely, and comfortably. History, too, plays its role in shaping the home of the present and the desired home of the future. Individual and collective historical experience of place enters this homemaking process as longing (sometimes nostalgic) for the sense of feeling at home, and sometimes as pain.[2] It is these longings, however, that do the most to shape the future, for every one longs for self-acceptance, a supportive family/community, and justice both in the home and in the homeland. Thus, the relationship between home and self is reciprocal: home defines the individual, yet the individual defines home through choices about values, human relationships, and self-expression. Individuals are both made by and makers of the ideological and emotional complex called home.

In joining the long-running discussion of home in African American literature, it is useful to situate Mosley alongside and between his contemporaries Amiri Baraka and August Wilson to understand his position in this rich and densely detailed tradition. Mosley, Baraka, and Wilson all "riff" on the trope of home—and its associated "blue notes," homemaking and homelessness—for purposes of sustaining and surviving as well as resisting and recreating. Like so many of their African American literary precursors and contemporaries, these three writers interrogate what Una Chaudhuri calls "geopathology," the "incessant dialogue between belonging and exile, home and homelessness . . . [that] centers upon the figure of America, explicating it, first, as a betrayal of place, and then finding in it a muted celebration of placeness . . . [and], by creatively confronting the problem of place, regarding it as a challenge and an invitation rather than a tragic impasse" (15).

Mosley, Baraka, and Wilson often respond to this problem by having their characters tap into memories of communities from their personal and historic pasts in attempting to recreate in their new urban presents the comforting and sustaining—if still far from perfect—social environments of those voluntarily or involuntarily forsaken homes. In doing so, they mirror a process of creative memory that both Charles Scruggs and Farah Jasmine Griffin have examined critically. Scruggs discusses the blend of idealistically utopian and realistically dystopian attitudes that pervade African American perspectives on the spaces to which they migrated upon leaving the South, claiming that "the idea of a visionary city is a durable and ongoing tradition within black urban literature. There may have been at times nostalgia expressed for some pastoral past, but since this century began a major theme of Afro-American writing has been a coming to terms with Afro-Americans' lives in the city. The city as a symbol of community, of civilization, of home—this image lies beneath the city of brute fact in which blacks of the twentieth century have had to live. This kernel has never been lost. It is one of the aspirations expressed in an ongoing dialogue that the Afro-American community has with itself, a dialogue that sets the city of the imagination, the city that one wants, against the empirical reality of the city that one has" (4–5). Griffin examines this dialogical state specifically in the context of the development of the blues after the first Great Migration:

> Prior to the development of a new and distinct urban blues, blues lyrics
> experience a transitional phase, a phase of confrontation and uncertainty.
> This uncertainty often leads the singer to question the wisdom of the deci-
> sion to migrate. . . . In this context, home, no matter how horrifying it
> may have been, is seen through a lens tinted with nostalgia. . . . [The blues
> performance] serves as a transitional space, making the transformation from
> migrant to urban dweller a little less harsh. It does this by providing the
> stability of "home" as well as offering a means to negotiate the "here." . . .
> [I]n the North, where the context in itself is the "stranger," the bluesman
> convenes the community and sets the atmosphere to invoke tradition. The
> blues performance therefore exists as a safe space where migrants are healed,
> informed, ministered, and entertained. (54–55)

It is our contention that Mosley's work as a whole serves as a novelistic version of this communitarian, home-creating blues, a notion that our volume's opening essay explores at length and all the others touch upon implicitly or explicitly.

Although differences in social and political stances separate Mosley, Baraka, and Wilson, all three explore the African American experience in terms of history, the vernacular, and the trope of home. When still LeRoi Jones, the degagé poet-king of Greenwich Village, Baraka's interest in the intersection of African American history, place, and identity became apparent in *Blues People: Negro Music in White America* (1963), his sociohistorical narrative of the evolution of black music and its ability to reflect, over historical time, the emotional reality, the invisible emotional history, of black people in America. Baraka chronicles myriad ways in which African Americans adapted to the dehumanizing condition of being property by asserting their humanity in music that changed with the times. African American music, rooted in the blues, then becomes both a reflection of historical change as well as a means for negotiating its cruel realities and creating a sense of home. Mosley echoes this contention in his long essay *What Next: A Memoir toward World Peace* (2003), in which he calls the blues "that musical home for the ironies and contradictions that Europeans strain to define in the philosophy of existentialism" (30).

Baraka continued his exploration in *Home: Social Essays* (1966). The black and white cover photo of the original edition visually reflects the reality revealed through Baraka's words: Two sets of eyes peer out at the reader through a rectangular slit in a weathered, dented, peeling metal-clad door bearing the address 23. Like Du Bois's "Veil" from *The Souls of Black Folk*, Baraka's door allows the faceless, identity-less "black" inhabitants to look out at the America beyond their confinement in a home that is at once prison and fortress, an enclosure that both oppresses and resists the lurking danger outside. This graphic image, like the essays inside, proclaims that "black is a country," a state of being inhabited by blues people. Baraka's energized prose attempts to make that country, that racial homeland, visible, much as *The Souls of Black Folk* attempted to do in taking its reader behind the Veil. Covering "Negro literature," soul food, historical stereotypes, and Harlem's history and emotional tenor, Baraka ranges across the vernacular and "high cultural" resources out of which African Americans constructed a homeland that is vibrantly human, albeit shadowed by poverty and racism. With these two books, Baraka begins his own lifelong quest for representing, razing, and rebuilding America as a home in which black individuals are free and fairly treated. "Cuba Libre," the opening essay of *Home*, marks Baraka's movement toward social engagement. Baraka recounts a trip he made to Cuba immediately after the 1959 revolution that liberated the country from the dictator Batista and opened up possibilities for a new world, a Cuban home remade in which all would ostensibly share equally in the country's wealth. Impressed by the fervor and commitment of the Latin American literary artists that he encountered, Baraka engages in the struggle to raze the old African American home as prison and find ways in which art and politics can conspire to produce a new, more humane home that lives up to the pledged promise of liberty and justice for all.

The metamorphosis from LeRoi Jones, latter-day Beat Poet, to Amiri Baraka, engaged artist, can be marked in his analysis of home in his two, now-classic short plays, *Dutchman* (1964) and *The Slave* (1964). Both invoke the trope of home to mediate and represent this transformation of identity. In *Dutchman*, Clay, a young black man, seeks to discover his place and identity (especially his manhood) on the subway, a contemporary figuration from two significant periods of African American history. Signifying ambiguously, the subway is both the "underground railroad" that carried black men out of the South's virulent, repressive atmosphere and the trains of the Great Migration that literally carried African Americans to a northern "Promised Land" where, ironically and tragically, racism and oppression still resided. Clay is a man in a liminal state, currently homeless but nevertheless moving toward an expectation of finding a home. Searching for individual identity, autonomy, and respect, Clay moves away from his bland, deracinated middle-class home where blacks hopelessly hope—to play on Du Bois's terminology—to achieve full status as Americans, the assimilative world rejected by Langston Hughes and anatomized by E. Franklin Frazier. He gets on the subway to move toward his own Promised Land, the sexually liberated and politically liberal Greenwich Village in Manhattan, where he can be free from his personal and ancestral history. Ironically, while middle-class black New Jersey pretends to be deracinated in hopes of enjoying the full promise of America, liberated Greenwich Village, represented by its seemingly mad representative, Lula, overdetermines Clay's blackness, appropriating it (and his identity) for its own resistance against American social and political mediocrity. Stripped of individual identity in both putative homes, Clay seeks home in his soaring monologue that finds refuge, identity, and resistance in black music and blues people. But rather than follow the logic of his emotional epiphany, Clay decides to mask this new identity, this new hopeful home in the blues, and is killed by Lula. The subway now reveals itself to be a veiled figure of the slave ship that initially stole black identity.

The Slave explores the alternative of black nationalism and revolution in the process of razing the old, oppressive American home as Walker Vessels, the central character, battles over a home in the figure of the family house and his mulatto children. The house in *The Slave* is under attack by Walker, its former owner, now leading a black revolutionary army to destroy his old house and all it represents and to move into the future with only the vaguest hope of constructing a new home for his identity. The house here stands for the West and its colonial impulses, the house of Western Culture; it is also an American home that once housed a multiracial family, attempting to be free of American history's endemic racism. In the end, the house is collapsing under shelling from the revolutionary black army that wears the symbol of a smiling slave as a sign of historical repression and resistance, and Walker is trapped inside under the debris with his dead white ex-wife and his white former professor, in death representing the emotional and intellectual ties that had furnished his old home.[3] Walker nevertheless achieves a kind of heroism amid the wreckage of home, and the twentieth-century character transforms into an old field hand, suffering but still standing.

After these watershed years, Baraka turned to agitprop drama and poetry in his home community, predominantly black Newark, New Jersey. He renames and refashions it as "New Ark," making it the figurative means to carry him toward a newly restored and humanizing home just as he sought refuge in black cultural nationalism to escape America's racism. Having exhausted the resources provided by black nationalism, Baraka's blues turned to reds as he studied Marxism to understand and undermine capitalism, which he came to see as the larger enemy of not only black Americans but of all humankind. His writing was mirrored by action: building a black arts theater and cultural center; roaming the streets during the 1967 riot/rebellion in Newark; writing impassioned polemical poetry attacking the forces of oppression; drafting manifestoes; and even engaging in the political process locally. Engaged in both revolutionary rhetoric and political action, Baraka has taken positions that have clearly placed him outside the American mainstream, even as he remains an inspirational and creative artistic experimentalist.

Unlike Baraka's "theater of cruelty" style in his plays, August Wilson takes a more Chekhovian view of home in his dramatic work, a richly nuanced representation of African American experience. Wilson's work draws on vernacular resources in providing a historical perspective of continuity and change over the course of several generations. His epic ten-play cycle of African American experience, one for each of the ten decades of the twentieth century, also emphasizes the importance of historical memory as a form of sustenance and resistance against whatever forces array themselves against the African American community at a given moment. All but one—*Ma Rainey's Black Bottom* (1984), which takes place in 1920s Chicago—are set in the Hill District of Pittsburgh, the neighborhood home for over one hundred years of the diverse African American characters that populate Wilson's plays. Two, the first and last in the cycle, center on the house of Aunt Ester, a former slave and soul-cleanser. In *Gem of the Ocean* (2003), set in 1904, she is already reputed to be 287 years old. Thus she is the sign and living symbol of a history of survival. It is the redemptive work done in her house, that, like Aunt Ester, recalls a slave past as it transforms itself into a slave ship to bring young Citizen Barlow to self-knowledge. The last play, *Radio Golf* (2005), set in the 1990s, focuses on the destruction of the now dead Aunt Ester's house by a black man fronting for a white developer, a man in danger of forgetting who he is and the value of his roots. Never itself visible in *Radio Golf*, the house and the communal history it stands for, the setbacks and striving, the suffering and joys of generations of marginal African Americans, are threatened with erasure by profit. Other plays in the cycle privilege other sites of community, like the restaurant in *Two Trains Running* (1990)—set in 1969—or the cab station in *Jitney* (1982)—set in the 1970s. Both of these plays suggest that the community's historical continuity is threatened by urban renewal. Set in the 1930s, *The Piano Lesson* (1987) pursues Wilson's theme of history as home threatened by the demands of survival as the family members struggle with one another over the sale of a piano linked both to slavery and the African ancestral past that has served to protect the household from haunts. And always in Wilson there is the blues sensibility, the ironizing humor that makes life bearable and valuable, and the literal blues that, like the piano, are threatened as pure cultural expressions and sources of communal strength by American capitalism and commercialism in *Ma Rainey's Black Bottom* and *Seven Guitars* (1996). Wilson's plays are not overtly political; they propose a rather conservative—and conservationist—approach to African American identity that values the cultural expressions and the history of survival and resistance that has served to create and sustain the African American sense of home, first against racial oppression and more recently against the homogenizing power of middle class materialism, the spawn of America's capitalist engine that first brought African Americans (perhaps even Aunt Ester) to Columbia's shores in the early seventeenth century. Wilson's political message is the injunction to keep the historical and cultural past alive to feed future generations' pride and identity.

With Baraka on one side and Wilson on the other (we might say far left and right) as foils, Mosley's art and politics stand out. Like Baraka, Mosley has been a man in motion politically. But in Mosley's earliest work, home is contested in rather traditional terms reminiscent of Wilson. The earliest Easy Rawlins novels— *Devil in a Blue Dress* (1990), *A Red Death* (1991), and *White Butterfly* (1992)—find Mosley rendering a detailed world—Los Angeles in the 1940s and 1950s—populated by a colorful array of characters drawn from the vernacular, often informed by folkloric types like the "badman," the "bad nigger," and the "conjure woman" who are sources of danger and strength for the detective hero. Although these novels provide the narrator with the opportunity to frame America of the time as seen from "behind the veil," the main struggle is within Easy himself as he struggles to define home. At first, he invests his energy in owning and keeping the quintessential element of the American Dream: a house. But over the course of these novels, Easy comes to reposition the defining element of home, vesting it in emotional capital, the human bonds that make a house a home, often associated nostalgically with his boyhood Southern home community. This struggle between the materialistic view of home and the one founded in community and family recurs in a variant form in the Fearless Jones series set in the 1950s. There Paris Minton represents a kind of intellectualized materialism owning and living in a bookstore; his co-protagonist, Fearless Jones, a version of the badman, acts out of loyalty and compassion for others.

Mosley's artistic concerns extend beyond representing the various modes by which African American characters negotiate a tentative home in the harsh realities of the historical past and/or present, though. He also attempts to create a sense of home that adumbrates a better, more humane and just home in the future. Mosley's ambition to reconstitute and renew not only the African American community but also the American community as a vital source of democratic power may best be seen in his periodic return to science fiction like *Blue Light* (1998), *Futureland* (2001), and *The Wave* (2006). Although they contain grimly dystopian and even apocalyptic elements, Mosley's speculations on the future are marked by a hopefulness akin to Easy's that some kind of self-determined and vivifying home *must* be possible, even in a world of technological panopticons, government-fostered drug addiction, and dehumanized toil like that of *Futureland*.

With the events of September 11, 2001, however, Mosley, like the Baraka of "Cuba Libre," was shocked into the role of the engaged artist, seeing his essays and fiction as a means not only of valuing African American history, vernacular, and community but also as an opportunity for providing a blue(s)print for transforming the larger American homeland. Even before September 2001, however, with the publication of his long essay *Workin' on the Chain Gang: Shakin' Off the Dead Hand of History* (2000), Mosley had begun to see the African American historical experience, marked by survival and resistance, as a model for all citizens subject to the dehumanizing forces of global capitalism. Thus, widely shared consciousness of African American experience could, in Mosley's mind, help Americans move toward a more humane sense of home; recognizing one's solidarity with and identity as a kind of slave would provoke change or new ideas for the future. As Mosley notes looking back on what he has written: "I see that I've crossed over from idealism to utopian thought" (107). Noting that he is embarrassed by this excursion into a better America, he encourages Americans to "treat the democratic process as a revolution of ideas, as if America is being formed and reformed every four years" (108). His fiction during this pre-9/11 period also foreshadows these tentatively hopeful moves toward refiguring the American home and, perhaps, the world. The Socrates Fortlow stories, published in the late 1990s, end with the protagonist, a violence-prone ex-con, moving out of invisibility to take on the role of a dissenting citizen through public protest to achieve justice.

In *What Next: A Memoir Toward World Peace* (2003), Mosley registers his shock at the terrorist attacks on September 1, 2001 as he watched the World Trade Centers towers collapse in fire and smoke. Recalling his father's experience in World War II, during which he discovered that he was an American by the violence the Germans aimed at him, Mosley reflects on American identity as seen by others oppressed by global capitalism's advances, often in opposition to traditional cultures, values, and communities. In particular, he urges black Americans to raise their voices against global capitalism's excesses, to assume the full responsibility of their identity as American citizens. With the publication of *Life Out of Context* (2006), Mosley has moved toward advocacy of grassroots citizen action. The subtitle of this slim volume reveals this new position: *Which Includes a Proposal for the Non-Violent Takeover of the House of Representatives. The Man in My Basement* (2004) brilliantly links African American heritage under economic pressure with the worldwide crimes of global capitalism. Perhaps his science fiction was a harbinger of this move. While he eschews the confrontational revolutionary harangue that has made Baraka so controversial, regrettably taking him largely out of the realm of public discourse on any level other than local, Mosley has clearly moved toward engagement in political debate and action. In other words, he inhabits a space somewhere between Wilson and Baraka, rhetorically and politically, but clearly he has taken a step toward the left. Mosley continues to write in popular genres, taking a different rhetorical strategy from Baraka's; Mosley entertains while he persuades, which keeps a wide, general American audience listening to his stories.

Reconstructing home in the mean streets of Los Angeles or New York, the locations in which most of Mosley's characters perform their homemaking activities, reveals not only their adherence to the material, homeowning tenets of the ideological American Dream but also to negotiating human relationships to recreate the warm sense of community developed in poor rural and urban African American communities: the Louisiana backwoods and the Fifth Ward of Houston,

Texas for Easy Rawlins, Paris Minton, and Soupspoon Wise; Indiana for Socrates Fortlow. How African Americans construct a home in an America that has historically oppressed them and denied their existence, and how they negotiate ways to survive in such conditions is one of Mosley's main concerns. His Easy Rawlins and Fearless Jones series, in particular, represent in artful detail the lives of the generation of African Americans from the Second Great Migration that took place in the wake of World War II (perhaps redeeming them from Wright's unblinking portrayal of the rootless, unconscious Bigger Thomas).

As Logan Hill notes, though, Mosley's larger vision has expanded significantly in response to the different conditions of twenty-first-century American life:

> As Easy has explored wider worlds, so has Mosley. His series recalls that of the playwright August Wilson, who devoted a play to African-American life in each decade of the last century. Mosley agrees that his work and Wilson's share a great deal—particularly the idea of showing black characters who aren't "pimps or shoe-shiners or Shaft, but regular guys sitting in a room talking over our problems." Like Wilson, Mosley says he'd like to extend his series into the year 2000 and can imagine exactly what the Louisiana natives Easy and Mouse . . . would do if they'd seen the recent damage. . . . "Easy'd just go right down there to help people," says Mosley. "Mouse would be shooting at the National Guard." (n. pag.)

Mosley's novels set in the 1990s and beyond remind readers that the problem of home and self-construction remains not only for African Americans but also for the oppressed former colonized peoples of the world (as pointed out by his discussion of Rwanda in *The Man in My Basement*). As a writer, too, Mosley is seeking a "home" for himself in terms of (sub)genre, language, social justice, politics, and even ontology at the same time that he tries to imagine meaningful constructions of home for his pantheon of characters within the various worlds they inhabit. Mosley's work presents alternative realities, both individual and collective, for his readers to contemplate and in which to find the means for rejuvenating—or perhaps more accurately, genuinely instituting—democratic community in the American homeland.

Over the past seventeen years, Walter Mosley has been prolific, producing work that has been both popular and critically acclaimed, all in the pursuit of defining and refining concepts of home. Henry Louis Gates and his editorial colleagues have included Mosley's fiction in the last two editions of the eminent *Norton Anthology of African American Literature*. In his introduction to these selections, Gates writes: "Mosley has swiftly entered into the company of contemporary American novelists whose work is expected to last." Our task in this volume is to add substantially to the small but growing scholarly commentary on Mosley, to assess through critical analysis exactly *why* his work might be expected to last.

While Mosley's work provides a rich field of study, as of 2007 only one introductory book—Charles E. Wilson Jr.'s *Walter Mosley: A Critical Companion* (2003)—and a handful of articles and chapters in anthologies have explored it critically. Most scholarly articles published to date have focused on Mosley's fiction from the perspective of genre, especially as an example of or response to hard-boiled fiction in the vein of Raymond Chandler and Mickey Spillane. In particular, critics have expended a great deal of effort in defining the specifically African American dimension that Mosley brings to detective fiction, either by comparing him against the putative standards established by white writers ranging from Edgar Allan Poe to Chandler and Dashiell Hammett, or by situating him within a tradition of African American detective writers such as Chester Himes. While the majority of this critical work has been insightful and articulate, it also has substantial limitations, both in terms of critical perspectives and in terms of which of Mosley's texts have been examined. The preponderance of extant criticism has focused on the Easy Rawlins series, and generally only the first three works in that series. In fact, only two published articles—Christine Levecq's "Blues Poetic and Blues Politics in Walter Mosley's *RL's Dream*" (2004) and David L. Smith's "Walter Mosley's *Blue Light*: (Double Consciousness)^{squared}" (2001)—depart from the Rawlins series. No critical work has yet appeared in print that examines in any depth the Socrates Fortlow stories, the Fearless Jones novels, Mosley's nonfictional writings, or his science fiction since *Blue Light*. To be sure, the rate and diversity of Mosley's literary output, especially in recent years, makes keeping up with him a challenging task. Nevertheless, it is an explicit goal of this collection of essays to expand and update the critical coverage of Mosley to include a broader sampling of critical approaches and to acknowledge the formal diversity within his *oeuvre*.

Toward that end, the twelve essays—from scholars representing four different countries—contained within this collection all in some way orbit around the notion of finding a home—whether material, social, cultural, or virtual. In doing so, they critically engage with all three of Mosley's detective/crime fiction series (Easy Rawlins, Socrates Fortlow, and Fearless Jones), his three books of speculative fiction, two of his "literary" novels (*RL's Dream, The Man in My Basement*), as well as nearly all of his more recent social and political nonfiction. In all, twenty-four of the thirty book-length works that Mosley had published as of mid-2008 receive critical attention within this volume (we briefly discuss the remainder in the epilogue), thereby nearly doubling the published coverage of Mosley's body of work. Moreover, the different vectors along which our contributors approach the theme of home not only allow for a rich theoretical discussion of the constituent issues that fit under that roof, but also give a sense of the ways in which Mosley's modes of expression have developed over the course of his career.

Daniel Stein opens the collection by examining Mosley's body of work—with special focus on *RL's Dream* (1995)—through Graham Lock's critical definition of *blutopia* as "an African American visionary future stained with memories." Stein claims that "Mosley enlists this blutopian philosophy as a conceptual framework through which he presents the human struggle for a physical, spiritual, and cultural home" and that he "offers the wisdom of the blues as a respite from communal dispersion and individual alienation in the American metropolis of the late twentieth century," language that resonates strongly with both Scruggs and Griffin (see above). Stein argues that *RL's Dream*, Mosley's first non-Easy Rawlins book, "can be considered a meta-novel, a text in which Mosley reflects most distinctly on the philosophical, aesthetic, and sociocultural presence of African Americanness in contemporary American life." Stein argues that Mosley does not simply use the blues to critique the inhuman vacuity of contemporary culture but also to seek to "mobiliz[e] the mythological potential of the blues as well as its universal human appeal as a spiritual answer to the maladies of the present."

Owen Brady follows this up by examining the quest for home motif in the Socrates Fortlow stories, accentuating a seeming paradox concerning notions of home: "Normatively, home signifies both a place and a feeling of domesticity: comfort, family, and security abide. . . . Historically for African Americans, however, home, both in the sense of the family house and the homeland's promise, has been severely limited, often denied." Drawing on Emerson's notion of an idealized, individualized concept of home, Brady reads the Fortlow stories as redemptive tales that "provide a new communal basis for reconceiving home in distinctively African American terms that transcends historic oppression and contemporary communal violence."

Keith Hughes's essay expands on Brady's essay, both in the sense that his work also examines the Socrates Fortlow stories and in the sense that it widens the context of Mosley's homemaking process from the local African American communities to the entire black diaspora. Hughes draws on Paul Gilroy's notion of the "black Atlantic" as a means of examining the cultural hybridity of the Fortlow series, arguing that "Mosley's narratives tap into a similar sensibility regarding the centrality of black experience in the whole construction of modernity." He notes that Mosley's work blends and recontextualizes a wide variety of European, African, and American cultural signifiers in a manner that gives them a new potency. Most prominently, he examines Socrates Fortlow's allusive first name in terms of the way he both is and is not a modern-day analogue of the Greek philosopher whose name he bears. In the end, Hughes contends that "Socratic methodology is adopted and adapted by Mosley and his protagonist so as to be answerable to the specific social and cultural traumas faced by Socrates Fortlow in 1990s Los Angeles."

Francesca Sautman expands the definition of home still further, placing it into a global context by looking at *The Man in My Basement* through the filter of human rights doctrine. Sautman interprets the novel as an outspoken humanistic, yet still inherently race-conscious, allegory, arguing that it "provokes serious reflection on a number of issues of international human rights, both immediately political and more broadly philosophical, including a compelling evocation of the disenfranchisement, abandonment, and lack of value ascribed to poor children in the world." Anniston Bennet's absurdly forced attempts at self-absolution through his voluntary confinement in the basement of Charles Blakey's house allow Mosley to illustrate the way white America can still exert power over a well-established African American home. Both Blakey's house—a material reminder of seven generations of free black life in America—and the artifacts of African American life that are recovered from his basement provide an anodyne to Bennett's controlling vision because "figuring out how to [save the house] by using the white man's scheme without being his tool becomes a major step in the conflict, and also in the ability to, at least this once, triumph over forces that seem unmovable, untouchable, all powerful."

Lisa Thompson's essay fills a major lacuna in the extant criticism on Mosley. She explores the ways in which the African American female characters in the Easy Rawlins series contest the mainstream stereotype of the strong, black matriarch as well as the conventional canons of female beauty and value. Thompson argues that Mosley's "downhome" women are part of "an alternative aesthetic in which they represent beauty, power, vulnerability, and Easy's own longing for home." Furthermore, she claims that Easy "not only concerns himself with saving black women's lives, but he also defends their dignity thereby expanding the meaning of black respectability." He sees beauty in physical and moral characteristics traditionally depreciated by the dominant culture; he also finds a source of rootedness—i.e., home—in African American women, in particular EttaMae Harris, whom he has known and loved since his adolescence in Houston. Taken collectively, Mosley's representation of African American women redeems them from the American cultural margin and reveals their complex humanity.

Each of the next five essays examines Mosley's work in terms of the ways in which issues of personal and/or racial identity relate to a sense of belonging (or, more to the point, exclusion) within American society. In the process, they comment on the prospects for self-definition, one of the most salient characteristics of what makes something into a "home" in which African American individuals can be both authentic and accepted.

As Brady notes in his essay, Mosley's African American male characters tend initially to be "enslaved by the nigger stereotype and at best can achieve invisibility and anonymity," and Kelly Connelly's essay compares the efforts of two characters—the narrator/protagonist of Ralph Ellison's *Invisible Man* (1952) and Mosley's detective Easy Rawlins—to escape this enslavement. Connelly contends that both the narrator and Easy "temporarily [don] the guise of the trickster, or the hustler, the man who uses the white man's expectations to manipulate both the black and white communities for his own gain," with the trickster/hustler role being represented by the characters of B. P. Rinehart in Ellison's novel and Raymond "Mouse" Alexander in Mosley's series. Connelly concludes that both Ellison's narrator and

Easy come to recognize "Rinehartism" as a form of "false visibility" that fails to liberate them and that both characters "ultimately seek to find their identity, their home, in some middle ground between their own invisibility and the fraudulent hyper-visibility of folkloric character types like the trickster."

Jerrilyn McGregory extends this notion further by examining the ways in which Mosley plays out some of the same dualities in terms of the process of masculine self-definition in both the Fearless Jones novels and in the Easy Rawlins series. McGregory uses the interrelated concepts of internal colonialism and *alterity* to probe the ways in which Mosley undermines the process by which he sees African American men being marginalized within American society. Like Connelly, McGregory argues that Mosley's characters find temporary, yet incomplete agency by adopting established roles: "There is a great deal of empowering potential in both the trickster and badman roles, but neither ultimately offers a fully liberating paradigm for the realization of an authentic self." She argues that both Fearless and Easy respond to their alterity—i.e., being assigned status as an "Other" outside the cultural norm—by "contest[ing] this status with an additional layer of intentional re-Othering. Through this self-initiated process they gain free agency, positioning themselves as sentient individuals deserving of recognition . . . not just as figures defined exclusively by their relation to the dominant culture."

Terrence Tucker also works with tropes of masculinity, specifically those found in the first two novels of the Fearless Jones series—*Fearless Jones* (2001) and *Fear Itself* (2003). His focus is on two particular African American archetypes, the "intellectual" and the "badman," as embodied in the series by Paris Minton and Tristan "Fearless" Jones, respectively. Tucker argues that "Mosley's interrogation of the intellectual and the badman recovers a time and culture, the American Negro of the 1950s, so that he can redefine heroism." The challenges facing African Americans during the time of the Second Migration—the temporal setting of the Fearless Jones novels—required new self-conceptions because the existing archetypes were formed in a substantially different cultural milieu that does not accommodate, for example, a working-class black intellectual like Paris. Tucker sees this process of redefinition as "lend[ing] voice to a community that actively formulates techniques and traditions to survive, resist, and transcend racist oppression."

Albert Turner revisits and revises one of the most frequent critical assertions made about Mosley, the idea that Easy Rawlins is an African American version of Raymond Chandler's "hard-boiled" detective. Turner contends that the Easy Rawlins series actually serves to break down some of the social and cultural assumptions codified in Chandler's formulation of the genre and, as such, represents "the alternative Mosley provides to exclusionary, hard-boiled ideological discourses that bolster masculinist, bourgeois, white social order." Turner makes the case that Easy's development from *Devil in a Blue Dress* through *Cinnamon Kiss* (2005) departs from the isolated and authoritarian nature of the conventional hard-boiled hero and instead "asserts the value of home, community, and collaboration . . . [and] provides a site from which to consider a means through which the hard-boiled hero can sustain African American communities."

Laura Quinn concludes this section in a related fashion by examining the role that formal parody plays in Mosley's work, arguing that Mosley's work is simultaneously a parody and an exemplar of "hard-boiled" detective fiction. Quinn begins by articulating a critical perspective that draws parallels between Henry Louis Gates, Jr.'s identification of "signifyin(g)" practices in African American literature and Linda Hutcheon's work on postmodern parodic techniques. Applying this perspective to several of the Easy Rawlins novels, Quinn argues that "Mosley uses the hard-boiled genre . . . at once to reiterate and to destabilize the formula. He makes rich use of its conventions while striving to bring its chickens home to roost by denaturalizing those conventions through a process of unmasking the undemocratic interests that they serve."

The final two essays in the collection expand the field of extant scholarship on Mosley's science fiction (or speculative fiction, depending on one's critical perspective and nomenclature). The publication of *The Wave* in late 2005 suggests that Mosley's interest in SF continues, thus adding to the potential relevance of this avenue of scholarship. Each of these essays examines *Futureland,* Mosley's second work of science fiction, at length within the critical context of utopia/dystopia. Nevertheless, the two essays arrive at substantially different conclusions about the nature of Mosley's appropriation of these techniques.

Juan Elices surveys Mosley's entire speculative fiction *oeuvre,* examining it within the predominantly twentieth-century tradition of dystopia and noting ways in which Mosley's work both draws on and departs from some of his predecessors in this category. He argues that Mosley's SF works simultaneously serve two purposes, one fictional and one metafictional. On the fictional level, each work corresponds to many of the usual genre conventions in "representing the efforts of a character or a group of characters to transcend a dystopian—or at least highly marginalized—existence." On another level, though, Mosley is writing SF explicitly to model "how African American writers might engage in discourses from which they have been traditionally marginalized," thereby entering "an arena of debate and contestation where durable clichés associated with African Americans can be dismantled."

Derek Maus concludes the collection by arguing that while *Futureland* does borrow from conventions associated with both dystopia and the more recent phenomenon of "cyberpunk" SF, it also contains a vision of a future in which racially and economically marginalized individuals might find a space (or, perhaps, a cyberspace) in which to live their own lives. Maus contends that Mosley not only "foreground[s] racial and socioeconomic politics much more explicitly, thus creating a level of social allegory that is rarely present in cyberpunk as a whole" but also transcends classical dystopia because, "[u]nlike Zamyatin's D-503, or John the Savage in Huxley's *Brave New World* (1932), or Winston Smith in Orwell's *Nine-*

teen Eighty-Four (1949) . . . most, if not all, of Mosley's protagonists in *Futureland* achieve a meaningful, albeit unconventional, degree of freedom from the metaphorical shackles of the system."

Although the essays in this collection represent a substantial expansion both in the volume of Mosley scholarship and in the range of Mosley's work that has been examined critically, we believe there is abundant critical work remaining to be done on what Mosley has already produced—to say nothing of the creative work still to come from his prolific pen. It is our hope that this volume will serve both to satisfy the growing interest in scholarship on Mosley and to stimulate others to investigate some of the critical "gaps" that such a collection inevitably leaves unfilled.

Notes

1. Cf. Scruggs; Sweeney Prince.

2. Cf. Ellison's notion of the "blues impulse" from his essay "Richard Wright's Blues" in *Shadow and Act* (1967) and Morrison's notion of "rememory" from *Beloved* (1987).

3. On the autobiographical level, of course, *The Slave* dramatizes the tension in the Jones/Baraka metamorphosis.

Abbreviations

AOAO	*Always Outnumbered, Always Outgunned.*
Bad Boy	*Bad Boy Brawly Brown*
BB	*Black Betty*
CK	*Cinnamon Kiss*
Devil	*Devil in a Blue Dress*
GF	*Gone Fishin'*
Killing	*Killing Johnny Fry*
LS	*Little Scarlet*
LYD	*A Little Yellow Dog*
MiMB	*The Man in My Basement*
RD	*A Red Death*
Six	*Six Easy Pieces*
Walkin'	*Walkin' the Dog*
Workin'	*Workin' on the Chain Gang: Shaking Off the Dead Hand of History*

Finding a Way Home

Walter Mosley's *RL's Dream* and the Creation of a Blutopian Community

—Daniel Stein

RL's Dream (1995), Walter Mosley's first non-Easy Rawlins novel, begins with bluesman Soupspoon Wise's grueling crawl from an old man's shelter to his Lower East Side apartment. Soupspoon is in agony—cancer causes "[p]ain [that] moved up . . . [his] hipbone like a plow breaking through hard sod"—but he is driven "toward home" by his desire to leave the shelter with its "disheveled . . . gibbering and farting men calling out to people who weren't there." By "imagining being home again" and by embracing his pain as a "new music," he finds the strength to make it to the apartment. Soupspoon decides that "he'd die singing and making music out of life"; totally exhausted, "he conjured up a young man with short nappy hair and one dead eye" (13–14). The music Soupspoon hears in his mind is a downhome blues, and the young man he conjures up is bluesman Robert Johnson, whom he had known in the 1930s. Soupspoon embraces the blues' dreamlike powers and Johnson's mythical resonance in his search for a physical and spiritual home.[1]

Mosley's depiction of Soupspoon's journey from the shelter to his apartment and the old man's recollection of the blues encapsulate an overarching philosophical framework that integrates the longing for a home with the hardheaded realism of the blues. A concept called *blutopia*, developed by Graham Lock in a study of Sun Ra, Duke Ellington, and Anthony Braxton, illuminates the philosophical outlook and narrative patterns of Mosley's blues novel.[2] According to Lock, "music [i]s an alternative form of history . . . [a] gateway to 'another reality'"; it initiates "two major impulses: a utopian impulse, evident in the creation of imagined places (Promised Lands), and the impulse to remember, to bear witness, which . . . relates to the particular history of slavery and its aftermath in the

United States" (2). Blutopia thus "signal[s] a utopia tinged with the blues, an African American visionary future stained with memories" (3). In this essay I argue that Mosley enlists this blutopian philosophy as a conceptual framework through which he presents the human struggle for a physical, spiritual, and cultural home. While this philosophy is deeply rooted in the African American experience, *RL's Dream* illustrates its applicability to Americans of every creed and color and offers the wisdom of the blues as a respite from communal dispersion and individual alienation in the American metropolis of the late twentieth century.

The blues are a regular feature of Mosley's literature, both as a musical expression as well as an outlook on life. *Gone Fishin'* (1997), the first novel Mosley wrote, already enters blues territory—Texas backcountry and its mythic places. During the trip with badman Raymond "Mouse" Alexander, Easy Rawlins meets blues guitarist and singer Sweet William and finds his personal blues when he becomes implicated in the murder of Mouse's stepfather, an event that keeps haunting Easy like the hellhounds in Robert Johnson's "Hell Hound on My Trail." *A Red Death* (1991) opens with an "*old blues refrain*": "If it wasn't for bad luck I wouldn't have no luck at all" (n. pag.) and *A Little Yellow Dog* (1996) employs the blues metaphor of the "dog" as a leitmotif (the title recalls W. C. Handy's "Yellow Dog Blues"). Chance, the protagonist of Mosley's speculative fiction novel *Blue Light* (1998), hears Robert Johnson's "Love in Vain"[3] on the radio; the new consciousness of people who have received the blue light is a blues consciousness (cf. Smith, D. 10).

Mosley connects this blues sensibility with his vision of African American quests for a home in a country not altogether sympathetic to this undertaking. Easy's response in *A Red Death* to the Garveyesque African Migration group's plans of relocating in Africa is telling: "I got me a home already. It might be in enemy lands, but it's mine still and all" (190). Finding ways to survive in these enemy lands and devising strategies that ensure the continuity of home are tasks Easy and others face.[4] While Easy "does make it here in America," as Mosley once explained, "he makes it . . . flawed and scarred" (qtd. in Kennedy 237). Bridging the discrepancy between utopian dreams of home and the knowledge of a diasporic past, the blues enunciate the dream of home—essential to spiritual survival—while recognizing the fallibility of this dream through reminders of alienation and discrimination.

In *RL's Dream*, the blues serve as a signifier of the longing for a home in enemy lands. Tracing them back through his protagonist Soupspoon's memories, Mosley turns to the Jim Crow South of the 1930s, when African Americans managed to survive—often "flawed and scarred"—the hardships of racial oppression by creating blues communities equipped to overpower the pain of physical, spiritual, and cultural homelessness enforced by institutional and individual forms of racism.[5] But this blues sensibility not only provides the ontological background to the characters' lives; it also emerges as subject matter and influences the narrative form of the story. This is why *RL's Dream* can be considered a meta-novel, a text in which Mosley reflects most distinctly on the philosophical, aesthetic, and sociocultural presence of African American-ness in contemporary American life.

All of Mosley's work negotiates in some form questions of spirituality, community, and the search for a home. Mosley routinely portrays "transplanted" characters, people who have fled their homes in order to assemble new lives elsewhere yet rely on their memories of a troubled past for spiritual sustenance and as reminders of their precarious social status. Ezekiel "Easy" Rawlins, for instance, Mosley's famous detective, relocates from Houston, Texas, to Watts. In *Devil in a Blue Dress* (1990), Easy enters an illegal nightclub: "When I opened the door I was slapped in the face by the force of Lips' alto horn. I had been hearing Lips and Willie and Flattop since I was a boy in Houston. All of them and John and half the people in that crowded room had migrated from Houston after the war, and some before that," Easy observes. "[B]eing on the bottom didn't feel so bad if you could come to John's now and then and remember how it felt back home in Texas, dreaming about California" (24). The displaced Southerners realize that Los Angeles is not a "heaven for the southern Negro," not a place where "you could eat fruit right off the trees and get enough work to retire one day." But while "the truth wasn't like the dream" (27), the music and the communal space of the bar evoke feelings of home, provide temporary shelter from realities of life in L.A., and create communal cohesion. As Liam Kennedy observes, "[t]his bittersweet commentary registers the need for a sustaining cultural life for the migrant community of Southern African Americans while recognizing utopian delusion in the dream . . . of opportunity and prosperity" (232).[6] When Cornel West speaks of African Americans as those "who could not not know" (qtd. in Fabre and O'Meally 3), he emphasizes the power of memory to determine a people's views of the future, and when Ralph Ellison detects a "boomerang" of history (*Invisible Man* 5), he reminds his readers of the essential flaws inherent in their American dreams of home.

The cultural life of African American migrant communities is sustained by the musical practices of the South. Music provides a sense of belonging, and it grounds performers and audience in a sense of self that is determined by the blues. As Mosley once told interviewer Frank Rizzo, "Anyone who knows my work . . . knows . . . there is going to be a black man at the center of . . . [the] story, and he's going to be struggling for identity, for redemption, for some kind of comprehension of who he is in a world which doesn't really care about that. And he has to create the tools to do the job that needs to get done" (qtd. in Wilson 19). This view implies a definition of the blues as an assertion of identity, a quest for redemption, and a coming to grips with one's situation in an uncaring world. According to this definition, Easy Rawlins is a "blues detective" in the truest sense, and it comes as no surprise that Socrates Fortlow, Mosley's good-hearted strong-man, finds "reason and deep purpose" (7) in his surroundings when listening to the blues and thinking about his past in *Walkin' the Dog* (1999).[7]

Mosley's characters recall experiences of the past in their struggle for a better future. This struggle typically involves the search for a home and the creation of a communal system characterized by the downhome values of support and sympathy. Easy, for instance, "was in the business of favors. I'd do something for somebody, like find a missing husband or figure out who's been breaking into so-and-so's store, and then maybe they could do me a good turn one day. It was a real country way of doing business" (*RD* 5). This "business of favors" awards Easy with a home in a double sense: It roots him in the black community in Watts, making him feel at home among its (displaced) people, and it generates the revenue he needs to become a homeowner. For Easy, owning property is a constant source of pride. "I loved going home. Maybe it was that I was raised on a sharecropper's farm or that I never owned anything until I bought that house, but I loved my little home," he confides in *Devil in a Blue Dress* (11). The house gives him a sense of social achievement: "I felt that I was just as good as any white man, but if I didn't even own my front door then people would look at me like just another poor beggar" (9). But Easy is forced to acknowledge in *White Butterfly* (1992): "The police could come to your house today and drag you from your bed. They could beat you until you swallow teeth and they can lock you in a hole for months" (270). Thus, Easy's home can never offer more than a temporary sanctum for his blended family; it can never be taken for granted.

The fundamental insecurity of the black home stands at the beginning of African American history in the sense that the transatlantic slave trade created physical, spiritual, and cultural homelessness on a massive scale, a homelessness institutionalized by the regime of American slavery and continued after slavery through Jim Crow laws, lynching, and Ku Klux Klan terrorism. In order to deal with this insecurity, people have again and again turned to the imaginative and affective powers of blutopia; and while all Mosley's fiction portrays versions of this turning, *RL's Dream* elaborates on the blutopian dream most forcefully. In this novel, the physical, spiritual, and cultural homelessness of the narrative present is addressed through a prominent dream motif, which appears throughout the novel and connects Mosley's characters to their pasts, and through call-and-response patterns, which connect present and past events and gradually make communication between individual characters possible. In learning to voice their dreams and nightmares within the structures outlined by the call-and-response impulse of the African American church and its secular expression in the blues, Mosley's characters manage to alleviate their pain and rebuild their shattered metropolitan community in the North.[8] Although they evoke the sounds and cultural practices of an African American past, the blues also prescribe an aesthetic that embraces, even necessitates, the ability to dream of a better world. They function as "the gateway to 'another reality'" (Lock, G. 2) and enable the novel's multicultural "blues people" (Amiri Baraka's term) to imagine a blutopian future by bearing witness to their nightmares and remembering the hurt of the past. *RL's Dream* thus offers one response to Toni Morrison's fundamental "question of how a dispossessed people, a disenfranchised people, a people without orthodox power, views the cities that it inhabits but does not have a claim to" ("City" 35).

Set in Reagan-era New York City in 1987, *RL's Dream* tells the story of Atwater Wise, better known as Soupspoon. Shortly after the old blues musician has returned from the shelter, he is evicted from his Beldin Arms apartment. Like Soupspoon, the apartment has seen better times; the mattress is fouled, the spigot tarnished, and a rat is claiming ownership of the place (14). Soupspoon is now homeless; about to die of cancer, he is standing at a crossroads, a situation reminiscent of Robert Johnson's "Cross Road Blues": He can either accept death and the meaninglessness of his life or use what is left of his strength and effect some final meaning for his own existence, reversing the old blues wisdom that "[y]ou looked good and died young, that was the way to play it, because an old blues-man was no better than an old dog" (27). He chooses the latter—"he'd die singing and making music out of life the way real men did it a long time ago" (13)—and begins to revive memories of the time when he was a young man in the Mississippi Delta and Johnson's musical companion. Like Johnson, Soupspoon makes a pact, but instead of selling his soul to the devil, as Johnson legendarily did, Soupspoon makes a pact with himself. "I followed him up to the gateway," he recalls, "but Satan scared me silly and left me back to cry" (144). Soupspoon translates the downhome blues to modern American city life, creates blutopian gateways for himself and others, and, in return, regains possession over his soul.[9]

Soupspoon's recollections of his time on the road with Johnson become more and more vivid as the narrative unfolds and as he gradually grows into a mythical blues character himself. Step by step, he enters a call-and-response relationship with the legendary musician. Johnson, simply called RL in the novel (his full name was Robert Leroy Johnson), represents the archetypal bluesman. He is always on the move, partly because his spirit is one of restlessness and partly because, as a visible and sexually "reckless" black musician in the Jim Crow South, he is hunted by racist white sheriffs just as he is haunted by jealous lovers, angry husbands, and his personal demons. What eventually distinguishes Soupspoon from his idol is his commitment to community, his recognition that the call-and-response procedure cannot remain confined to his individual exploration of the past but instead needs to "enable . . . both individual and community to define themselves" (Werner xviii).[10] Instead of living the life of an eternal rambler, Soupspoon comes to realize that he has to quit dreaming about the past and start applying its lessons to the predicaments of the present.

In blues historiography and popular culture, Johnson figures as folk hero, devil incarnate, musical genius, and supernatural lover: as an open canvas that can be painted with images of a powerful past. It is no coincidence, then, that Mosley picks Johnson as the organizing metaphor of his novel. Barry Lee Pearson and Bill McCulloch note that "[t]he image of Johnson prevailing today—the Johnson legend—borders on allegory," but rather than seeing the literary potential of this allegory, they attempt to separate fact from fiction and find the "real" Johnson (2–3; ch. 13). It is more productive, however, to approach the Johnson of *RL's Dream* as a "site of memory," as Patricia Schroeder suggests (128). For Geneviève Fabre and Robert O'Meally, the theory of the *lieux de mémoire* (developed by French historian Pierre Nora) connotes the "interaction between history and memory . . . the interplay between the personal and the collective" (7). The novel's prologue effectively identifies both Johnson and the blues as sites of memory in which the personal meets the collective and history comes alive through musical memory: "RL wasn't no real man" but someone who "wasn't never born an' couldn't die." Like the blues itself, Johnson can never be fully captured in words, nor can he be completely identified and defined—after all, he is a blutopian character, unreal because his legendary powers are imagined by his admirers, and all the more real because Soupspoon is bearing witness to Johnson's violent life and demise. "[U]s po' fools lookin' fo' his story is lost 'fore we begin," the prologue continues. "He was the blues; he is today. Ain't no start to his misery. An' death could not never ease his kinda pain" (9).[11]

Soupspoon's recollection of RL is symptomatic of contemporary myths about Johnson's life and music: "We were the lowest kinda godless riffraff. Migrants and roustabouts, we was bad from the day we was born. Blues is the devil's music an' we his chirren. RL was Satan's favorite son" (140). But Mosley's Johnson also embodies the blutopian spirit. He gives Soupspoon the strength to integrate the preacher-to-congregation ethic of the church with the blues singer-to-audience ethic of blues communication (Jones 46). These ethics imply an intellectual and emotional exchange from congregation to preacher, from audience to blues singer, and vice versa. Craig Hansen Werner notes about the relationship between the religious and the secular variants of the call-and-response phenomenon: "If the blues impulse can be described as a three-stage process—brutal experience, lyrical expression, affirmation—then the gospel impulse can be described in parallel terms derived from the sacred vocabularies of the African-American church: the burden, bearing witness, the vision of (universal) salvation" (xxii). The blutopian impulse unites the blues and gospel impulses. Rejecting the vision of universal salvation (a heavenly home), it shoulders the burden of brutal experience, encourages lyrical expression and bearing witness, and motivates the affirmation of self through community (a physical, spiritual, and cultural home).[12]

Mosley's use of Johnson combines the scant reliable historical information about him with the blutopian qualities of the blues and thereby foregrounds a philosophy of home and community that has deep roots in the African American literary tradition.[13] Mosley recognizes the cultural centrality and affective power of the Johnson legend as "an African American cultural product [that] has been appropriated and exoticized for the thrill of white audiences" (Levecq 240). He reclaims Johnson and his music for African American readers but also offers them as spiritual resources to a multicultural and multiethnic readership.[14] The notion of blutopia is therefore not primarily linked to Robert Johnson. For Mosley, the blues function as the paradigmatic expression of the blutopian search for a home, and the Johnson myth serves as a welcome allegory for this search.

Mosley's literary application of the blues as a spiritual allegory follows Albert Murray's views on the blues: "They are absolutely noiseless at all times. Their movements make no sound whatsoever. And they are evidently voiceless. They are said to speak, but only in the silent language of spirits. So even when they are quoted as if verbatim, you know the speaker is paraphrasing, because the accent and tone and even the volume and timbre are always very obvious stylizations of a voice all too obviously his own. Moreover, no matter how concrete the references, you already know very well that the statement is meant only to be taken as allegorical" (4). Soupspoon's search for RL becomes the search for the "silent language of spirits" Murray describes, for a spiritual home that is coded musically and allegorically and only exists as a paraphrase.[15] The blues compel him to imagine a home even if it is stained with the painful memories of the past, but Soupspoon has to undergo a process of learning before he can understand this. Seeking information on Johnson, he visits his ex-wife Mavis decades after they have separated. Soupspoon is not really interested in Mavis; he never wonders about her all-white apartment and its excessive lighting but only wants to hear about the one night she spent with RL and about what she knows about his legendary deal with the devil.[16] Mavis recognizes the futility of Soupspoon's quest, deriding it as "Mo' shit about Robert Johnson's all it is" (189). Undeterred, Soupspoon asks: "He tell you about how he sold his soul?" But Mavis denies him an answer. Instead, she explains Johnson's music as his reaction to lifelong alienation: "He told me how everybody hated him. . . . Everybody was jealous of him. They stole his music and blamed him for all kindsa things. Maybe they blamed him for sellin' his soul" (195). Soupspoon is so enthralled with the Johnson of the past that he is not yet able to recognize Johnson's imperative to overcome alienation by creating a blutopian community that should, for instance, provide a spiritual home for Mavis.

Like Mavis, those who knew Johnson cannot provide Soupspoon with the blues musician's essence since the answer lies within the blues themselves. They are of a spiritual nature, gateways to a blutopian state of mind rather than material objects and concrete geographical spaces; they cannot be found but only invited to visit. When Soupspoon finally takes up playing again, he makes a first step toward realizing that the bluesman, though a notoriously lonely figure, can only exist if he meets an audience, if he ties people together in a communal bond by offering them his words and music. The blues are thus a medium through which a temporary state of mind—a feeling of being home—can be induced. "He told you about far-off places in the world and played music that was stranger yet. He made songs that were deep down in you," Soupspoon recalls about RL. "He took something of yours that you didn't even know you had . . . [a]nd taking it away he left you with something missing—and that something was better than anything else that ever you had" (44). Filling this vacuum by expressing his own blues, making others see his vision and affecting their lives, Soupspoon eventually realizes RL's unvoiced dream. We can witness this in the depiction of the night of his death, when Soupspoon plays the blues at Rudy's bar. His new girlfriend, the eighteen-year-old Chevette, is among the listeners. She is mesmerized by the performance, which includes the following lines:

> *You know I seen the Lord an' he seen me.*
> *Say, Soup, have you lost your mind?*
>
> *He had twenty angels and a big white car*
> *table set with crawfish pie.*
>
> *He say this here could all be yours*
> *just kiss these breathin' blues goodbye.* (253, italics in original)

The old man's blues prepare Chevette for what is to come: Soupspoon will die and leave her a grieving woman. He will not renounce his allegiance to the blues and will thus go to hell, but he will also leave music that "filled her heart. Music that scurried like a scared dog cowering and dashing underfoot. It was a towering world of heavy blows that brought a song of yelps and cries; of a hard pounding heart" (253). The humanity expressed in the yelps, cries, and pounding heart of the blues equips Chevette with the strength to accept Soupspoon's death, described as a homecoming: " 'What am I doin' here?' the music whines. 'Nowhere, baby. I'm comin' home,' the same song replies. If you heard the words they made no sense. But if you felt the music it could make you cry" (253). In this realization lies the beauty of the music; Chevette, too, feels at home with the blues. Like the young Soupspoon, who "heard things that he never heard before" (74) the first time he listened to the blues, and like Robert Johnson, who "might break if he didn't holler it off with a song" (131), Chevette discovers a sanctuary in the blues.

The dream implied in the novel's title connects the realm of the real with various states of blutopia. For the dying Soupspoon, RL's spiritual appearance signifies a paradoxical relation between life and death: "*Chilly death pass through me like a rill through the woods, like maybe I'ma wake up and all this I been goin' through is just a dream. The kinda dream that somebody like RL would have. A evil long-lastin' dream about all the bad things could happen here*" (266, italics in original). The nightmarish elements of life call for the blues as a release. These blues represent a creatively imagined mechanism for dealing with adversity; they find their expression in Ralph Ellison's conception of the blues impulse, which enables people "to keep the painful details and episodes of a brutal experience alive in . . .

[their] aching consciousness, to finger its jagged grain, and to transcend it, not by the consolation of philosophy but by squeezing from it a near-tragic, near-comic lyricism" ("Richard Wright's" 129). Near-tragedy and near-comedy are the means with which life is transformed into blutopia; as Soupspoon explains: "[I]t's all just a dream. Day in and day out all the things that ever happened, just like they happened. . . . It's like you're asleep and can't wake up. Because if you could wake up you would change it" (258). Life in the 1930s South meant the omnipresent threat of death, but singing the blues meant dreaming of a better place, even though the "freedom" demanded by the blues singer was always temporary: "You could demand freedom in the blues. But it wasn't so much freedom a poor black man wanted but release. That's a slave's freedom; a sharecropper's freedom. Release from his bonds and his bondage. . . . And when we asked for release we knew that it . . . meant death too. We was bound for nowhere. Bound for a heavy iron ball on the chain gang or just at work on the plantation. Bound to die—that's what we was" (202–3).[17] For those who migrated to the North, however, "nowhere" could be, if not a utopian place, at least a blutopian space where people found homes in enemy lands and made it through life, flawed and scarred, by tapping into their hurt-stained memories of the past.

Soupspoon's blues and his attempts at community building are not simple steps toward a better world. The past with which Soupspoon is dealing and which is both the cause and result of his blues is an ambivalent one that informs and shapes his understanding of the present. On the one hand, it is dominated by memories of lynching, violence, and poverty in the Mississippi Delta in the 1930s and 40s—"It was a hard life back then" (91), he recalls—but on the other hand, it is a home "full of colors and smells and music" (72). It keeps alive in Soupspoon's aching consciousness, by way of the blues impulse, the tragic-comic experiences that shape his struggle for a home in the city and his relationship with the people of his neighborhood. It is neither authenticity or realism, nor nostalgia and romanticism, as some critics have argued, that drives Mosley's portrayal of the Southern blues past. Instead, it is the power of the blues that enables individuals like Soupspoon to conjure up the stained, bittersweet memories of the past and mobilize them for the creation of a blutopian community.[18]

Among the displaced people of New York, Soupspoon searches for a home and the communal ties he knew in the Delta, a quest shared by all of the novel's other characters. Everybody is trying to escape the past by repressing the painful details of their lives: Mavis is pained by memories of her son Cort's death; Kiki Waters, a white woman in her thirties born and raised in the Delta region, suffers from the trauma of sexual abuse by her father; Soupspoon is haunted by the lynching of his substitute father, Bannon Tripp. It is looming death itself that makes Soupspoon realize that an unfingered jagged grain means a betrayal of the blues ethic, a betrayal of the imperative to help others and make the best out of life even if things look terribly bleak. The pain of the present drives Soupspoon and his friends out of their homes and away from their realms of security: Soupspoon loses his apartment and becomes temporarily homeless; Kiki hides from her father; Randy denies his African ancestry. Nonetheless, the blues connect these Americans beyond race, sex, and class: "Music and style in black America are so vibrant because they are barely veiled codes that express the pain . . . that is common to *all* women and men, black and white" (13) as Mosley maintains in *Workin' on the Chain Gang* (2000).[19]

Soupspoon was orphaned as a boy; his condition of homelessness is thus a chronic one. Not only does he grow up without his parents, but living in the Jim Crow South condemns him to another state of homelessness, one that renders black Americans noncitizens in their own country. Soupspoon's blues are a result of the forced flight of African Americans from the physical and emotional violence of the racist South. *RL's Dream*, then, covers more than the emotional and temporal dimensions of Soupspoon's life. Geographical "mobility," the movement from place to place within the South and eventually to the North (or California, in Easy's case), appears as another central motif. Michael Shapiro writes about "the special meaning of geography for black America" by connecting geographical issues with modes of survival and the development of the blues: "For many African Americans in the twentieth century, geography has been a practice of place that is inseparable from strategies of survival rather than a disinterested mode of description, a simple mapping of distances and boundaries. . . . [T]he development of the blues . . . is inextricably tied to a dynamic African American territorial experience, a domestic black diaspora which resulted from a combination of locally and federally generated economic policies . . . and white discriminatory practices, ranging from the inscribed, legal and administrative to the tacit, extralegal and violent" (n. pag.). The blues are a testament to Soupspoon's final realization that he cannot run from death but must face his demons. Having lived in the Lower East Side for decades, Soupspoon has become immobile in geographical terms but begins to learn that he can move back and forth between past and present, South and North, through his music, tapping into the blues as a strategy for survival.

The racial, musical, and spiritual geography inscribed in the blues resurfaces in the novel's call-and-response structure; it is enacted through Soupspoon's dreams of the past and his wish to collect his memories on tape (a permanent "home" for the music). According to Werner, the "call and response" process "begins with the call of a leader who expresses his/her own voice through the vehicle of a traditional song, story, or image. This call, which provides a communal context for exploration of the 'individual' emotion, itself responds to a shared history. . . . If the community . . . recognizes and shares the experience evoked by the call, it responds with another phrase . . . which may either affirm or present a different perspective on the initial call" (xviii). Most significant for Mosley's blutopian vision is that the call-and-response "process requires individuals not to seek a synthesis, to deny the extreme aspects of their own experiences, but to assert their subjectivity in response to other, equally personal and equally extreme, assertions of experience" (xviii). Thus, it provides room for Soupspoon's temporal and geographical explorations as well as for Kiki's struggle with the violent memories of past abuse, which she can only confront because she realizes that she can share the pain with Soupspoon. Together, they manage to "[get] so close to pain that it's like a friend, like somebody [they] love" (182), and are able, in a phrase reminiscent of Zora Neale Hurston, to "lap up the gravy while [they] can still lick" (167).[20]

When, at the outset of *RL's Dream*, Soupspoon finds himself unable to walk and talk with all of his possessions thrown out onto the street, he is picked up and taken in by Kiki. As the narrative unfolds, the young woman and the old bluesman establish the core of a communal bond that resembles black working-class communities of the pre-WWII South: They help each other in times of need, they share what little they have, they make new friends and bring them into the bounds of their relationship, and they manage to squeeze occasional pleasure from the fruit of life through music and stories. They finally create a network of people in the Northern city that evokes what Robin D. G. Kelley terms "the pleasures and politics of black communities under segregation" and revives the communal ethics of the black South according to which people "not only helped families with basic survival needs, but created and sustained bonds of fellowship, mutual support networks, and a collectivist ethos" (35, 38). Kiki accepts the call for creating sustained bonds of human fellowship when she organizes an alternative relief system for the ailing Soupspoon by deceiving the insurance company for which she works. She invents insurance records for Atwater and his "wife" Tanya Wise, as whom she poses whenever Soupspoon goes in for chemotherapy.

Kiki's family name recalls Delta blues guitar player and singer Muddy Waters, which places her within the Southern blues tradition gone North. Kiki provides Soupspoon with the kind of support he only knew in his past life. When she takes him in, finds him a wheelchair, and cooks him breakfast, Soupspoon "was amazed again. All the years he lived as a poor man among poor people and it always happened like this. You might know somebody for twenty years and never know their first name or what their feet looked like. But then one day something happens and somebody you never even thought of is there in your life closer than family. You know their smell and their temper. . . . That's how it was with Robert Johnson" (44). Kiki can only save herself by providing a home for Soupspoon— her humanity becomes meaningful once she grants humanity to Soupspoon, who is barely alive and even declared deceased by Social Services. Fighting the moving men, who intend to leave Soupspoon on the street in front of his apartment, Kiki screams: "You put an old man out 'cause he's sick! You motherfucker!" (30). She expresses the communal ethos of home as well as a cultural ethic of care: "I don't think somebody should just stand by if something is happening and they know it's wrong" (35). This blues-inspired transformation from abandonment to community, from homelessness to home, represents a blutopian vision of a future that acknowledges the pain of the past, indeed embraces it and finds consolation in it because it reminds people of their humanity and the need to enter into communion with others.[21]

In *RL's Dream*, the blutopian call-and-response appears on a philosophical and on a formal level. In the standard blues form, the call is issued twice, always with slight variations, by a singer who acknowledges that each telling of an event and each perspective from which it is viewed is slightly different, despite being tied to a shared humanity. In Mosley's novel, the first call usually describes a situation in the present that demands an answer to a problem. The second, restating call is both a response and a parallel call that recaptures scenes from the past. In this way, the present echoes the past by expressing a related event removed in time and place. The final answer is provided by the blues' third line, the traditional response to the double call. For Mosley, this line is represented by the blutopian qualities of the blues themselves, the realization that past and present need to be identified as related spheres of one's emotional landscape and the recognition that the blues have something to say to everybody at any time. Kiki's devotion to helping Soupspoon not only recalls Johnson's "Kind Hearted Woman Blues"—in which he sings: "I got a kind-hearted woman, do most anything in this world for me"—but also illustrates this tripartite structure. Having herself benefited from Hattie's and Hector's selfless help, Kiki immediately empathizes with Soupspoon. Her readiness to support the old man spurs Soupspoon's reminiscences about his childhood, the time when Ruby and Inez, two equally kind-hearted women, took him in and nursed him back to health after influenza had claimed his parents and little brother. Utilizing the call-and-response structure of the blues, Mosley repeats statements in altered form: Ruby and Inez saved Soupspoon's life as a child (first blues line); now Kiki accepts the burden of caring for him (second blues line). Finally, the blues' third line finishes the call voiced in the preceding statements. In *RL's Dream*, this third line is Soupspoon's pledge to give back to the community, to reciprocate the love and care others have lavished upon him.

A key sentence connecting a dream of the past with the realities of the present exemplifies the novel's recurrent blues structure. Soupspoon is dreaming of Ruby kissing him during his childhood days, a reminiscence evoked by Kiki's kisses: "The young boy fell asleep but the old man came awake" (73). Past and present, childhood and old age, reside on a continuum of human experience that is expressed by the cyclical structure of the blues, its progression away from and back to a root chord. This musical return to the root is bound to a notion of place and time. "[T]he word *down home*, it mean back to the root, which mean where it all start at," blues singer Jo Jo Williams explains (qtd. in Titon 3, italics in original).

When Soupspoon begins to play the downhome blues again and adapts them to his present-day life, he becomes Ellison's "link in the chain of tradition" ("Charlie Christian" 267). The music not only encodes and transports Soupspoon's past and the lives of the Mississippi Delta people to the present; it also speaks to the younger generation. Past and present therefore enounce consecutive and parallel calls.[22] This parallelism resurfaces in the stories and recollections Soupspoon commits to tape and gives to Sono's boyfriend, Gerald Pickford. They find their way into *Back Road to the Blues*, an oral history compiled from Soupspoon's tapes that reflexively provides the epigraph for the novel and thus insinuates that *RL's Dream*, Mosley's work of fiction, is echoed by Soupspoon's own memories in book form. As Wilson concludes, the epigraph manipulates time; dating it a year before (1986) the events in the novel are said to take place, "Mosley suggests that the very text of *RL's Dream* . . . is just that, a dream. . . . [I]t defies being fixed in only the present moment" (99). In this sense, the novel follows Murray's understanding of the blues as a paraphrase, a tribute to the silent language of the blues spirit as well as blutopian dreams of home.

Mosley's expression of hope for late twentieth-century America and beyond in *RL's Dream* lies in the transformation of a devalued and barren city life to a humane blues collectivity. Suggesting neither a grand vision of remodeling the American metropolis nor solutions to the urban crisis drawn from the social sciences or political theory, Mosley digs up an older value system, one developed out of necessity by a people reduced to the very essentials of life. Turning lack into possession by casting one's pain into creative expression makes possible the sharing of burdens; it invests life with meaning, sows the seeds for communal living, and provides an immaterial, blutopian home. The blutopian theme of home and community is integral to Mosley's literary view of African American life in the city, particularly Soupspoon's New York, but also the Los Angeles that Easy Rawlins, Socrates Fortlow, and Paris Minton inhabit. Mosley proposes, via Soupspoon's blues, a spiritual answer to the urban crisis that takes its inspiration from the communal practices and informal networks of the Depression South. In Mosley's fiction, and especially in *RL's Dream*, blues-induced dreams remind individuals to retain their ability to dream of a physical, spiritual, and cultural home and to strive toward communal harmony in a country that has proven its inhospitability to the dream more than once.

Notes

I thank Micha Edlich, Owen Brady, and Derek Maus for advice and suggestions.

1. Titon defines *downhome* as "a spirit, a *sense* of place evoked in singer and listener by a style of music" (xv) as well as "both a place in time and a state of mind" (29). Soupspoon's struggle to find his way home is therefore a physical and a spiritual quest; his music provides others with "a taste of down home" (*RL's Dream* 154).

2. Lock takes the term "blutopia," a contraction of *blues* and *utopia*, from Duke Ellington's composition of the same title. See *The Duke Ellington Carnegie Hall Concerts: December 1944* (Prestige, 1977).

3. "Hell Hound on My Trail," "Love in Vain," and all other Johnson recordings discussed in this essay are anthologized on *Robert Johnson: The Complete Recordings* (Columbia/Legacy, 1990).

4. In *The Man in My Basement* (2004), Charles Blakey is forced to rent his basement to the white Anniston Bennet in order to pay his mortgage. Blakey's family has owned the "beautiful home for seven generations or more" (4), which makes them homeowners since the early nineteenth century and ties them to a tradition of black property ownership, signaling that black lives were lived throughout American history in homes other than slave quarters and cabins.

5. These different forms of *homelessness* add complexity to Cornel West's recognition of *invisibility* and *namelessness* as the central effects of the modern black diaspora (27).

6. Kennedy notes that the Easy Rawlins novels "look both backwards and forwards from the present tense of narrative time, situating Easy Rawlins in a continuum of black diaspora experiences" (229). He emphasizes Mosley's treatment of social spaces as "the loci of black culture as a way of life, a normative system of behavior and expression, attitudes and values" (232). Arguing that Mosley "interrogate[s] utopian and dystopian features of black experiences in Los Angeles" (237), Kennedy describes the blutopian philosophy without labeling it as such.

7. I take the term "blues detective" from Soitos, who mentions Mosley but does not examine the significance of the blues in the Easy Rawlins series.

8. Levecq overstates the discontinuities between Soupspoon's rural Southern blues and his modern city blues. "What the novel seems to endorse . . . is a concept of community completely different from the one left over from the Delta days" (247). And: "[T]he new vision of community espoused by the novel entails a new vision of the blues as well" (249). Instead of discovering a "completely different" blues vision, however, Mosley seems to be arguing—via the call-and-response structure of his text—that the blutopian vision of the present evolves directly from the blues ethos of Soupspoon's Delta past.

9. On Mosley's treatment of Johnson's alleged pact with the devil, cf. Levecq 240–41; on the pact's significance in blues historiography, see Guralnick, Pearson and McCulloch, Schroeder, Wald.

10. Southern working-class societies from Reconstruction onwards, Kelley notes, "were structured in a democratic manner that allowed all voices to play some kind of role in constructing a vision of the community" (39).

11. Schroeder views both Johnson and Mosley's version of the blues as sites of memory (132).

12. Levecq calls the blues in *RL's Dream* an "incarnat[ion of] communities" and sees them "as holding the possibility to foster a vision of future social change" (240); Schroeder recognizes "the sustaining powers of the blues and its importance in creating community" (128).

13. The authors evoked in this essay—Ellison, Hughes, Hurston, Morrison, and Wright—but also James Baldwin, Amiri Baraka, Alice Walker, and August Wilson, are exponents of this tradition. Levecq's assertion that Mosley's fictional use of Johnson "clearly points toward romantic simplification" (241) only makes sense if we compare Johnson's biography with the fictional portrait. Johnson's mythical potential seems to be of greater importance to Mosley than the search for historical "truth." I agree with Elijah Wald's argument in *Escaping the Delta* that our understanding of the musical and social cultures that birthed the blues have no separate existence from the stories, legends, and myths surrounding the music.

14. Schroeder connects *RL's Dream* with Cornel West's "new cultural politics of difference," which "neither romanticizes nor idealizes marginalized peoples . . . [but r]ather accen-

tuates their humanity" (West 34). As the narrator of *RL's Dream* remarks, "Soupspoon's music was for everybody and everything" (211). Schroeder further suggests Alan Rodgers's *Bone Music* and Sherman Alexie's *Reservation Blues* (both of which feature fictional Robert Johnsons and were published in 1995) as intertexts for Mosley's novel (113–14).

15. As such, it differs from historical inquiries like Guralnick's *Searching for Robert Johnson*.

16. Mavis's urge to illuminate her home recalls the 1,369 light bulbs of Ellison's narrator in *Invisible Man*, who hibernates in an underground hole/home in Harlem.

17. Soupspoon recalls further: "People died in the Delta; they died all the time" (74). Playing the blues "was the only way we could bear the weight of those days" (140). On the blues and the plantation system, see Woods.

18. Levecq identifies instances of Southern pastoralism in Mosley's representation of the Mississippi Delta, for instance in Soupspoon's recollection of "days and days down by the river with his little boyfriends—fishing, rafting, swimming among the catfish and carp" (73). These images are, however, presented through the consciousness of a dying old man. To speak of "rural exceptionalism" and "pastoral bliss," as Levecq does (243), and to read Mosley's vision of the Delta as a romantic creation of "a place of true, real, unadulterated black identity" (244), is to confuse character perspective with narrative/authorial perspective and to miss the blutopian vision of the novel—Levecq merely notes that "Mosley gently criticizes" Soupspoon for his enthrallment with the Delta blues life (240). Lipsitz faults Mosley for depicting "Johnson's music nostalgically as an art form that involved its listeners in depths of feeling unknown to today's audiences. . . . Once again, the blues are deployed as an antidote to the shallowness of contemporary commercial culture, as an art form precious because it is unapproachable and unknowable, locked in the past but superior to anything we can imagine in the present" (121). But *RL's Dream* is less concerned with contemporary commercial culture's shallowness than with mobilizing the mythological potential of the blues as a spiritual answer to the maladies of the present.

19. Thomas Stein's conclusion about the Easy Rawlins series—"the reader knows that Easy thinks neither 'black' nor 'white' but like an American" (203)—fits *RL's Dream*, which imagines the blues as a trope for an American community beyond racial boundaries.

20. Kiki was rescued from her father by the two black adults Hattie and Hector but grows up with feelings of physical and emotional insecurity. The friendship between Soupspoon and Kiki fills a gap Morrison finds in black urban fiction: "What is missing in city fiction . . . is the . . . advising, benevolent, protective, wise Black ancestor" ("City" 39). Soupspoon takes on the role of this wise ancestor, but others, such as Kiki and Mavis, are equally responsible for imparting knowledge about life to neighbors. The blues community, including Sono, Chevette, Gerald, Rudy, Randy, is itself a village within the city; it gives voice to "the affection of Black writers . . . for the city . . . [through an embrace of] the village within it: the neighborhoods and the population of those neighborhoods" (Morrison, "City" 37).

21. The three major themes Wilson identifies in *RL's Dream*—the "blues condition," the "validation of self," and the "interconnectedness of human experience" (89–90)—are tied together by Soupspoon's blues.

22. I disagree with Levecq's assertion that *RL's Dream* "contrasts . . . [Soupspoon's] present blues, as a commercial performance in an ignorant environment, to yesterday's blues, as the direct expression of emotion and the sharing of it with a knowledgeable public" (248). Soupspoon is sowing the seeds for a new generation of musicians and listeners, who must yet learn how to tap into the blutopian powers of the blues. Their search is of a spiritual, not commercial, nature.

Socrates Fortlow's Odyssey

The Quest for Home and Self

—OWEN E. BRADY

> Every spirit builds itself a house; and beyond its house a world; and beyond its world,
> a heaven. Know then that the world exists for you. For you is the phenomenon per-
> fect. What we are, that only we can see. All that Adam had, all that Caesar could, you
> have and can do. Adam called his house, heaven and earth; Caesar called his house,
> Rome; you perhaps call yours a cobbler's trade; a hundred acres of ploughed land; or a
> scholar's garret. Yet line for line and point for point, your domain is as great as theirs,
> though without fine names. Build, therefore, your own world. .
> —R. W. EMERSON, *Nature*, Lecture (48)

Using the trope of the house to signify the more encompassing concept of home, Walter Mosley participates in an American literary tradition that has given central place to the image of the house.[1] Mosley's entire corpus from his Easy Rawlins mystery series (begun in 1990) to his more recent *The Man in My Basement* (2004) to his nonfiction such as *Black Genius* (1999), *Workin' on the Chain Gang* (2000), and *What Next* (2003) may be read as an extended reflection on this theme of home as the site for self-fashioning and rebuilding a sense of community.[2] Like Emerson, Mosley uses the house to suggest the more expansive term of home, a total environment or world, that moves outward from the self in concentric "circles of hominess," ever-widening social relationships: from family, to neighborhood, to nation as homeland (Hollander 33). Each of these social relationships serves as a site for refashioning individual identity and rebuilding the shattered African American community. In *Always Outnumbered, Always Outgunned* (1997) and *Walkin' the Dog* (1999), the trope of house as home unifies the two volumes into the picaresque odyssey of Socrates Fortlow. A former criminal guilty of destroying human bonds through murder and rape, Socrates relocates himself both spatially and morally. In the process of seeking a home, he transforms his identity from the violent "bad nig-ger," a threat to the security of the African American community, to the heroic "badman," whose aggressive action serves the community's "dreams of freedom through political action" (Roberts 177).³ Moreover, Socrates's self-transforming actions provide a new communal basis for reconceiving home in distinctively African American terms that transcends historic oppression and contemporary communal violence.

Mosley's use of the house/home trope signifies on the normative understand-ing of home. Normatively, home signifies both a place and a feeling of domestic-ity: comfort, family, and security abide. In American culture, the family home, the occupant-owned house, is central to popular conceptions of the American Dream. Ownership of the family home signifies individual success. On the individual level, the house/home is a haven, a private retreat from society.⁴ On the larger scale, it represents the fulfillment of the homeland's promise of life, liberty, and the pursuit of happiness—a site where justice, in the form of prosperity, is available to all. The pursuit of this dream of possession of a house that is also a home is common to all Americans. Writing of the African American experience, Valerie Sweeney Prince comments in *Burnin' Down the House: Home in African American Literature* (2005): "The search for justice, opportunity, and liberty that characterized the twentieth century for African Americans can be described as a quest for home" (1). Historically for African Americans, however, home, both in the sense of the family house and the homeland's promise, has been severely limited, often denied. Thus, Socrates is representative, experiencing life in America as homelessness or exile, a feeling of being unfree, a slave or a criminal. As Orlando Patterson notes in his discussion of home, "The slave, in short, is the quintessentially homeless person. Homelessness in the most fundamental sense of the term: kinless, rootless, a stranger forever, cut off not only from our ancestors but from descendants. . . . The slave is absolutely alone, outside of history, outside of community" (162–63). To represent this bleak state, Mosley focuses not on one dwelling but on multiple sites for house/home as Socrates moves from alienation to social integration, from bad nigger to badman, from criminal to American citizen.

Socrates's house of origin is the Big House, an Indiana penitentiary with his-toric overtones of the slave plantation, chief symbol of white hegemony. Whether penitentiary or plantation house, the Big House is the inherently deficient home where the black criminal/slave originates and belongs, but can never own or feel secure within. The personal and historic memory of the Big House appears as the Indiana Department of Correction's "Certificate of Final Discharge" ending Socrates's twenty-seven-year sentence, a document that takes on almost metaphys-ical significance in its placement before *Always Outnumbered, Always Outgunned*'s table of contents. Like the slave pass or manumission papers,⁵ the certificate pro-vides the criminal with a marginal degree of freedom but little material prosperity and less security, little sense of feeling at home. An ever-present dysfunctional home, the penitentiary recurs in flashbacks reflecting Socrates's self-identity marked by guilt and violence. In the Big House, Socrates, like the slave, performed socially transgressive acts to survive or achieve justice that confirm him to the white authority as the nigger stereotype. For example, in "Midnight Meeting," the brutality and dehumanizing atmosphere of prison causes Socrates to seek a rough kind of justice in secretly killing Fitzroy, a brutal black inmate, who terrorizes his cellmate, Clyde (*AOAO* 29). In both versions of the Big House—plantation and prison—home is experienced as displacement and alienation, housing a divided self.[6]

As Socrates moves from the Big House to a cell-like hovel in Los Angeles, he carries with him the divided self that embodies Du Bois's warring double consciousness of self as Negro and as American. As Negro, a socially imposed identity, "Socrates was guilty, guilty all the way around. He was big and he was black, he was an ex-convict and he was poor" (*Walkin'* 111). Yet, as an American longing for the homeland's promise of individual self-fulfillment, Socrates moves west to reject the stereotype that creates feelings of being enslaved by his own skin, of not feeling at home: "I ain't no niggah" (*AOAO* 62). Socrates moves to the American urban frontier, whose "ideological work" in the pursuit of the American Dream is "the production of individualism" (Crooks 69). But unlike the mythic western frontier for the European-American self, Socrates finds himself on the wrong side of the frontier, cast as one of the ghettoized savages of South Central Los Angeles. There he contends with the dangers of the Watts "wilderness" as well as those posed by the agents of American civilization, the Los Angeles Police Department. Assigned to keep the savages on the other side of the frontier, the police hover in helicopters over South Central. Thus, Los Angeles inverts the frontier's promise of individuality. Like his African American neighbors, Socrates continues to be enslaved by the nigger stereotype and at best can achieve invisibility and anonymity: "[Socrates] learned in prison that L. A. was a big rambling bunch of towns and that everybody was in too much of a hurry to remember faces, places, times, and events. An ex-con would need that kind of anonymity" (*AOAO* 110).

Appropriately, Socrates dwells invisibly for almost nine years in a cell-like house that initially reflects his impoverished self-identity. While it serves the need for shelter, the house possesses little homey comfort, either physical or emotional. It is a rental, hardly bigger or better outfitted than a prison cell; its size, spare furniture, and condition emphasize his feelings of alienation and loneliness: "The kitchen was only big enough for a man and a half. The floor was pitted linoleum; maroon where it had kept its color, gray where it had worn through. There was a card table for dining and a fold-up plastic chair for a seat. There was a sink with a hot plate on the drainboard and shelves that were once cabinets—before the doors were torn off" (*AOAO* 14). Like Socrates, the building has become invisible, lodged between abandoned buildings, forgotten, with an owner long dead. Though Socrates sends regular rent checks for months none are cashed. The house also represents his criminal identity and homelessness. He comes "[h]ome to his illegal gap. Home to a place that had no street address, a jury-rigged electrical system, plumbing that turned off every once in a while, sometimes for weeks. It was a hard place. . . . It was a place he slept in, a place to read or drink or almost cry. But it had never been home" (*Walkin'* 22–23). Socrates Fortlow is a nowhere man in a nowhere home: an absent presence, "the subject who is denied status or selfhood by the culture" (Weinstein 5).

The only memento decorating his stark house is a picture of an angry woman standing, glowering in front of a dark house. It defines Socrates's guilt and alien- ation, his metaphoric homelessness. The sign of the absent home-defining femi- nine presence,[7] the picture negates positive feelings of home. The angry woman barring the door represents Socrates's grieved mother or his lost love, Theresa, who cut him dead when she learned of his crime, the rape and the murder of two friends. In heinously sundering the bonds of friendship, Socrates has rejected the domesticating feminine. Indeed, the narrator tells us that the woman in the picture "stared her disapproval of men" (*AOAO* 21)—especially the aggres- sive bad niggers, like Socrates, who "indulged in gratuitous violence and bullied and preyed on other blacks" (Roberts 179). The motif of the pained and disap- proving woman, most often a grieving mother, recurs in several stories, remind- ing Socrates of his guilt and violation of a core idea of home: caring human relationships.

During his nine years in his invisible house, Socrates tries to resolve his home- lessness and the tension of his double consciousness by creating a sense of family and community, places where people care for each other. To do so, Socrates trans- forms his impoverished house into a home that is a refuge for those hungry and hungering for justice. In "Crimson Shadow," the opening story of his two-volume odyssey, Socrates catches Darryl, a young boy, stealing and killing an old rooster. Sensing a person to be ransomed from a future of crime, Socrates feeds Darryl's body and mind even as he punishes him. Forcing the boy to clean, cook, and eat the tough old bird, Socrates teaches him a useful skill and provides a lesson in responsibility that turns wasted life into nourishing food. The black boy and black man forge a bond of mutual identity as Socrates correctly senses Darryl's guilt for murdering a retarded young boy. From bitter experience, Socrates knows that to incarcerate a boy who does not yet accept his guilt wastes potential; however, teaching him to be a man by taking responsibility for violating human bonds may help society become better. Socrates tells Darryl, "If you learn you wrong then maybe you get to be a man. . . . We all got to be our own judge, li'l brother. 'Cause if you don't know when you wrong then yo' life ain't worf a damn" (*AOAO* 22). Opening the cell-like house to Darryl any time he feels the need for support be- gins to domesticate it, a step toward a home, that starts to ameliorate Socrates's alienation. Through a bond of guilt, Darryl and Socrates have become family, the lost son found and the surrogate father.

Locating Socrates's invisible house in the larger social circle of the African American neighborhood, Mosley stresses the importance of communal bonds and justice in constructing a home. "Midnight Meeting" literally brings the neighborhood inside Socrates's cramped house. A community watch group meets to discuss dealing with a dope-head killer jeopardizing the neighborhood. Surrounded by abandoned buildings, closed businesses, and mean streets, the residents see no recourse in the police, who loiter above in helicopters patrolling the urban frontier. In the meeting, Socrates bonds himself to his neighbors' interests and organizes a visit to the criminal's house to intimidate him physically and force him to vacate the neighborhood. Though Socrates accepts responsibility for protecting his neighbors, he rejects their suggestion to kill the criminal because "we're not animals" (*AOAO* 29) and "killing ain't no answer for civilized men" (30). Once the violent bad nigger, Socrates now morphs into the badman, seeking justice in terms that transgress law but are acceptable to his African American neighbors, though not to his own conscience.

While in his penitential cell-like house, Socrates manages to forge a new positive sense of identity in two ways. First, he bonds himself to the needs of his crime-ridden contemporary African American community that, like Socrates, needs redemption from historical oppression and self-inflicted degradation. Second, Socrates experiences the power of roots in vernacular culture and historical knowledge. His sense of mission and valuing cultural memory enlarge the impoverished house. It thereby transcends its limits becoming a home invested with "family" and furnished with memories. Mosley also employs specific African American cultural referents to broaden our understanding of home—an archetypal ancestor figure, a blues man, and a personal memory that connects Socrates with African American literature and historical achievement.

In "Marvane Street," an overpowering dream figure, a gigantic jet-black man appears: "A man with a broad broad nose and sensual big lips. The man's eyes were stern and his shoulders were wide as a sail" (*AOAO* 94). He charges Socrates with a hard but potentially transforming mission that might redeem him and his community. In the dream, Mosley signifies on the term "blood," transforming it from its common metaphoric sense as a sign of guilt into the positive "blood" ties that reconnect Socrates to his African American community. The powerful black man resonates with history and archetype; he is the folkloric African forebear, the rebel slave, John Henry, a gigantic symbol of power and liberation, the badman.[8] When he orders Socrates to dig up all the black people "that had died from grief" in an enormous graveyard where each "grave was marked by a small granite stone, hardly larger than a silver dollar" (*AOAO* 94), Socrates protests that the job would kill him. The giant replies, "We all die!" (94), a blues joke that wakens Socrates with painful laughter but invests him with a sense of mission: to resurrect South Central's dead souls, which will transform the guilty blood on his hands into the basis for a new sense of community built on racial identity and communal responsibility.

In "that smell" from *Walkin' the Dog*, the blues figure as an ambiguous sign of both communal degradation as well as potential transcendence in Socrates's odyssey. His redemption of the derelict blues trumpeter, Hoagland Mars, obeys the ancestor figure's command to dig up those who have died from grief. The weak, drunken, self-soiled Mars and the blues he carries within him serve as a communal and cultural metonymy. Mars is a metaphoric vessel carrying the communal weight of painful historical experience, including self-inflicted violence, and the music that has the power to transcend it. Walking home after a discussion group on a quintessential blues topic, the battle between black men and women, Socrates finds Mars literally housed in "a small wooden structure that was once meant to house trash cans for the weekly dump truck. The graying pine cube now contained the life of a man" (*Walkin'* 136). Covered in his own excrement and vomit, smelling up the area, Mars figures the historically imposed and self-inflicted condition of life in the African American 'hood. Recognizing that "[m]y daddy . . . [d]ied on the street just like Mars was gonna do" (139), Socrates empathetically identifies with this representative of the historical waste of African American lives and talent, especially males. Digging Mars out of the trash, Socrates carts him to Luvia Prine's big boarding house for rehabilitation and love. Moving Mars from his cryptlike pine cube house to Luvia's foreshadows the transformation of the house/home trope, with the Big House now positioned as a site of communal concern ruled by a woman. Thus key elements of a new sense of home—communal responsibility and the domesticating feminine presence—are available for the final movement of Socrates's odyssey.

Acquiring knowledge of African American history and literature also enlarges Socrates's sense of home by engendering cultural pride. In "History," riot swirls in the streets fueling Socrates's anger at white oppression and his sense of alienation. To calm the feelings that resonate with the rebellious rioters' rage, Socrates recalls an earlier time, shortly after his arrival in Los Angeles, when he "was on a path to violence" and spent days "roaming the streets . . . waiting for somebody to give him a look so he could break their face for them" (*AOAO* 154). A chance visit to Oscar and Winnie Minette's Capricorn Bookstore, however, defuses his sociopathic violence. The Minettes' bookstore offers a civilized alternative to the rioting in the streets. There neighbors could read, disagree, despise, or love each other as they discussed civilly, in colloquial terms, African history, foreign relations, the media's role in Vietnam, or the war of institutional wealth against the citizenry. Moreover, the Capricorn Bookstore represents a repository of African American historical memory that poses an alternative site of cultural origin. Socrates browses African American literature and a history of racial achievement: "Black cowboys running roughshod in Oklahoma. Black scientists and war heroes and con men" (*AOAO* 155). The Minettes also provide a living conduit to African American culture, having met James Baldwin, Langston Hughes, "both Martin Luther Kings" and "gone to Africa with Louis Armstrong in the sixties" (161). Socrates's feelings of anger and guilt, characteristic of his homelessness, dissolve in a visit to their humble home where "[h]e felt himself relaxing in their home. It was a comfort that he'd given up on years before he went to prison" (161).

For the most part Socrates's growing sense of home resides in his relationships with an African American community. Socrates does, however, move toward a visible place within the larger American homeland. In doing so, he attempts to resolve or ameliorate the tension between the two warring ideals Du Bois articulated: Negro and American. Socrates's commitment to helping African American neighbors and his cultural pride have begun to make him more at home in his Negro identity. Midway through *Always Outnumbered, Always Outgunned*, Socrates begins a parallel move toward fuller participation in the broadest circle of home, the American homeland, where Socrates can, at least tenuously, experience identity as an American citizen. Socrates's place in the African American neighborhood results primarily from transgressive actions in which he breaks laws to achieve justice denied friends or community members; however, through his self-conscious use of law and the exercise of a civil right, Socrates moves from the savage section of the frontier, where he has developed a positive but necessarily tribal sense of community, and into the larger circle of American civil society. But in crossing the frontier, Socrates again evokes the bad nigger stereotype in the eyes of the white power structure when his assertion of legal rights appears transgressive. In his legal transgressions, however, Socrates goes some way toward wresting a place in the widest circle of home, as a fully franchised American citizen.

Socrates's quest for a place in the large circle of the American homeland begins as he tries to achieve dignity through work. Rather than consciously transgressive behavior, he uses the law in seeking a job with ironic consequences. After eight years of attenuated, invisible freedom, Socrates gives up the demeaning work of collecting bottles to eke out a meager existence because he can no longer abide the assaults on his human dignity heaped upon him by the employees of Ralphie's supermarket where he redeems the bottles: "They made him wait and checked after him like he was some sort of stupid animal" (*AOAO* 41). At great effort, he seeks employment as a stock boy in the Bounty supermarket located in a distant white community. When he asks a white assistant manager for an application, Socrates's looming, lowering physical presence and threadbare camouflage jacket conjure fear in the white man's mind. Denied the application, Socrates invokes the equal opportunity laws. Despite his best efforts and despite the intent of the law, he is seen as threatening and ultimately the supermarket security force intervenes. Though denying him the job, the security men, both former cops, decide as a sort of joke to test the liberal inclinations of a Hispanic manager of a Bounty branch on Santa Monica Boulevard, asking him to employ Socrates. In an ironic twist worthy of the blues, invoking the law has produced injustice and, at the same time, a job (*AOAO* 77). Getting a job immediately changes Socrates's identity by providing dignity; and Socrates's newfound sense of identity is reflected at his celebratory party, bringing the community into his small house.

In "moving on," Socrates reflects on how work and repositioning his alienated criminal self in a surrogate family and a circle of friends has created a sense of domesticity, making him feel at home: "[H]e was almost completely satisfied with life. He had a good job and friends who he could talk to when he was lonely and a door that he could unlock any time he wanted. He had a girlfriend and a telephone and new shoes that didn't hurt his feet. He was a free man, just as long as the police didn't know about his hidden handgun and no one found out about a fight or two he had had in the streets. There was a young boy who looked up to him and even though they lived under different roofs everyone who knew them thought of Socrates and Darryl as father and son" (*Walkin'* 199). But the story suggests the always-tenuous position of the African American sense of home in America. Socrates's house/home comes under pressure characteristic of the American frontier where the forces of civilization, driven by an individualistic capitalism, raid and exploit the allegedly savage side. His invisible house becomes a visible object of desire for a black capitalist developer, Ira Lomax of the Cherry Hill Development Company (*Walkin'* 204). Socrates's "illegal gap" of a home and he himself have become legal targets because Lomax sees the property as ripe for profitable development and forcibly tries to dispossess Socrates.

The legal struggle for Socrates's house/home reinforces the ambiguity of his African American identity, sharply delineating its doubleness: the Negro and the American. Despite help from Brenda Marsh, a black, female lawyer, the police still treat him as a bad nigger/criminal, assume his guilt, and imprison him briefly for assaulting the goons sent to dispossess him. Nonetheless, through Marsh's perseverance and a compassionate white judge, Socrates becomes legally visible as an American citizen with individual dignity and property rights. His house is momentarily safe as it achieves the juridical definition of home—"legal domicile" (203).[9] The forces of capitalism, however, resort to extralegal intimidation as Lomax threatens to hire hit men to eliminate the house and, if necessary, Socrates. Justice ultimately relies ironically on Socrates again assuming the bad nigger stereotype as he uses indirect threats of violence worthy of a mafia don to intimidate the pusillanimous Lomax, who agrees to provide Socrates a monetary settlement. Thus, in this episode, both Socrates and his house become legally visible. But Socrates's visibility reveals his duality: he is an American deserving justice but also the hated, violent stereotype that becomes necessary to actually achieving it.

Mosley represents Socrates's dignity and new legal visibility as an American in the Edenic garden house that the settlement allows him to rent. Both setting and interior contrast sharply with the bleakness and cell-like character of his former house: "It was a small garden house in the middle of a green lawn. . . . There was a large lemon bush in the center of the lawn. Five feet high and wider still. Golden bees buzzed around the tiny white flowers. A snow white cat flitted in among the leaves of roses that lined the high redwood fence circling the yard" (*Walkin'* 211). The interior, too, contrasts sharply with the worn and dingy cell-house. The garden house has oak floors, painted walls, a fully equipped kitchen, and a large bedroom (212). While he brings his personal guilt with him in the form of "the photograph of a painting of a disapproving woman dressed in red" (216), the king-sized bed, twelve folding chairs, fancy folding table, cot for Darryl, and telephone represent his widening sense of home as surrogate family and connections to community. The garden house becomes the home of debate and pride as neighbors visit to discuss communal issues and admire Socrates's new dwelling. As for Socrates, he smiles at his newfound sense of domesticity and comfort; but his smile also recognizes ironically how tenuous a black man's sense of home is because he knows that he may have to leave it and reassume homelessnes and invisibility to survive: "He had a home that he loved but still he could disappear leaving nothing behind" (216).

In "rogue," the last story in Socrates's odyssey, Mosley brings together the characteristics necessary to resolve the problem of dual identity and to establish the foundation of a new sense of home. Though asserting his rights as an American, Socrates embraces the homely feminine principle of compassion and rejects socially disruptive male violence, literally abandons invisibility, and claims solidarity with his African American community. Witnessing the grief of yet another African American mother over the killing of her teen son by a policeman under dubious circumstances moves Socrates to public protest. In protesting, Socrates makes himself literally visible and tentatively resolves his dual identity as Negro and American. Motivated by compassion, Socrates chooses to act rationally, a decision that frees him from guilt, fear, and anger that so often called the bad nigger into existence. He reasons that he can either shoot or not shoot a rogue L. A. cop who has brutalized the African American community by beating, raping, intimidating, and killing its members in the name of law. This choice to eschew violence and the stereotypical identities it would impose on him frees Socrates for a next step in his progress toward becoming "a civilized man," and toward a new meaning of home—an America where even the marginalized find justice under law. Socrates relates his feeling of liberation from anger and from guilt to his surrogate son, Darryl, in terms that associate self-identity with feeling at home: "I felt free. . . . All my life I ain't never felt like that. I was ready to die along with that man [the rogue cop]. My life for his—you cain't get more free than that. . . . I just stood there—smiling, thinkin' 'bout how good it felt to be in my own skin" (*Walkin'* 241).

Like Frederick Douglass, who agrees to be the silent text witnessing slavery's legalized brutality, Socrates becomes the literal and figurative sign of social injustice. Socrates dons a sandwich board sign that details the cop's history of brutal behavior and his identity—"an enlarged photocopy of the public record" of allegations of police brutality and a photo of "Matthew G. Cardwell Jr., POLICE

OFFICER *and* KILLER" (*Walkin'* 245). In an ironic twist, Socrates's protest reveals the invisible history of law enforcement in L. A. as well as the dual identity of the cop. This visible demand for justice ends Socrates's alienation as he literally houses himself in a cell-like space and stands up for the cop's African American victims. The national and international media amplify Socrates's silent message drawing attention to the riot that ensues his unwarranted arrest for exercising his rights. In another irony, invoking his rights under the law has brought Socrates seemingly full circle back to prison, his house of origin. Unlike his first long incarceration for violating the human bonds to satisfy his own rogue desires, this time he is imprisoned for three days because he has accepted responsibility for human bonds and a group identity, his own blood.

Socrates's victory is not without cost; but, even though he loses his house, he intuits a sense of home rooted in community and civic action. Although media attention forces the police to act against one of their own and free Socrates, he has lost his job and consequently his bright, roomy garden home. Reflecting on his experience, he talks to Darryl not about his loss of the garden house but rather dwells on the power of people acting together for justice when they rallied to protect him from the police bullies: "It was so much power, like fire out of nowhere. There was somethin' to that. Somethin' I always knew was there but I never really thought about it" (*Walkin'* 254). In taking the power to be a man, standing up and being responsible rather than killing like an animal, Socrates has escaped the "niggah" stereotype he verbally rejected earlier and freed generations from its stigma too, as the dream giant had enjoined him: "All [Socrates] thought was that he had to stand up without killing. Because killing, even killing someone like Cardwell, was a mark on your soul. And not only on you but on all the black men and women who were alive, and those who were to come after, and those who were to come after that too" (*Walkin'* 254). Urged to use his international notoriety and power, Socrates only intimates what social good might come of people's power rightly used. He tells Darryl that he can't quite articulate yet what he will do because first "[y]ou got to dream it. You got to make it up. And when you get it right then it'll be there" (*Walkin'* 259).

Emerson encouraged his fellow Americans to dream large and build a metaphoric house and thereby a world, the all-encompassing and comfortable home. Dreaming about harnessing people's power to transform the world into a just American home, Socrates stands at the end of the story a quintessential American dreamer. But Mosley differentiates this dream as distinctly African American, for Socrates's success is tinged with blue notes, the sense that home is still in the making, not yet perfect and still housing pain and the anxiety that one can lose what is cherished, can still be dispossessed. While Iula is Socrates's lover, she is not a wife; while he is Darryl's spiritual guide, he is not his true father; while he has created for himself in his African American identity and community a place to feel at home, he has lost his cherished garden house. Socrates's final move from prison to Luvia Prine's group home, a transformed Big House, both renews old ideas of home and presents a new dimension to the American home. The scorn of the absent woman in Socrates's picture is replaced by the living presence of Luvia, the proper Christian woman, the domesticating and ruling feminine presence central to the idea of home. Having rejected Socrates for his criminal past as a bad nigger, Luvia now grudgingly accepts him into her Big House. The story ends with an African American signed domestic image of homey comfort: Socrates in bed, happy, listening to the blues trumpet of the formerly derelict Hoagland Mars,[10] whom Socrates redeemed from a garbage dump.

Luvia's Big House accurately marks Socrates' progress toward a new conception of home that Mosley has explored in other works like *RL's Dream* (1995).[11] Unlike the archetypal single family house/home central to a version of the American Dream based on individualism, Luvia's Big House seems more akin to what Tamara Harevan identifies as the pre-industrial household that "served the entire community by taking in dependent members who were not related to the family and by helping maintain the social order" (229). The social relations that define home now were then "not restricted to ties of blood and marriage" (229). In Mosley's transformed version of the Big House, Harevan's "ties of blood," a term referring to the bourgeois family, is transformed as Socrates comprehends the more extensive African American meaning of blood to suggest communal identity. Rather than a haven of privacy and privilege, the Big House refigured becomes a place of social intercourse and communal service, redeeming those most in need. As Emerson claimed[12] and Mosley here seems to suggest, the physical dimension of the house is merely the necessary location for the human intercourse and mutual concern that is central to home as world.

Notes

1. As Marilyn Chandler writes, "Our literature reiterates with remarkable consistency the centrality of the house in American cultural life and imagination." In novels it functions "as a unifying symbolic structure that represents and defines the relationships of the central characters to one another, to themselves, and to the world and raises a wide range of questions starting with Thoreau's deceptively simple 'What is a house?'" (1).

2. In writing about *Blue Light*, David Smith notes Mosley's use of the house as home in a number of his novels: "These places—these homes with their gardens—embody the possibility of a balance between private aspirations and public forces, freedom and fate, transcendent hopes and historical limits. They provide a space for life to thrive momentarily in the face of death and social decay" (21).

3. Roberts provides a historical explanation of this important distinction in his chapter, "'You Done Me Wrong' The Badman as Outlaw Hero" (171–219).

4. Both Witold Rybczynski and Tamara Hareven note these characteristics of home in a historical context.

5. Mary Young notes Mosley's use of elements from the slave narrative, specifically the slave pass, in his first three Easy Rawlins novels. In this essay, I extend the catalogue of signs from the narratives of slavery, especially the master's Big House or the slave cabin, to illuminate the present.

6. The Big House inverts the normative understanding of home, creating a sense of geopathology: "an incessant dialogue between belonging and exile, home and homelessness" that "centers upon the figure of America . . . as a *betrayal* of place" (Chaudurhi 15).

7. Historically, the emergence of feminine control and the centrality of the woman (mother) to the concept of domesticity or hominess appear as formative moments in the development of the idea of home. Tamara K. Harevan notes that women were "custodians of the home" (236). Witold Rybczynski writes that the house as it became more intimate gained a special atmosphere: "It was becoming a feminine place, or at least a place under feminine control" (75).

8. Toni Morrison notes the importance of the appearance of the ancestor figure in the development of what she calls village or tribal values: "[T]he ancestor is not only wise: he or she values racial connection, race memory over individual fulfillment" (43). Levecq uses Morrison's concept effectively in her discussion of community formation in *RL's Dream*.

9. See Hollander's discussion of the legal definition of home: "where simply you are at legally, as a citizen, as a social agent" (30).

10. In naming the blues man, Mosley plays on his interest in science fiction and in the possibility of new worlds. Any internet search of Hoagland's Mars will lead to Richard Hoagland's theories about space exploration and possible worlds as well as to his theory about the ancient intelligent society Mars once housed.

11. See Levecq.

12. In his essay "Nature," as in his lecture on the topic, Emerson reflects on the house as a necessary material dwelling for the instantiation of the concept home as a communal site to develop humans' highest potentials. This view resonates with Mosley's in his representation of the house/home. Reflecting on the functions of the house/home, Emerson notes: "Thought, virtue, beauty were the ends; but it is known that men of thought and virtue sometimes had the head-ache, or wet feet, or could lose good time whilst the room was getting warm in the winter" (552). Hollander closes his essay with reference to Emerson's sense of home that transcends the material house (44–45).

Walter Mosley, Socratic Method, and the Black Atlantic

—KEITH HUGHES

In "The American Dream and the American Negro" (1965), one of his many essays on the difficulty of merely *being* a black American, James Baldwin identifies a systemic and historical resistance in American culture to the African American's right to belong: "It comes as a great shock to discover that the country which is your birthplace and to which you owe your life and identity has not, in its whole system of reality, evolved any place for you. . . . You are 30 by now and nothing you have done has helped you escape the trap. But what is worse is that nothing you have done, and as far as you can tell nothing you *can* do, will save your son or your daughter from having the same disaster and from coming to the same end" (715, italics in original). It is a strange "system of reality" indeed which gives you identity while, simultaneously denying you a space in which to live out this identity, a space just to be. Baldwin represents African American experience as primarily an experience grounded in an existential problem; this problem is, quite simply, how to survive in a society that has as its basic premise your nonbeing. The struggle to exist—from Frederick Douglass's fight against the slave-breaker Covey, via the (in)famous "Battle Royal" scene in Ralph Ellison's *Invisible Man* (1952), onto Celie's self-creation through writing in Alice Walker's *The Color Purple* (1982)—is confounded by what W. E. B. Du Bois termed "this double-consciousness, this sense of always looking at one's self through the eyes of others" (Du Bois, *Souls* 364). This resonant phrase from Du Bois's *The Souls of Black Folk* (1903) figures the divided African American self as being forced to fight against both the prejudices of the white world and its own internalization of those prejudices.

One of the myriad ways in which this double consciousness is realized in African American writing is the existence of what we might term an economy of violence. That is to say, violence is deployed and understood as a medium of exchange in the African American narrative tradition, both as a form of resistance (Douglass) and as a form of acquiescence (Ellison's invisible narrator). The acquiescent violence significantly connects to W.E.B. Du Bois's notion of "double-consciousness," the ontological predicament in which one is "measuring one's soul by the tape of a world that looks on in amused contempt and pity" (Du Bois 364). Predominantly black-on-black, this acquiescent violence is a displaced product of rage against the white supremacist world, as in this passage from Richard Wright's *Black Boy* (1945): "The fight was on, against our will. I felt trapped and ashamed. I lashed out even harder, and the harder I fought the harder Harrison fought. Our plans and promises now meant nothing. We fought four hard rounds, stabbing, slugging, grunting, spitting, cursing, crying, bleeding. The shame and anger we felt for having allowed ourselves to be duped crept into our blows and blood ran into our eyes, half blinding us. The hate we felt for the men whom we had tried to cheat went into the blows we threw at each other. . . . I could not look at Harrison. I hated him and I hated myself" (245). In this passage, Wright identifies the self-loathing engendered in the "black boys" who turn on each other. Reduced to mere fighting animals by the white men, both Wright and Harrison turn their loathing of their white oppressors against each other. Such internecine violence, produced by and for white society, is a central concern of Walter Mosley's art in the collection of stories *Always Outnumbered, Always Outgunned* (1997), and fuels the heightened tension encountered by the reader throughout the book.

In *Always Outnumbered, Always Outgunned*, Mosley lays bare the struggle for selfhood, a struggle involving both racial and gendered conflict. Mosley's protagonist, Socrates Fortlow, an ex-convict guilty of acquiescent violence—murder and rape—embodies the striking predicament of the African American subject looking, and fighting, for a place to be. An economy of violence permeates this text, acting as a narrative glue and signifying the tenuous and strained relationship which Socrates has with the social world. However, this endemic violence and threat of violence is not always self-directed, or acquiescent; at times, it is deployed as a kind of countermeasure to the deeper ontological and societal violence perpetrated on Socrates and his fellow inhabitants of Watts: a way of achieving justice, denied by the institutional agents of the law, by alternative means.

In "Midnight Meeting"—the second story in the collection, and thus one of the reader's earliest encounters with Socrates's relationship with violence—confronted with a threat to his community, Socrates considers the necessity for physical confrontation, as the police have no interest in black-on-black crime, and besides "Goin' to the cops ovah a brother is like askin' for chains" (*AOAO* 32). In the claustrophobic "small living room" of his own home (*AOAO* 25), Socrates and some male neighbors debate what is to be done about a violent drug-dealer in the neighborhood, whether to use violence and how much to use; and, "it wasn't the first time that he'd had such a problem" (*AOAO* 29). Recalling his killing of a brutal fellow prisoner, Socrates confronts the present neighborhood situation as an ethical problem, problematizing retributive justice: "I'm sayin' . . . that killin' ain't no answer for civilized men. I'm sayin' that bein' right won't wash the blood from your hands" (*AOAO* 30).

The final confrontation with the drug-dealer, Petis, while seeking the Socratic ideal of justice, ironically resolves itself in what appears to be acquiescent violence, the antithesis of Socratic method. With his demand for silence and obedience to the threat of force, Socrates's voice reveals the limits of Socratic dialogue: "Don't talk, Petis. Nobody wanna hear what you got to say. We come here to talk to you. What you got to do is listen. . . . [I]f I see you anywhere but on a bus outta Watts I'm gonna kill you. Kill you." (*AOAO* 34–35). Acting pragmatically, in a way that Socrates knows compromises his own humanity, he beats Petis to force his compliance and achieve a modicum of safety for the Watts community.

Living in Watts, Los Angeles, at the time of the Rodney King riots of 1992, Socrates inhabits the heart of America's contemporary racialized polity, struggling to find a place to exist, "striving," in Cornel West's ringing evocation of Du Bois, "to survive and subsist . . . within the whirlwind of white supremacy" (West 101). To survive in Watts, Socrates must act pragmatically, thus perpetuating the acquiescent violence resulting from white denial of black existence. If James Baldwin is correct, and the USA provides "no place" for the African American to be, then where *can* the African American exist? Perhaps even more importantly in terms of the Socrates Fortlow stories, *how* do African Americans prevent their descendants from, as Baldwin states, "having the same disaster and from coming to the same end"? How do they end the cycle of acquiescent violence? This essay will explore some of the means by which Mosley seeks correspondences beyond the American homeland, attaching African American cultural and social experience to European and African culture, while simultaneously demanding new, specifically black, cultural spaces in which to operate. In this way, Mosley's writing in *Always Outnumbered, Always Outgunned* echoes Paul Gilroy's attempt in his paradigm-shifting study *The Black Atlantic* (1993) to illuminate the ways in which many black writers have managed to "complicate the exceptionalist narrative of black suffering and self-emancipation in the United States" (Gilroy 121).

Gilroy's argument for the centrality of "black Atlantic" aesthetics and sensibilities in the project of modernity is a compelling one, and Mosley's narratives tap into a similar sensibility regarding the centrality of black experience in the whole construction of modernity. The economic and cultural pressures brought to bear on the black subject from the early expansion of the European slave trade down to the urban poverty and violence of 1990s Los Angeles motivate Mosley's most powerful writing, both in fiction and nonfiction. In *What Next: A Memoir toward World Peace* (2003), a polemical call for African American leadership in the struggle for global peace, Mosley calls African Americans and their slave ancestors "the first pure slaves of mass production, and therefore we are the first bona fide members of the modern proletariat" (29). In his earlier nonfictional book, *Workin' on the Chain Gang* (2000), Mosley places African American experience at the center of the experience of capitalism felt by *all* the exploited of the world. Like Du Bois, Mosley sees African Americans as holding a unique vantage point from which to critique the world, a vantage point gained through suffering, as "[o]ver hundreds of years, black people developed identities designed to deal with the tyranny of capitalism in its most naked state: slavery" (*Workin'* 42). This elevation of African Americans into the vanguard of a class-based politics allows Mosley to establish linkage between the undeniable specificity of African American experience and the generality of the experiences of the working and workless classes globally. For Paul Gilroy, as for Mosley, "black history" is only useful if it is seen as part of a larger struggle. From such a perspective, slavery needs to be understood as "part of the ethical and historical heritage of the west as a whole," rather than being what the black Briton Gilroy terms "special property" (Gilroy 49).

Clearly, any reading of *Always Outnumbered, Always Outgunned* looking to explicate traces of European culture within the text will necessarily have to consider the protagonist's name, a name which allusively associates him with not only the entire legacy of European philosophy, but also with large swaths of European polity and social living. This essay deliberates on the name Socrates, but at the same time warns *against* reading Socrates Fortlow as too directly analogous to the Greek philosopher. Rather, Socratic methodology is adopted and adapted by Mosley and his protagonist so as to be answerable to the specific social and cultural traumas faced by Socrates Fortlow in 1990s Los Angeles.

One of the principal motivations behind the genesis and development of Socrates Fortlow as a character is spelled out early on in *What Next*. In a personal account of his development as a thinking human being, Mosley notes with irony a philosophical black hole: "When I went to school, there were no Black philosophers, at least none that I was aware of, who were recognized by Western universities. All of the philosophers I studied were white (with a few eastern exceptions), and, for that matter, they were all male. Africa, the cradle of civilization, seemed to have no footing in the highest form of human thought. Even the few philosophers who were obviously born on the Mother Continent were most often represented in white face" (11–12). This whitening out to the point of invisibility of black philosophy brings to mind the argument put forward by Charles Mills in *The Racial Contract* (1997) and developed by Bill Lawson and Frank Kirkland in their important reevaluation of Frederick Douglass as a *philosopher*. Adopting Mills's notion of the silent agreement over racial boundaries in culture, Lawson and Kirkland argue for the existence of a "Racial Contract" in philosophy, "in which 'black/colored' voices and texts are to be regarded as philosophically 'dumb' and 'whited out' respectively" (1). Seen from this angle, Mosley is himself being excluded from the label of philosophical novelist. For the "black" writer—not only the African American—the universalist assumptions of Enlightenment philosophy, predicated as they are on a white worldview, already and always present a barrier as much as a key to understanding any African American sense of home.

Recognizing the young Mosley's isolation from a black philosophical tradition, we see him turn to another figure, a more traditional and domestic one, for authority and self-recognition: the father. The relatively complex issue of patrilineal descent is key not only to *What Next* but also to *Always Outnumbered, Always Outgunned* and Plato's Socratic dialogues. Although the topic is deserving of an essay-length examination in its own right, it is worth briefly noting for the purpose of this essay that these works include three examples of literal fatherly relationships: "father" Mosley and Walter Mosley; Socrates Fortlow and Darryl; and Socrates and Plato. Additionally, we also have multiple metaphorical and/or literary fatherings: Mosley as the creator of his father (through writing about him); Mosley as the literary creator of Socrates Fortlow; and Plato as the creator of Socrates (who wrote nothing himself). What is at stake in the mentoring process throughout these texts is the reception and transformation of knowledge *and* method. Whatever wisdom is passed on by the father includes the means of reproducing that wisdom: the sons learn how to learn, and in turn how to teach that inheritance, which invariably will be tempered by their own experience.

In *What Next*, Walter Mosley figures his father as a mentor and guide, but also, crucially, as a philosopher. And not just any philosopher: "I would have been completely brainwashed by this lopsided and racist view of the world if it weren't for my father. He was a deep thinker and an irrepressible problem solver. He was a Black Socrates, asking why and then spoiling ready-made replies. He laughed when things got really bogged down, but he was no Sophist. My father cared about the world he lived in, and so he admitted his confusion about his place in America because he didn't want me to make the same mistake in my life. Or, if I did make a mis-step, he wanted to make sure that I could find the remedy in his great treasury of tales" (*What Next* 12). The focus on the business of self-critical living, of helping Walter avoid making "the same mistake in [his] own life" (cf. Baldwin) is precisely *why* Mosley's father is described as a Black Socrates. The dual sense that identity emerges from behavior and that self-worth is a product of social living, is a crux of Socratic thinking in Plato's major dialogues. In the *Gorgias*, for example, Socrates asserts that "there's nothing which even a relatively unintelligent person could take more seriously than the issue we're discussing—the issue of how to live one's life" (Plato 500b10–500c5).

This struggle to come to grips with the most serious of philosophical questions—how to live one's life—is of course carried out dialogically by the Greek Socrates; and this dialogical approach—an approach reliant upon movement, dynamism, openness to contradiction—finds its analogue for Mosley in his father's dialectical thinking. The dialectical nature of his father's approach to self-awareness strikes a chord with Mosley, and the dynamism of Mosley senior's search for "how to live one's life" is spelled out clearly: "The first thing that I had to work out was that his story unfolded in three stages: First the fearless ignorance that blinded my father to his real place in the world and the real threat of the war; then the violent and frightening experience that made him see that he had been wrong all those years; and finally the wisdom he gained, which showed him that he had to break away from the world he had known, and the world that knew him, in order to act on the knowledge he had gained. His was a path set out in ideas and a system of thought based on a unique experience" (*What Next* 12–13). Mosley senior's path towards "self-recognition" is highly dialectical: broadly speaking it involves, firstly, "fearless ignorance," followed by knowledge gained through the "violent and frightening experience" of war.[1] Lastly, the "wisdom" enabling him to act on the "knowledge" gained.

Mosley's father becomes American, as it were, at a point of crisis. Trapped in the "violent and frightening experience" of war, he embraces a sense of nationhood that Du Bois's notion of double consciousness might interpret as necessarily excluding him. In doing so, there is a certain dogged refusal to bear the ontological strain of "his two-ness,—an American, a Negro; two souls, two thoughts, two unreconciled strivings" (Du Bois 8). For Mosley's father, being American becomes an act of resistance: "Those Germans wanted to kill me as much as they wanted to kill every other foreign soldier. As a matter of fact, them shooting at me was what made me realize that I really was an American" (*What Next* 10). This ontological rupture, a kind of rebirth at the death scene of war, has a dialectical trajectory for Mosley's father, as he weighs up the implications of his Americanness. The implications are heavy in their social and political ramifications, redefining not only his relationship with white America, but also his relationship with himself: "They were shooting at *me*, Walter. . . . I could hear their bullets cutting through the air. When I picked up that rifle, I knew that I had just as much on the line as all those white soldiers. And when I thought about it afterwards, I realized that if I had just as much to lose, then I deserved all that any white man deserved. I became an American in France, under fire and afraid for my life" (*What Next* 15–16).

In a sense, this life-and-death experience destabilizes Du Bois's notion of African American "double consciousness," which Gilroy sees as paradigmatic of modernity. The separate African and American identities constituting the "double" become subsumed in a politically charged demand that the white world accept his Americanness: "That's why, when I was discharged, I left the South and came here to Los Angeles. Because I couldn't live among people who didn't know or couldn't accept what I had become in danger and under fire in the war" (*What Next* 10). However, far from undermining the black Atlanticist notion of the African American as a paradigm subject of modernity, the position adopted by Mosley's father—making his wartime European experience a motivating factor in his resistance to white hegemony—can be usefully read as analogous to Gilroy's in its insistence upon the centrality of black experience to formulations of cultural and political modernity. Mosley senior self-reflexively casts an inflected shadow over the Socrates Fortlow stories, thereby providing a useful framework within which the Socrates stories can be read as textual evocations of an insistent cultural hybridity. Importantly, however, for Mosley—as for Douglass, Du Bois, Wright, and others—this hybridity is not to be achieved at the expense of political relevance. It is not something to be celebrated for its own sake; rather, it is a weapon with which to fight against the ontological erasure.

Having earlier considered Mosley's vision of his father as Socratic in his self-critique and his teaching, this essay will now consider the ways in which the characterization of Socrates Fortlow reaches beyond the dominant paradigms of African American writing towards a more culturally complex black Atlantic rendering of the African American experience. I contend that Mosley adapts Socratic forms of thinking, speaking, and acting to the specificities of Socrates Fortlow's daily experiences in a way that creates new hybridized forms appropriate for 1990s Los Angeles. Put simply, no amount of "self-knowledge" or "knowing how to live" will allow Socrates Fortlow to transcend the racist social environment he inhabits; work, home, even leisure, all are poisoned by the effects of day-to-day discrimination.[2] As Du Bois implies in the magisterial opening chapter of *Souls of Black Folk*, the "problem" is not the black person (7), the problem is the invocation of a "color-line" (15). This problem is not susceptible to individual transcendence, only to negotiation.

The idea of learning lessons from experience, of reflecting on one's own experience in order to better understand both one's self and one's political homeland, and of passing on these lessons to a younger generation, is a central tenet of Socratic philosophy and methodology, as it is also the principal lesson gleaned by the young Mosley from his father: "My father always taught by telling stories about his experiences. His lessons were about morality and art and what insects and birds and human beings had in common. He told me what it meant to be a man and to be a Black man" (*What Next* 10). And it is precisely this pedagogical model that motivates the narratives of *Always Outnumbered, Always Outgunned*.

Before considering the ways in which Mosley's Socrates articulates a pedagogical approach informed both by his European namesake and by Du Bois's idea of double consciousness, we need to recognize that Fortlow is himself a pupil in the process of becoming a philosophical teacher. In "History," Socrates is given license to speak by the proprietor of the Capricorn Bookshop, Winifred Minette, whose "soft voice was ethereal" (*AOAO* 157). Just "sixty-two days and four weeks" out of prison, Socrates is nervous about entering into the heated political and cultural discussions which take place in the bookshop, "shy of the men and women at the Capricorn because they were readers. No prison-yard lawyers or bullshitters. These people studied the history of black-folk because they loved to learn" (157). Interrupted first by the men he is with, then by the doorbell ringing, Socrates seems powerless to speak further, until Mrs. Minette urges him on three times:

"Let him talk, Roland" (157)
"What were you saying, Mr. Fortlow?" (158)
"What were you going to say, Mr. Fortlow?" (158)

He receives further encouragement upon the arrival of Oscar Minette, who enters the bookstore in the midst of the discussion and asks, "What did you say, Socrates?" (159). Encouraged to speak—and to think before speaking—Socrates becomes adept himself at encouraging, at times cajoling, others to do the same; the purpose is to bring about self-recognition.

Socrates's memories of his education at the Capricorn Bookshop surface during the riots that followed the 1992 acquittal of the LAPD police officers responsible for the brutal attack on a black man, Rodney King. Crucially, in resisting the temptation to go outside to "the blocks burning around him" (*AOAO* 153) and become involved in the troubles, Socrates's self-reflexive behavior gives the occasion for the memory, a memory located in the tension between violence and discourse. The initial recourse to the Capricorn Bookshop comes just as the recently imprisoned Socrates is "waiting for somebody to give him a look so he could break their face for them" (*AOAO* 154). Initially, the bookshop offers an almost accidental sanctuary from his own violent passions. Socrates first enters the shop because it may have air conditioning, thereby establishing a metaphorical linkage of climatic heat and incipient violence reminiscent of Spike Lee's film *Do the Right Thing* (1989); in an important sense, the Capricorn offers an alternative to acquiescent black-on-black violence; it offers dialogue, historicization, and an opportunity to acquire greater context for the social strife he witnesses and lives each day.

Reading across *What's Next*, Socrates's decision to stay indoors in 1992 is paralleled by the one Mosley's father made while the Watts Riots of 1965 took place outside his L.A. home. Mosley senior explains to his son that such reactive behavior is, ultimately, self-defeating: "It's not a *real* war, Walter. It's just a bunch'a people tearing down their own stores and their own neighborhood. Most of the people getting killed are Black people, and they're outnumbered. They're right to be mad, and they *should* fight. But those stores are *theirs*. Once they burn down, they're not coming back" (*What Next* 64, italics in original). This sense of an ill-directed rage, inward-looking and constrained in its options by the racially constructed urban polity, echoes the sense in "History" of a chaotic, history-less present.[3] However, standing against this chaotic present is a past that is borne into the present as a treasured counterweight; and its weight comes from expansiveness and hybridity. One key scene, Socrates's dinner at the Minettes' home, formalizes the difficult relationship between the proactive, Atlanticist and internationalist culture of African American progressivism, and the insular enslavement to violent reaction from which the recently released Socrates is seeking to free himself:

The Minettes had met James Baldwin and Langston Hughes and both Martin Luther Kings. They hosted plays on the weekends and had gone to Africa with Louis Armstrong in the sixties.

"We don't have any money in the bank," Winifred said. "But our lives are like treasure chests." She looked at her husband and they linked hands across the table. (*AOAO* 161)

The Minettes's world is distinctively a black Atlantic world, the African American subject connecting deeply (if also perhaps in a somewhat exilic fashion) with Europe—Baldwin with France, Hughes with Spain and Russia—and traveling to Africa to validate the African roots of American music. Indeed, the mention of "both Martin Luther Kings" suggests the even broader cultural boundaries of the tradition of nonviolent resistance; King Jr. looking to Gandhi, Gandhi looking to Thoreau, Thoreau looking to ancient Indian scriptures. Just as Winifred sees their lives as "like treasure chests,"[4] so the Minettes' home and their bookshop are repositories for Socrates, repositories of a hope constructed through dialogic interaction. Like the Greek Socrates, whose "interlocutors are invited to join him in the pursuit of wisdom, rather than to be passively 'instructed' in whatever Socrates has already learned himself" (Brickhouse and Smith 4), Mosley's Socrates creates a discursive space for his mostly younger companions to enter into self-reflective discussion. The teenage boy Darryl, the principal receiver of Socratic wisdom in 1990s Watts, is initiated into the method through main force, but is then allowed space to interrogate his own behavior and to understand the possibilities of change. Having killed Socrates's neighbor's rooster, Darryl is forcefully taken into Socrates's small home, where "Socrates made Darryl sit in the chair while he turned over the trash can for his seat. He read the paper for half an hour or more while the rooster simmered on the hot plate. Darryl knew how to keep quiet" (*AOAO* 18). The enforced silence gives way to dialogue concerning Darryl's killing of a helpless boy—evoking in Socrates a recognition of his younger self in Darryl—in which the "lesson," as it were, is made to grow out of Darryl himself, after initial moral prompting from Socrates:

"You murdered a poor boy couldn't stand up to you. You killed your little brother an' he wasn't no threat; an' he didn't have no money that you couldn't take wit'out killin' 'im. You did wrong, Darryl. You did wrong."

"How the fuck you know?' Darryl yelled. He would have said more but Socrates raised his hand, not in violence but to point out the truth to his dinner guest.

"I ain't your warden, li'l brother. I ain't gonna show you to no jail. I'm just talkin' to ya—one black man to another one. If you don't hear me there ain't nuthin' I could do." (21–22)

The dialogue here forces Darryl to confront his own acquiescent violence in the killing of a handicapped boy; methodologically, Socrates's approach emphasizes self-knowledge, not punishment, and is dialogical not monological.

The skill with which Mosley interweaves the more straightforward "Socratic" approach of spoken dialogue with other cultural forms, to create a hybrid narrative form adaptable to the interconnected world Socrates inhabits, is startlingly realized in "The Wanderer," in which Socrates encounters Gordo, a Vietnam veteran and, like Socrates, a killer. Here, Socrates experiences an immediately recognizable symbolic moment in black American writing: that of being faced by another black man with whom he may have to fight. Gerald Early reads the fight scene in Richard Wright's *Black Boy* (see above) as an ironic reflection on Douglass, arguing that Wright asserts that black manhood *cannot* be attained through direct confrontation with white manhood/white power (Early 26). I would suggest Mosley makes an even bolder move in "The Wanderer," completely disrupting the reader's expectations of the content of the symbolic moment of violence. Socrates—whose name itself suggests cultural hybridity, and dialectical possibility—finds the appropriate image for his experience from far beyond the "black American" world:

> "You got a car?' Gordo asked.
> Socrates felt prickles across his bald scalp. "You sure you ain't killed nobody in twenty-six years?" he asked.
> Gordo's white smile flashed on his dusky face. He let out a low chortle.
> Socrates felt his weight against the soft, giving ground. If he rose up quickly his feet would sink in the sand. The image of a painting that he'd seen in the prison library came into his mind. It was in a book called *The History of European Art*. He didn't remember the painter's name.
> It was a dark scene. Two men, sunk in the ground up to their knees, were hitting each other with cudgels. They were bloody and tired but they were stuck in the ground and had to keep on fighting forever. They were big men too. Bigger than the mountains that lay behind them." (*AOAO* 122)

The painting referenced here is surely one of Goya's so-called "Black paintings," painted by the artist onto the walls of his home *Quinta del sordo*, and now hanging in Madrid's Prado museum.[5] It has no formal title—though it is frequently referred to as *Duel with Cudgels* or *Fight with Cudgels*—and depicts two men fighting with heavy clubs, seemingly knee-deep in mud. Locked inside the nightmarish vision of black-on-black violence, Socrates here finds temporary release in the otherness of European Art. Crucially though, there is a knowledge gap as Socrates can recall "the image of [the] painting" but cannot recall the salient detail of the painter's name.

The anonymity of the picture and its painter (for Socrates) provides its strangely liberating force, giving it a transcultural, hybrid valence. Resisting closure, the picture remains, as one art historian notes, "unresolved . . . incomplete . . . since lacking any intended textual elucidation" (Muller 12). This incompleteness produces both a "lasting disquiet" (Muller 12) and a space to which other texts—including the narrative of an African American ex-convict—can append themselves. The namelessness of the painting is a kind of abdication of control, and it is possible to say that, in one sense, Socrates *creates* it himself (or at least re-creates it) with his movement on the beach.

However, the painting can also be interpreted as a warning against internecine conflict. As Priscilla Muller notes, Goya's painting "has in fact been thought to illustrate the sin of Civil Discord. Its combatants, seen as possibly Aragonese peasants, would represent two highly polarized factions of the time . . . liberals and monarchists. These opponents indeed fought bitterly during the 'civil war' affecting Spain in the early 1820's while Goya created the *quinta* program" (Muller 94). That the painting *can be* interpreted as having a specific Spanish historical theme in no way lessens its relevance for Mosley's story; quite the opposite, as it is the very self-destructiveness of internecine violence among African Americans that haunts Socrates's American homeland. Additionally, Gilroy's contention that African American experience is paradigmatic of the experience of modernity, suggests that Socrates would of course associate with the scene. The ironies of Socrates's encounter with Goya's painting are numerous: the tension between prison and artistic expression, between a black ex-con (socially stigmatized forever by this label) and high European art, but above all the irony that the appropriate image for Socrates's confrontation with Gordo is a painting by a dead white European.

In using a painting from European art to elucidate a vision of African American entrapment, Mosley discovers and develops avenues beyond America's borders in which to situate Socrates Fortlow's ontological struggle. Similarly, Mosley's father specifies that it was his wartime experiences in Europe which initiated his process of self-evaluation This linking of the specificities of black American experience with events and cultural forces from elsewhere, and most distinctly from Europe, is what allows much of Mosley's writing to be considered from a productively black Atlantic angle.

Of course, the third point of the Atlantic triangle upon which Gilroy constructs his paradigm is Africa. One particularly powerful counterpoint to the Goya painting, representative of European culture, is the appearance of an African Ancestor figure in the dream sequence at the end of "Marvane Street." He is described in the text as "a towering, jet-black man. A man with a broad nose and sensual big lips" (*AOAO* 92–93). The figure leads Socrates to "a graveyard that went on for hundreds of miles," which he claims is the burial place of "all the black people that had died from grief" (94). This figure introduces a clearly

Africanist element to the narrative; invoking the alterity of African culture, and particularly manifestations of African wisdom which can compete with dominant European discourses of knowledge, the Ancestor figure has transcultural complexity as it is imported from one home (Africa) to another (America), as a means of resistance and even of explication. The figure ultimately orders Socrates to help dig up the bodies, and Mosley's text here evokes a line of the spiritual, "My Lord, What a Morning": "You'll hear the trumpet sound, /To wake the nations underground." The invocation to bring back the African dead, an invocation which lies at the heart of black liberation theology, seems particularly apposite here as it links Socrates back to one of the earliest African elements in American culture, namely slave spirituals; it also echoes Du Bois, who uses this very spiritual as "the source of his epigraph to the chapter 'Of the Dawn of Freedom' in *The Souls of Black Folk*" (Sundquist 1). For Du Bois, the spirituals are aesthetically one half of the notion of double consciousness he introduces, and which is taken up by Gilroy. Thus, this dream image from the African past helps Socrates focus his life, aiming now at redeeming black people, his home community, from the grief caused by centuries of acquiescent violence to which Socrates had contributed years before.

In *Always Outnumbered, Always Outgunned*—and the succeeding volume, *Walkin' the Dog* (1999)—the triangulation among Africa, Europe, and America settles on the figure of Socrates Fortlow himself; he embodies the hybrid, anti-essentialist matrix of the black Atlantic world. In creating Socrates Fortlow, Mosley has arguably come as close as any contemporary writer to imagining and representing the modern world "from the slaves' perspective" (Gilroy 55). To be sure, Socrates is not a literal slave; however, the perspective he adopts, and is forced into adopting, articulates the ontological nightmare of slavery, in which human identity is stripped away, in which the individual self is objectified so it can be stolen. Indeed, each of the graves of "all the black people that had died from grief [was] marked by a small, granite stone, hardly larger than a silver dollar" (*AOAO* 94); the "silver dollar" acts to forge a symbolic connection between the murderous "grief" and the workings of capitalist economics, most particularly the commodification of human beings—not just black ones, although their position in the "vanguard" gives this scene added force— into units of labor.

This reading of the world from the point of view of one who has to fight to regain and retain his identity, indeed his very being, is compellingly dealt with in the story "The Thief." This story centers on another example of Socrates facing a dilemma in an encounter with a black man. In this case, the man, Wilfred—whose name mirrors Winifred, just as his character inverts hers—is encountered in Socrates's favorite eating place, boasting of his prowess as a thief, riling Socrates into calling him "a fool." It is not, however, the theft of material things from white people which riles Socrates, but the theft from himself of something much more valuable:

"You don't see that you walkin' all over me like I was some piece'a dog shit. An' you don't care. You just put on a monkey suit an' steal a few pennies from some po' woman's purse. You come down here slummin', flashin' your twenty-dollar bills, talkin' all big. But when you all through people gonna look at me like I'm shit. They scared'a me 'cause you out there pretendin' that you're me robbin' them."

Wilfred held up his hands in a false gesture of surrender and laughed. "You too deep for me, brother," he said. He was smiling but alert to the violence in the older man's words. "Way too deep."

"You the one shovelin' it, man. You the one out there stealin' from the white man an' blamin' me. You the one wanna be like them in their clothes. You hatin' them an' dressed like the ones you hate. You don't even know who the hell you is!" (*AOAO* 49)

Paul Gilroy sees Du Bois's notion of "double consciousness" as critical in the development of transatlantic black aesthetics, and in this scene from "The Thief" we have this writ large. Not only is Socrates aware—like Du Bois, like Wright, and like Baldwin—that he necessarily views himself partly through the prism of white racial typography and stereotyping (hence "they scared'a me") but he is also aware that the younger man's sense of self is predicated entirely on the wish to be other than who he is. Socrates has doubts throughout the book regarding his own ontology, and the narratives are expressions of these doubts. He accuses Wilfred (the eponymous "thief"), however, of having both embraced the white world's vision of itself as desirable and its denial of Wilfred's self when he says "you don't even know who the hell you is." Knowing "who the hell you is" takes us back to Mosley's description of his father's dialectical autobiography and then further back to Plato's rendering of Socratic philosophy in the dialogues.[6] There is a certain pointed irony to the fact that Wilfred exploits white stereotypes of the black male for economic gain, although the brunt of the exploitation is borne by other black males who Wilfred is "pretendin'" to be.

Lifting himself up on the beach, Socrates Fortlow can avoid a violent confrontation with Gordo, his mirror image in "The Wanderer." He can negotiate the situation. But, as the Goya painting, which seems to inhabit Socrates's body as a part of the nervous system, attests this is merely the temporary avoidance of a problem stretching beyond his own self-regard. The "trap" identified by Baldwin at the beginning of this essay is not amenable to individual escape; socially constructed, bulwarked by racial discourse, it can only be disentangled through coherent and collective social and discursive struggle. This is the clear message of Mosley's historicist rendering of American racial polity in *Workin' on the Chain Gang*, and it is what lies behind the seemingly endless struggle of Socrates Fortlow to live well. Ironically, it is also the seemingly impossible struggle that makes Mosley's fictions so powerful, so lacking in tidy and convenient answers. The struggle that Mosley, like his father and like Socrates Fortlow, engages in is one for self-identification; self-knowledge. Confronting a violent world, including their own violence, they exploit their experience in order to create a sense of worth for themselves. For Mosley's father this means demanding his rights as an American citizen and refusing to be drawn into the lose-lose world of communal violence. For Socrates Fortlow, it means serving the community as a mentor to Darryl and others, and in *Always Outnumbered, Always Outgunned*'s final story, "Last Rites," enabling his terminally ill friend Right to die "'Drunk an' high'" (*AOAO* 208), like a man. The racialized world offers them no home, as Baldwin points out; so they create their own, out of the disparate cultural resources of a transatlantic world.

Notes

1. Perhaps tellingly, Mosley's father shares these traits with two of Mosley's most famous literary creations, Ezekiel "Easy" Rawlins and Tristan "Fearless" Jones.

2. This is why Easy Rawlins places such importance on owning his own property; despite the fact that it does not always do him much good (and, in fact, makes him vulnerable at times). The same can be said of Socrates Fortlow.

3. His father's emphasis on the rioters being "outnumbered" hardly seems accidental given the title of Mosley's first Socrates Fortlow collection.

4. This statement resonates with the description of Charles Blakey's house in Mosley's *The Man in My Basement* (2004), which proves to be a treasure trove of ancestral and personal history that the protagonist of that novel only gradually comes to recognize as significant to his identity (see Francesca Sautman's essay in this volume).

5. My recognition of the painting as one of Goya's "black" paintings owes a debt to another contemporary writer, the Scottish novelist James Kelman. In his novel *A Disaffection* (1989), Kelman refers to "these amazing paintings done by Goya when he was quite old. . . . They were actually astonishing. Incredible pieces of art. And gruesome" (Kelman 8). In one of these paintings, Kelman tells us, two men, up to their thighs in mud, batter each other with cudgels; seemingly unable to get away from each other—"Stuck fast in the mud, the miring quicksand. . . . Belabouring each other with those stout sticks" (Kelman 10). I sought out the painting, and then, when I read "The Wanderer" shortly afterwards the amazing coincidence of a proletarian Scottish writer and an African American writer using the exact same nineteenth-century Spanish painting to give an image to social struggle jumped out at me. Mosley quite clearly had the same picture in mind. It is very infrequent that "literary detective work" can be so comfortingly easy, and I have no idea if Mosley has read Kelman.

6. And, of course, the quintessential Socratic maxim, "Know thyself."

Devil with the Blue Eyes

Reclaiming the Human against Pure Evil in
Walter Mosley's The Man in My Basement

—FRANCESCA CANADÉ SAUTMAN

Walter Mosley's *The Man in My Basement* (2004) begins with the simplest of questions: "Mr. Blakey?" (3). Intoned by Anniston Bennet at the door of Charles Blakey's family home on Sag Harbor, Long Island, that question, filled with sinister undertones, seems familiar to the reader of Mosley's Easy Rawlins series; the less-than friendly white man, peering at the hero-narrator from his doorway, announces trouble. A small white man endowed with a substantial bank account, a mysterious profession, and undisclosed power, Bennet pressures Blakey to rent him the basement of his three-story home for the summer for an unusually large sum of money and for unknown reasons. Bennet arrives armed with full knowledge of all the details of Charles's life, which he uses as blackmail so that he can remain in Blakey's basement several months. In the basement, Bennet plans to confess his many crimes against humanity and elicit or, if need be, coerce a sort of "absolution" from Charles (120–21; 174).

As the confession unfurls in a vast array of egregious human rights violations, it becomes a potential trap, the site for a struggle between the two protagonists over what constitutes good and evil; truth and lies; the value of human compassion; the entitlements of greed and power; the meaning of history; and, most significantly, what it means to be human. That seemingly abstract debate—actualized in a dramatic conflict over competing narratives of African American history—raises questions of origins, responsibilities, and (implicitly) reparations. That the conflict is verbal makes it no less deadly, as it pits Charles's struggle to attain dignity, community survival and purpose against Bennet's sneering affirmation of power. In the end, bested in the contest, Bennet takes his own life. But one particularly haunting item of his confession recurs, engraving itself in Charles's consciousness all the way to the last words of the novel: "[A]nd whenever I think about children, I remember that there was once a boy who was sold to a dog" (249).

The Man in My Basement provokes serious reflection on a number of issues of international human rights, both immediately political and more broadly philosophical, including a compelling evocation of the disenfranchisement, abandonment, and lack of value ascribed to poor children in the world.[1] There are clear allusions to the destructive impact of a global economy driven by Western and U.S. imperatives, specifically in Africa, where Western schemes have elicited untold misery under the guise of cultivating the "global village." In Mosley's novel, there are numerous references to the 1994 genocide in Rwanda (214, 215, 219, 227), where close to a million Tutsis were killed in a matter of months by Hutu nationalist militias supported by a large segment of the Hutu population, fired up to settle old economic and political scores.[2] Mosley also recounts "crimes . . . fantastic and sick" (240); coups and acts of terror that can potentially destabilize nations; and bombings "that could level a city block or blow a jetliner out of the sky" (233–34).[3] The right to overcome poverty—elusive in most government-driven definitions of human rights, and one whose implications affluent Western powers particularly fear—is blithely quashed by Bennet's apology for the forces of global capitalism.[4] The poverty of millions is maintained through Bennet's "reclamations" business that appropriates their resources, strips them of means of subsistence, and fosters the acquisition of more wealth, including symbols such as the stolen Picasso (187–88). In his harrowing litany of crimes, Bennet recounts: "I once gave a nine-month-old infant as a present to a man's dog" (215); the sacrifice of the infant to a beast then stands for other acts of inhumanity perpetrated as whims or business obligations by agents of the "clean" and democratic West.

The Man in My Basement, an allegorical novel built on the psychomachia that pits the narrator against the self-jailed Bennet and couched in the stylistic frameworks of both the detective novel and the political thriller, is adumbrated by thinking on the place of human rights in today's brutal world. The "new humanity" that the novel theorizes is profoundly shaped by the impetus of race, and thus critical race theory interfaces with human rights doctrines. The importance of human rights as a theme in this novel is deeply inflected by the main character's relationship to a place—at once a house, and a home, and then a community space. Yet *The Man in My Basement* meshes the themes of the cruelest rights violations on a global scale and of the place of home in African American lives in particularly rich and creative ways.

In the global picture, absences of home (e.g., homelessness, exile, being uprooted, chased and hunted down, etc.) are some of the most glaring forms of human rights deprivation for untold numbers of people in the early 21st century. The persistent and detailed references to the Rwandan genocide in Mosley's novel illustrate the power of home as it was denied to hundreds of thousands who had to flee, face massacre, and live in camps. During those events, as Hutus were prompted to kill Tutsi family members, the ethnic terror unleashed battered down all pretense to the permanence of home.

The novel's reminders of the loss of home in Rwanda sets the narrator's struggle to maintain his home on Long Island in a global perspective. As Charles sees his threadbare subsistence unravel and is close to losing house and home, he faces a familiar specter in the poorest sections of the larger African community: homelessness. And his embezzling at the bank, apparently known to employers and others on the Island, proposes not only this loss of home but also creates other familiar specters associated with homelessness: prolonged joblessness and prison, a place that awaits disproportionate numbers of black men in American society. Can Charles, anxiety ridden and marked by a lingering sadness, be unaware of these specters? Charles keeps these terrifying shadows of an existence stripped of rights at bay through the conservation of his home, in which he learns to nurture the representation and spirits of his own ancestors,[5] eventually expanding the notion of home from the individual to the collective as a community museum.

Charles's house is not merely a place to live; it is home in every sense. A quasi-recluse, Charles has built a private universe of memories that sustain him through visual and tangible clues to his deceased parents' presence. Also haunted by the painful and unreconciled memories of Uncle Brent, the house is at once a refuge for him and a place of mourning. And it is mourning that returns the concept of home in *The Man in My Basement* to the burden of intense human suffering inherent in the desecration of human rights. Mourning and sadness are heavy and diffuse in Charles's daily countenancing of the world around him, personal, intimate, pervasive yet incompletely explained. As the novel unfurls, Charles increasingly confronts the explicit social and racial horror he had, perhaps, been able to eschew before Bennet's arrival. It becomes difficult to disassociate his emotions from what has been called "racial grief" and "racial melancholy," applied to authors such as John Edgar Wideman. Gerald Bergevin's remark about Wideman that "[t]ransformative politics comes on the other side of grief, not in resting upon grievance " (76–78) applies to the new Charles that emerges in the narrative. Having heard enough of Bennet's atrocities, he is moved to action, both immediate, to curtail his boarder's indifference to human deprivation, and long-range, to sustain community and ancestral memory.

The Man in My Basement is distinctive within Mosley's *oeuvre*. The relative value and danger of truth, the absence of a classical detective, the realization that what one knows may hurt more than unknowing, all relate it to what Jeanne Ewert calls "metaphysical detection" (179). By using the detective genre as a vehicle to uncover and denounce acts of gross inhumanity on a large scale, *The Man in My Basement* makes it function at another level. The self-incarcerated Bennet notably states: "I am here answering for crimes against humanity" (134). The genre is frequently concerned with politics and political intrigue, something particularly evident in African American detective novels where a strong consciousness of race, black identity, and social injustice is markedly present (Soitos 27, 31–33). Belgian writer Didier Daeninckx's *Meurtres pour Mémoire* (1984), a relentless exposé of the massacre in 1961 by the Paris police of Algerian demonstrators at the Richelieu-Drouot station, is another model of metaphysical detection. With over 200 dead Algerians in the streets of the "city of lights," the massacre was carefully hidden from history for decades, until historians themselves resorted to Daeninckx as a deferred testimony to bring it to light.

In the developing critical awareness of the rich possibilities of linking the discourses of human rights advocacy and the creative work of literature, *The Man in My Basement* makes an important and original contribution. Exposing and denouncing social and political ills is certainly not a new calling for literature. African American literature has nobly held the field in this respect since its inception. The most despairing and angry vision of American society and its racial injustice is evident in the later noir/thrillers penned by Chester Himes, with such violence that the conventions of the genre exploded (Soitos 164–78). Yet, since the 1980s, other writers, especially outside of the Western hemisphere, have forged a new understanding and practice of writing as a tool to denounce injustice and human oppression. They have also translated into a postmodern aesthetic of the fragmented and the disheveled a profound out/rage at the unbearable and the unspeakable. In the face of immense human tragedies like famines and epidemics, and of human destruction wrought by dictatorships and genocide, writers in Francophone Africa, for instance, have undertaken a duty to come to terms with the immensity of grief, the immeasurable in human suffering, with horror that remains beyond what can be spoken, and thus to struggle with the capabilities of the act of writing itself (Canadé Sautman 108–11). Out of the monstrous events of the Rwandan genocide, international writing projects have been born, such as "Ecrire par Devoir de Mémoire" (Writing as a Duty to/of Memory) group.

The Man in My Basement contributes to such a project by evoking Rwanda with a crude brutality of lapidary detail: bodies rot, becoming "deflated bags of maggots," as plunderers like Bennet systematically collect the victim's diamonds, then hide "them safely in a titanium box in the Alps" (215). This scene is an inescapable echo of the reification of the exterminated during the Holocaust that is as uncharacteristic of the novel's general style and tone as it is unforgettable in the narrative of human rights violations. The memory of Rwanda is firmly inscribed in the novel through direct evocations, allegorical figuration, and an eloquent reflection on the importance of remembering that transcends Rwanda proper and becomes vastly allegorical. The violent obliteration of people, individuals, and places flashing through Bennet's confession contrasts sharply with Charles's slowly surfacing, sustaining memories of home and community as the novel weaves back in time. Refusing to forget the death of the infant, the atrocities in Rwanda, and the African American cultural past becomes urgent because forgetting would be complicit with crimes against humanity. But the desire to actively forget Bennet's gruesome memories, his complacent narratives, and his calculating ideology can also be a survival tactic, in effect, asserting the right to be free of impending terror. Such conflicts propel *The Man in My Basement* into a spiraling movement towards political denunciation of the unspeakable.

Bennet also conjures the unspeakable in what he does not speak but implies. His story is shadowed by the specter of a massive human rights violation, situated in the historical past but ever present: slavery. Because of its immensity, some scholars of human rights advocate recognition of the transatlantic slave trade as another holocaust worthy of reparations and contest the unique quality of the terms "unprecedented" and Holocaust applied by Arendt and others as having currency only in relation to the extermination of the Jews by the Nazi apparatus.[6] Allusions to slavery in the novel are veiled, assumed, questioned, and reformulated. Charles's family history and the historical narrative of daily life among free blacks conveyed by the artifacts in his basement turn their back on slavery as the defining feature of African American history as proposed by Bennet's implicit narrative of slavery. Yet Bennet's version of slavery's legacy is evident in his caged performance and in his choice of Charles's home to hide in, ponder his life, and exact the absolution he expects. Charles angrily challenges this choice: "Why here Mr. Bennet? Why my house?" (173). The shallowness of Bennet's repentance is evident as he lists the many benefits of his "reclamations" business ascribed to wars, poverty, and exploitation of labor in Africa; and to Charles's astonished objection, "My house isn't in Africa," Bennet answers simply, "But you are a black man. You come from over there. I need a black face to look in on me. No white man has the right" (174). Later, he adds: "I'm supposed to be down here. Trapped by a Negro, a black man" (237). It is as if centuries of African American history did not exist, as if Charles had no ancestors whatsoever and he had just "arrived" from Africa, unchanged—and unchangeable—reduced to an archetype, a "black face," a silent mask, created solely for Anniston Bennet's performance. Thus, not only are two versions of humanity in conflict in *The Man in My Basement* but two historical memories as well.

Bennet's static narrative of slavery is supported by an artifact. Bennet brings along a lock, the rare artifact of the powerful collector,[7] acquired in Mali, "an original lock used to hold down a line of slaves in the old slaving ships" (125). The white man Bennet's ownership of the slave ship lock is at the very least distasteful; but its implications are serious. They simultaneously write the narrative of slavery onto Charles's consciousness and obfuscate the narrative of slavery itself. Presented like some quaint, harmless antiquity, the lock recalls slaves and "the old slaving ships"—blithely referred to by their function, like whaling ships, not as ships with enslaved human beings peopling them—and works to constrain the narrative. The lock's figuring of the historical Middle Passage becomes a static point. Here the enslaved are denied any form of motion or emotion and imagined as the chattel to which James Baldwin alludes,[8] a state in which confinement denies individuality and humanity. Narrative or poetic representations of the Middle Passage by black writers, on the other hand, place the enslaved between sky and sea, propelled towards an unknown. These dynamic narratives have the capability to search and dig, to reconstitute the consciousness of the enslaved through full awareness of horror. This process is evident, for example, in the burning, eloquent prose of Edouard Glissant's introduction to his *Poetics of Relation* (1990). While Charles has not thought of slavery much before, his imagination, reformulating the lock as a "vicious thing" (125), reacts to the immensity of slavery's horror: "I could imagine that ugly device holding down twenty men in the cold fastness of the Atlantic" (125).

Thus Bennet has formulated Charles's identity as the purported descendant of African slaves, a genealogy he assumes for all African Americans, and one which Charles obdurately resists. Charles Dodd-Blakey is in fact scion to an established and respected African American middle-class family, who have owned a venerable home in Sag Harbor for over seven generations, and whose ancestors had *never* been slaves (125). Bennet's production of the lock is an aggressive interpellation, foisting on Charles a version of history, which is really a discourse of whiteness forged in decades of slavery and colonialism. It is the kind of version Derrick Bell has deplored in discussing African American identity, denouncing the way African Americans are "shaped, molded, changed, from what we might have been . . . into what we are" (75). At the same time Bennet makes slavery the all-encompassing point of reference in Charles's identity, he also wants to obliterate the importance of race in individual destiny and to advocate "color-blind" relations: he dies with this conceit, chiding Charles in his departing letter for worrying about the race of those killed, "as if death had a race" (246)—missing the point that in his (and our) society, it has.

Bennet's banter and apparent friendliness conceal his subsuming of complex African American history through pat narratives; if this particular black man can be brought to appreciate the subtleties of Bennet's fine logic, to see things his way, and purvey the absolution Bennet covets, his performance will be complete. Coolly, Bennet explains his ritual; he invented "Anniston Bennet, the whitest white man I could think up, [who] would be jailed by a black man who really was a blue blood in American history" (219) and receive absolution. Imposing his one-dimensional narrative on a black "blue blood" is even more meaningful, evoking that "old slaving ship"—the residual pretension of unassailable white privilege to mastery, perpetuated in a dominant historical narrative. When Bennet's voluntary caging game is recognized as the obverse of a sinister historical form of capture and lock-up, white privilege becomes clear. He playfully calls Charles his jailer or warden and knows that he can leave whenever he decides to. The cynical performance underscores the underlying presence of racism in the weight of a dominant slavery narrative, wherein African American history is passively inherited and generalized rather than communally constructed. Thus, Charles finally characterizes Bennet as "a slaver of souls in the twentieth-century," and adds, "*I* didn't want to be another one of his slaves" (234–35, italics in original).

The proposition that the history of slavery is inseparable from the genealogy of all African Americans is common enough. Dubbed inescapable by James Baldwin (*Fire* 84), this one-dimensional history is still lamented as belief rather than fact by contemporary activist and journalist Randall Robinson (16). The novel, however, shows history to be much more complex. For example, Charles's family descended from free Africans, while his friend Clarance has a double history: his family has been in Sag Harbor for centuries, "but they came from slaves down in Georgia" (164). African American genealogies do *not* fit one template, and Bennet's deaf ear to a multifaceted African American history and his mouthing of the blanket model of ancestral slavery reaffirm his investment in that "property" of whiteness identified by critical race theorists like Derrick Bell, Cheryl Harris, and Ian López.

Charles Blakey nevertheless succeeds in reclaiming agency for himself and his diverse African American home community represented by individual human types, bourgeois to blue-collar, in his neighborhood in Sag Harbor, Long Island: wise elders, fun-seekers, cab drivers, bank employees, teenagers, homeowners, and antiquarians.[9] The narrator's face-to-face with the horrors of a conflict-ridden, globalized world is imbedded in a close and affectionate connection to a local community threatened, too, by Bennet's whitened history. Charles eventually turns the conniving white recluse into a real prisoner and warps the mandate to secure his perverted legacy, facilitating Bennet's suicide (244–45). But these actions are merely the playing out of the deferred violence of the tale, the generally "male-centered" combat zone inscribed in the *noir* genre. In contrast, victory in *The Man in My Basement* is achieved in an unassuming manner, under the gentler auspices of a cultural activist, the seductive and erudite Narciss, who mentors Charles in salvaging his family heirlooms as pieces of African American history and the memorial material out which the concept of home emerges.

In this struggle, Charles musters the shadowy yet powerful presence of the Ancestors— reified or human, such as the African masks (145, 153); the vengeful and critical Uncle Brent; the benign and watchful eighty-year-old Irene Littleneck, whose face, like a mask, is only visible through the red flicker of her cigarette in the dark; or Charles's protective, deceased parents. They intervene decisively in the psychomachia between Charles and Bennet around the reconstitution of African American history and the affirmation of competing versions of humanity and the human. Inscribed in the novel's very title, the house is central to this network of strength and support associated with the notion of home, and to lose it is more than a sentimental or economic matter for Charles and by extension the diverse African American community. Ironically, Bennet provides the unexpected financial means to keep the house because its basement is essential to his plans for historical whitewashing and recuperation. Charles Blakey's Sag Harbor house is thus fully mobilized as an actor in this war of narratives. For Charles, it is a place of living memory, resonating with his parents' traces: the closet with his father's suits; his mother's sewing room on the top floor; her slippers; and the bag of quilt pieces he sleeps on that audibly elicit her comforting voice for him (129), far from the demonic rage of the man in the basement. There is also a parallelism between the artifacts in the basement—recoverable, valuable in the public eye and highly salable—and those on the top floor. The mother's slippers and sewing basket with quilt pieces are private, domestic and intimate with no salvage value other than for the son in his search for self and identity. Saving the house becomes part and parcel of securing the local African American past through an independent narrative of family history; figuring out how to do it by using the white man's scheme without being his tool becomes a major step in the conflict, and also in the ability to, at least this once, triumph over forces that seem unmovable, untouchable, all powerful.

Bennet does not merely rent space in a house; he intrudes into a complex space, a real home, Charles's home, as the word "my" in the novel's title underscores. Bennet's intrusion makes the refuge unsafe, contaminating the serenity of ancestral and communal presence in this home with his own dangerous and evil presence. He transforms the space of the house, and thus the contours of home, as one part of it—the basement—becomes his, and thus a place to which Charles journeys with apprehension. Ultimately, after failing several attempts at reading himself into Charles's intimate genealogy of lost fathers, as a grotesque Father/mentor, Bennet transforms his part of the house into a tomb. Thus, in the agonistic struggle between Charles and Bennet, the structure of the house—a three-story building—creates a poetics of ascent and descent marked by a quasi-religious symbolism of good and evil: Bennet, the personification of evil, ensconced in his privately crafted little basement hell; Charles, troubled and in search of the good in himself and the world, escaping to the higher reaches of the house. Escaping to the top floor even before Bennet's arrival, Charles remains, at the novel's end, attached to the innocence and comfort of his room: "And I still live up in my childhood room" (249). The ascent/descent contrast reaches its final point with Bennet's suicide and disappearance beyond the basement. Charles quietly buries him behind the house and proceeds to destroy his tapes and, with them, the monument he had wished for: his self-absorbed confession.

Thus, Walter Mosley's articulation of the problems of human rights—their elusiveness, their fragility, their constant violations—is deeply marked by race, history, and the always-in-question status of black rights and existence in today's world. That this shadow reaches the quiet, historically established, black community in Sag Harbor renders it even more ominous and reflects the continued menaced state of the African American home.

"Detecting the text" (to paraphrase the title of Patricia Merivale and Susan Sweeney's study of the metaphysical detective story) of Bennet's half-truths is a matter of both dignity and survival. The contest of wits stands for much larger contested issues: victim status versus that of a free people staking a claim, reparations versus reclamations, being without history versus protecting and transmitting one's own, being a powerless witness to crimes versus hearing a case and being its judge. Bennet admits to human rights violations only after many layers of pseudo-truth have coiled around it, recondite yet trivial in their complacent overuse of moral clichés and canonical Western texts like *The Story of Civilization*, *Wealth of Nations*, and *The Prince* (111–12, 130–34, 146–51, 168–69). Painstakingly, Charles succeeds in unraveling the pseudo-truths, even taping the confessions, but they nevertheless remain ambiguous. Bennet's crimes are at once his own and, as he is quick to underscore, those of our entire society, merely enacted through him (217); they are at once petty in their aims but much larger having global objectives. Bennet acknowledges this when he speaks of the mass consequences of his actions; but he does so in a self-aggrandizing mode, as if drunk on his own power, holding the fate of humanity in his hands. On several occasions, he justifies murder and complicity in genocide by stating that these are actually the means to saving humanity as a whole (229). The home, and specifically, the African American home, seems a fragile opponent for such global mustering of power and evil. Yet, as a metonymy for that elusive and dreamed-of safe space for all human beings sought by Human Rights advocacy, it is one that the novel mobilizes with effective force. A narrative catalyst appears to be the story of the sacrificed infant: it is as if this story had attacked and desecrated the bond between home and childhood at a level so deep that Charles could no longer tolerate it, moving him to action.

In the end, even the "reasonable" expectation of human rights advocacy, a binding quality of the human,[10] has been questioned by the purchase and sacrifice of an infant. Personal enrichment becomes the justification for all actions and the basis for some of Bennet's most cynical disquisitions. The novel thus addresses fundamental ethical questions at the root of human rights: What are the effects of the definition of the human being eradicated, left open to question? What are the implications of an animal being given fuller status and rights than members of the human race? *The Man in My Basement*'s dialogues struggle with the very definition of evil, while recognizing that discourse cannot adequately render it and that attempts to do so lead to more lies (155–57). Naked horror is not merely the violation of human rights, but their complete absence, predicated on the denial of the human itself, a quality that is neither intrinsic nor given, as much of human rights advocacy suggests, but expendable, relative, deniable by power centers to those outside them. The instance of the hapless baby, bought and given to a dog to devour (215–16) merely as an experiment that piques a rich man's curiosity, is crucial in the novel's exploration of humanity and rights. It originates in famine and the action of a mother who sacrifices one child to save the others (238), and

Bennet mentions it for the first time in a list immediately followed by his presence in Rwanda (215). At the other extreme of the monstrous events that led Hannah Arendt to elaborate her theory of the "unprecedented" (Baehr 823) in regard to the the Nazi extermination camps, the lone destiny of the eradicated child, betrayed by fellow humans and given over to the unpredictable behavior of a mere beast, is also a form of the unprecedented. Culminating a list of crimes against groups, in particular the massacres in Rwanda, comes the incident of the most defenseless of human creatures placed in harm's way, beyond human compassion, and deadly force becomes, literally, brute.

In a novel darkened by the conflict between competing interpretations of history and by the place of slavery in history, the unprecedented quality of the example of a baby given to a dog becomes an event that stands allegorically for all the evils and human rights violations perpetrated by states, corporations, interest groups, and their operatives. Charles relentlessly brings up this crime and questions Bennet on his role in Rwanda and the killing, mutilation, torture, and rape (amply retold by witnesses, and retransmitted by journalists and writers). In his memorial to those exterminated, Abdourahman Waberi relates one witness's story about dogs: the usually famished dogs that ran rampant in villages and towns were suddenly overfed, for the number of the dead and dying was such that the dogs feasted on cadavers, and even finished off the wounded (Waberi 60–62). The story of the infant sacrificed to a dog to entertain a rich man is thus allegorical, not farfetched. As such it takes on the power of catastrophe, and thus it is read by Charles.

If whiteness is to be assumed a foundation for these sorts of lethal privileges, the novel mercilessly deconstructs it. As Harris, Bell, and López suggest, the historical and contemporary implications of a conflation between being "white" as a status and being outside of slavery make "whiteness" a proprietary identity. Whiteness as "property" is an illuminating concept in a novel where free enterprise, like Bennet's reclamation business, by any and all means generates an inextinguishable desire for material things, and runs parallel to the importance of being a homeowner in one's own community, exemplified by Charles and his friends.

Thus, a startling twist in the novel is that Bennet, the whitest of white men, turns out not to be what he seems at all. His transformation illustrates what López calls the "plastic" nature of race (194). Bennet's blue eyes are the result of a cosmetic change through contacts lenses; his bald pate is crafted so that "black locks" will not grow apparent; his paleness is borrowed as well as his Anglo-Saxon name (195). He epitomizes what Ian López calls "racial fabrication" (196). His actual name is Tamal Knossos; he is the bastard son of a Greek mother and a Turkish father, a murdered drug addict, whose real name he does not even know (242). Tamal now embodies Charles's earlier statement that white men wear lies like clothes. Because he hails from the borderlands of the Mediterranean, at the confines of the "Orient" and Europe, he is incompletely "white" by the standards of the historical racial hierarchies of the United States, a marginal figure, a transnational noncitizen, a fake "white-man." Working unquestioningly in the service of the rich and powerful, he remains their "precision tool" (229), albeit one that is precisely not "precise" because blurred, unstable, uprooted. The gradual, conscious rooting of Blakey in his family heritage thus stands—as he does not fail to remind Bennet—in stark contrast: "'You're passing as a blue blood,' I said. 'But you're really nothing. You don't even know if your father was Turkish. He could have been Arab or even African'" (195).

Bennet/Knossos thus embodies both the tool and the privileged group membership, and the latter remains racially marked by the lingering stranglehold of whiteness, "that dominate[s] every major economic sector" (Chua 189). It has been pointed out that narrow in-group membership is directly proportionate to more permissiveness towards those who are excluded, relegated to being part of a "different human species altogether, who can be treated with impunity and for whom conventional norms of restraint no longer apply" (Baehr 816). Thus the stakes for Tamal Knossos's crafting of whiteness are high indeed. They stretch from the personal and material advantages of buying into white privilege, to the granting of the needed permissiveness to do harm to others, to acting in concert with powerful "white-men" the world over, who exact their demands, visit their wrath, and exercise their violence on the "homeless"— the vulnerable and dispossessed.

The most compelling response to naked power and destruction in the novel is to provide a different reading of survival. Survival then means circumventing cultural erasure, in this case, the past of Charles Blakey's ancestors that came close to being summarily thrown out on the street by Bennet's narrative of slavery. This reads as a subtext of human rights talk, as the right of a people to its cultural past is increasingly recognized as an urgent form of human rights as Peter Schmidt argues in *Plundering the African Past* (1996). This is not the first time Mosley makes the protection of the African American past a focal point. In *Fear Itself* (2003), published one year earlier, the search for an invaluable manuscript that told a centuries-old black family history was at the center of the plot. To the obliteration, silent and slow, of the African past and that of Charles Blakey its African American descendant, *The Man in My Basement* effectively opposes a quiet resistance, the salvaging and conservation of an unassuming but remarkable African American cultural past that emerges from Blakey's basement, where it had been, literally, mute for years. The increasingly powerful presence of these remnants thus overrides Bennet's dominant narrative of homelessness, of forceful removal and subjugation into slavery. The small ivory masks are not only extraordinarily rare and valuable artifacts—"It's the history of your history," whispers Narciss as she opens their box (63)—not only traces of a lost material culture, but they speak strongly through ritual and representation. They are, as Narciss points out, the real spiritual connection between Charles and his American and his African ancestors. Thus, Charles treats them with great care, as he finds a haven from the white man's awful revelations in communion with his masks and the imagined ancestors he has ascribed to them (145,191). They are the most dramatic device in the novel's recovery of the African American past, not only because of the charge held by masks in African cultures as sacred and untouchable mediums loaded with the voice of Ancestors, but because they do not come alone. The American family objects—clothing, letters, dolls, and other artifacts—Narciss lovingly catalogues and preserves are a testimony to the cultural past of a people blithely assumed by the dominant white mainstream discourse to have no history, or merely one "crushed under" what Randall Robinson calls "the remorseless commerce of slavery" (27). To the muted voicing of these artifacts, the rescue returns both speech and the written word, providing a resistant reading of the past, at odds both with Bennet's banalized slavery narrative and with the literal erasure wrought by time and neglect. In contrast, Charles finally buries the records of Bennet's confession—forty tapes' worth of it—in his basement (248), condemning him and his deeds to an oblivion inseparable from and symmetrical to Charles's role in bringing his family's past and that of the community out of the basement and back to light.

In *Burnin' Down the House* (2005), a study of the theme of "home" in African American literature, Valerie Sweeney Prince refers to Houston Baker's remarks on the politics of space and the importance of setting one's own boundaries on a place, lest one becomes circumscribed by others and literally "placeless" (21). Baker's observation illuminates the struggle for control of place and meaning at once between Charles and Bennet. Sweeney Prince's statement, referring to Morrison's *Song of Solomon* (1977), that "The novel declares that home is untenable—yet, it must be defended, even at the cost of our lives"(9) is a remarkable cipher for the conflicting emotions elicited by home in Charles and the urgency of his final actions. Far from being a narrow, rearguard action, defending and freeing Home, in the context of diverse African American perspectives, brings together the consciousness of human rights and of racial justice that Charles comes to embody.

The Man in My Basement thus links the recovery of the full cultural past of African Americans, in one local community, to the denunciation of global crimes that include expropriation, murder and genocide. In the end, the peaceable, quotidian traces of a family and community past endure in Charles's home museum and overcome the chilling presence of global terror. Though the act of resistance is small, it has vaster implications.[11] *The Man in My Basement* handles the unspeakable of human rights destruction through taught allegorical mechanisms that contrast memory and eradication, spaces (the small tightknit Sag Harbor versus the world at large; the basement and the top floor), objects (the lock versus the masks), and books (the pseudo-philosophy of the terror operative Bennet versus Charles's futuristic fantasy works). The novel resolves the problem of the unspeakable by making it very palpable and oppressive through the wordy flow of Bennet's complacent narrative of inhuman acts and then burying it. To achieve this tour de force with an economy of means, Mosley has forced that unspeakable from the basement up to full exposure, returning to Home its vocation as safe haven and a place to be somebody. He forces silence to speak and condemns to silence that persistent, dominant voice. Thus he confers voice to the invaluable residue that could have remained, in the present system of world power imbalance, forever, the unspoken.

Notes

1. The rights of children are a surprisingly underrepresented area of human rights writing and advocacy, one that is now garnering more attention, in part because of the tragic condition of the child soldier (Ishay, 301–5).

2. See Mamdani, Taylor, and Chua for details of the Rwandan conflict.

3. The jetliner may refer to an actual event: The death of the dictatorial Hutu nationalist president, Juvenal Habyarimana and members of his government, when his plane was shot down near Kigali on April 6, 1994 (Taylor 83, 178 n. 2).

4. Poverty is, for Pogge, at the root of "most of the current underfulfillment of human rights," and could be eradicated against a minimal amount of the "disposable income" of affluent nations (151–52).

5. It is such a negation of home that the poet Etheridge Knight envisions in his poem "The Idea of Ancestry." The poet sees the faces of all his ancestors on the wall of a prison, whose barred exit also symbolizes a personal destiny drawn by a history of racial and social injustice that reaches beyond the individual.

6. Max Du Plessis, a scholar of international human rights, examines the case for reparations on a global scale in "Historical Injustice and International Law: An Exploratory Discussion of Reparation for Slavery" (2003).

7. In his denunciation of the pillaging of Africa's artworks and destruction of its archaeological sites, McIntosh exposes a vast, rotting "tree" of complicities, aiming at Western museums, galleries, dealers, scientists, and "collectors-for-profit": "Collecting art in the international arena has always involved showing power—personal and national—over others" (51–53).

8. Baldwin notes: "I am, then, both visibly and legally the descendant of slaves in a white, Protestant country, and this is what it means to be an American Negro, this is who he is—a kidnapped pagan, who was sold like an animal and treated like one, who was once defined by the American Constitution as "three-fifths" of a man, and who, according to the Dred Scott decision, had no rights that a white man was bound to respect" (*Fire* 84).

9. Sag Harbor is a longstanding free black settlement, dating to the early 1800s when it was a whaling port; it was a known stop on the Underground Railroad. Black professionals began to build their homes there in the 1920s, and since, it has seen flourishing upper-class black neighborhoods (Graham, 168–69), quite different from the ones evoked by Mosley in Charles's world.

10. Among advocates for a philosophy of human rights, there is a desire to establish an internationally "shared understanding" of what human rights are, especially as "moral rights"

(Pogge 158). Human rights should largely be seen as the result of natural law, according to which every human being derives such rights by the mere fact of being born human (Marks 509–14).

11. Deborah F. Atwater and Sandra L. Herndon discuss the importance of the community museum's role in upholding cultural memory.

Easy Women

Black Beauty in Walter Mosley's
Easy Rawlins Mystery Series

—LISA B. THOMPSON

I n the summer of 2006, HBO Films shocked many by casting
Jeffrey Wright as Ezekiel "Easy" Rawlins in their film adaptation
of Walter Mosley's novel *Little Scarlet* (2004) instead of Denzel
Washington who originated the role on the big screen in 1995.[1] Also of note
was their replacement of Don Cheadle with Mos Def as Easy's friend Raymond
"Mouse" Alexander. African American actors seek these roles because Mosley creates complex, strong black male characters that are a rarity in American cinema.
Yet I found myself equally compelled by the question of which actresses the studio
planned to cast in the film, especially in the role of Nola Payne or Little Scarlet.
The roles Mosley writes for black women are as intriguing as those for black men.
Instead of allowing Nola to become just "victim number thirty-four" (13), an-
other dead black woman, Mosley depicts her as a figure so magnetic that Nola
comes to life in Easy's imagination. Nola's beauty, symbolized by her red hair,
haunts Easy with the same intensity experienced by detective Mark McPherson
(Dana Andrews) in Otto Preminger's film noir classic, *Laura* (1944). Unlike Laura
Hunt (Gene Tierney), the wealthy svelte blonde beauty who preoccupies the detective in *Laura*, Mosley's victim occupies the margins of American society. While
Mosley undoubtedly presents refreshing portraits of African American masculinity, what also makes the prolific author's work so compelling is his championing
an atypically complex representation of African American womanhood. In his
Easy Rawlins mystery series, Mosley's protagonist champions women who fall
outside traditional norms of beauty and value—they are rarely white, middle-
class, slender, or blonde. Instead his African American female characters are often
large, working-class women with dark skin and thick lips. In this essay I discuss

how Mosley's rendering of African American women, particularly EttaMae Harris, a recurring character in the Easy Rawlins series, presents an alternative aesthetic in which they represent beauty, power, vulnerability, and Easy's own longing for home. I conclude with a reading of *Little Scarlet*, the ninth installment in the series, because it exemplifies Mosley's reconsideration of black womanhood, challenging both representations of black women in African American literature and views of them in mainstream society.

While Mosley's mystery series celebrates a distinctive beauty aesthetic, his books rarely fetishize one type of black woman. Easy champions women who range from the sophisticated, fair Daphne Monet to his longtime live-in girlfriend, the dark Caribbean flight attendant, Bonnie Shay. Easy also contests the traditional view of black women by defending those who live outside the boundaries of society—the forgotten, dispossessed, and disrespected. Many of them are kept women, prostitutes, grifters, or bar girls. Instead of representing only professional, morally respectable black women, Mosley's series values women with questionable sexual histories and criminal pasts. In one instance in *Little Scarlet*, Easy scolds a police officer for absentmindedly calling a crime victim a "girl," explaining that "I don't like bein' called boy. . . . I don't like our Negro women to be called girls" (239). Mosley's detective not only concerns himself with saving black women's lives, but he also defends their dignity thereby expanding the meaning of black respectability.

Easy's affinity for black women makes a particularly strong statement since American society rarely considers black women valuable enough to defend or avenge. While recent news programs have been accused of fostering a climate of hysteria about missing or murdered white women, it seems society typically regards the violent deaths of black women as normative.[2] It is as if America is inured to the plight of black women; because of their race, and sometimes their class background, society rarely grants them the same worth. Valerie Smith's essay "Split Affinities" (1998), which addresses the Central Park Jogger case, suggests that poor black women who suffer violent ends find themselves particularly neglected by the media which, like the dominant culture, assesses the victimization of women differently depending on their race and socioeconomic status: "The relative invisibility of black women victims of rape also reflects the differential value of women's bodies in capitalist societies. To the extent that rape is constructed as a crime against the property of privileged white men, crimes against the bodies of less valuable women—women of color, working-class women, and lesbians, for example—mean less or mean differently than do those against heterosexual white women from the middle and upper classes" (9). Mosley's hero subverts the dominant paradigm that Smith identifies by consciously imbuing black women's lives with more worth than others typically grant them. Instead of accepting the devaluation of black women's lives and bodies, Easy Rawlins considers black women meaningful parts of his life and the broader African American community.

Mosley's objection to the violence toward and disposability of black female bodies works in concert with his effort to challenge dominant portrayals of African American womanhood. In *Saints, Sinners, Saviors: Strong Black Women in African American Literature* (2001), Trudier Harris argues: "[T]he black female body—with passing connection to reality—was manufactured for white public consumption, whether in print or visual media, or on the stage. Even more fascinating is how such images, especially that of the strong black woman, were embraced within African American culture and eventually found their way into and dominated female portrayal in African American literature" (1–2). Harris goes on to suggest that the rendering of strong and asexual heroines governs the presentation of African American women in twentieth-century black literature. In her assessment of characters ranging from Lorraine Hansberry's urban matriarch Lena Younger from *A Raisin in the Sun* (1959) to the pioneer Sophie Washington from Pearl Cleage's play *Flyin' West* (1992), Harris reveals how black writers have adopted a representational strategy to endow African American women with "suprahumanity" in order to combat demeaning stereotypes of them as licentious, aggressive, and unattractive. Harris rightly discerns that these black female characters operate as isolated figures who are so vigorously self-reliant that their strength often alienates others. In these cases the virtue of strength repeatedly becomes another burden and stifling stereotype:

> These suprahuman female characters have been denied the "luxuries" of failure, nervous breakdowns, leisured existences, or anything else that would suggest that they are complex, multidimensional characters. They must swallow their pain, gird their loins against trouble (the masculine image coincides with the denial of traditional femininity to them), and persist in spite of adversity (they "keep on keeping on"). Black female characters have so frequently been called upon to be strong that strength has repeatedly overshadowed their tenderness, overshadowed their softness, overshadowed the complexity of their femininity and humanity. . . . With strength as their primary trait, they exist in isolated, unchallenged realms of authority where their morality and physical prowess are all they have to comfort themselves. (12–13)

The literary iconography of strong black womanhood that Harris details ironically supports the findings of the Moynihan Report of 1965. These female characters maintain the "tangle of pathology" in the African American family—a set of problems derived from what the report defines as the overbearing black matriarch.[3] The infamous study regards black women as too strong for their own good: their independence is detrimental to the African American man and the nuclear family. Harris's assertion also concurs with Michele Wallace's landmark book *Black Macho and the Myth of the Superwoman* (1978) that suggests that images of black women as "too strong, too aggressive, too outspoken, too castrating, too mascu-line" continue to reign as the prevailing image of black womanhood in American culture (91). This one-dimensional rendering in both literature and public policy discourse dehumanizes African American women, and Mosley's Easy Rawlins se-ries directly addresses this problem, as I hope to demonstrate.

Continuing her analysis of literary character, Harris identifies not only the emotional strength of black women characters but also demonstrates how their physical power distinguishes them. She suggests that their commanding bodies and masculine strength helped the black family and by extension the black com-munity to survive. Harris correctly argues: "Large size in black communities fre-quently brought with it an authority of sorts. . . . Larger women who had the physical prowess to back up their directives with physical force usually held sway" (9); unfortunately, large black women fall completely outside of the parameters of American beauty. In *Venus in the Dark: Blackness and Beauty in Popular Culture* (2005), Janell Hobson contends that "beauty becomes a significant site for politi-cal resistance and aesthetic transformation in which black women, whose beauty has been contested in dominant culture, strive to redefine their bodies by means of reasserting their womanhood and, possibly, their humanity" (7). This notion of beauty is important because, as Hobson continues, "all women are judged by their physical attractiveness and evaluated in comparison to particular standards of beauty based on white supremacy" (7).

In Easy Rawlins's world those notions of beauty are based upon an alternate aesthetic that values African American women of various ages, skin tones, and sizes. Hobson suggests that "[s]omehow, the creation of a black feminist aesthetic must challenge dominant culture's discourse of the black body grotesque and ar-ticulate a black liberation discourse on the black body beautiful" (15). In the Easy Rawlins series, Mosley adopts just such a black feminist aesthetic. Easy's apprecia-tion for all varieties of black womanhood challenges both prevailing beauty ideals and notions of black worth. In this way, Mosley's fiction participates in the kind of political resistance that Hobson advocates in her book. Once a reader enters Easy's world, she encounters standards of beauty that stand in sharp contrast to those that exist outside Mosley's prose. While he could easily subvert dominant stereotypes by depicting black woman as passive, weak, and vulnerable, he opts for a more subtle approach. Rather than simply reviving images of super-strong black womanhood, his characterizations also often suggest a vulnerability and ten-derness lurking behind the tough veneer of black women that exists in so many mainstream representations.

In the Easy Rawlins mystery series, Mosley dispels the myth of the suprahu-man black woman through alternative representational strategies that also allow for a resourceful yet soft, vulnerable, and sensual black woman. Mosley populates his crime novels with black women who occupy the role of the "damsel in distress," a position most often reserved for white women. Black women are the innocent crime victims who either require rescue or need Easy to avenge them. While Easy finds himself attracted to many of the women he encounters, that is not his only response to African American women. At times Mosley presents loving portraits of older black women otherwise forgotten by life. While that demographic is rarely depicted as interesting or dynamic in other contexts, Mosley portrays them as complex women with full histories and intriguing personalities. While on a case, Easy calls upon an elderly black woman; his respectful (and sometimes flirtatious) treatment helps her to remember better times. For example, while pursuing a lead in *Cinnamon Kiss* (2005), Easy must ask the elderly, former restaurant owner Lena Macalister for information. Before he arrives at her home, a caring and prescient Easy purchases groceries, for which she is grateful because "[h]er refrigerator was empty except for two hard-boiled eggs" (141). His visit makes her feel cared for and relevant again. Over all, Mosley's African American heroines humanize the over-determined superwoman stereotype identified by black feminist scholars such as Harris, Wallace, Hobson, and others.[4]

While society rarely deems black women vulnerable, weak, or needy, Mosley endows his black female characters with both vulnerability and strength. Acting within the hard-boiled detective's code of behavior, Easy considers himself a protector of the weak. What makes Easy so compelling is that he often protects black women. Black women characters such as Elizabeth Eady from *Black Betty* (1994), a dark-skinned woman who "had something about her that drove men wild" (14), and the young Juanda in *Little Scarlet* demonstrate how Mosley uses Rawlins to challenge mainstream views about African American women as unattractive, masculine, and super strong. But, most importantly, it is Mosley's EttaMae Harris, Easy's one-time lover and Mouse's wife, who especially disrupts unsophisticated renderings of black female strength and attractiveness.

Easy initially mentions EttaMae in the opening novel in the series, *Devil in a Blue Dress* (1990), but she doesn't actually make her appearance until the second installment, *A Red Death* (1991). Remarkably, although EttaMae appears in most of the Easy Rawlins mysteries, she barely merits a mention by most critics of Mosley's work.[5] In fact, she garners far less attention than Daphne Monet, who appears in only one book. Although Daphne passes for white, EttaMae cherishes her culture and community. Moreover, in her connections to "down home," Easy's past in Houston's black fifth ward, she comes to symbolize important aspects of domesticity for Easy. The omission is also striking because EttaMae may be one of the most compelling black female characters in African American fiction. EttaMae is a prime example of how Mosley defies the literary convention of suprahuman black womanhood critiqued by scholars such as Harris. Mosley depicts EttaMae as a woman of multiple and sometimes conflicting attributes. Alternately strong, weak, seductive, and maternal, EttaMae plays a myriad of roles in Easy's life: lover, confidante, assistant, advisor, and friend. On occasion she needs Easy's help, and at other moments she rescues him. For instance, in *A Red Death* Easy helps

EttaMae navigate Los Angeles. In contrast, in the short story "Lavender" from *Six Easy Pieces* (2003), while Easy works on a case at her behest, EttaMae returns the favor by shooting a villain and saving his life.⁶ In *Cinnamon Kiss*, when an assassin threatens Easy's children and girlfriend, he instructs his loved ones to contact EttaMae if they need to speak with him and before they consider returning home. When arrested Easy also calls on EttaMae for assistance instead of one of his many male friends. He trusts her completely and she provides the kind of safety net that often makes Easy's detective work possible. EttaMae's multi-dimensionality produces an image of black womanhood that defies monolithic renderings of black female strength and power. Her repeated appearances throughout the series allow readers both to observe her character unfold in unexpected ways and to chart the ways her relationship with Easy develops his characteristic longing for home. Alternately soft and powerful, EttaMae persists as Easy's icon of black womanhood's beauty and domesticating power.

Mosley creates a character in EttaMae that defies predictable notions of Western beauty. Easy describes her in *A Red Death* as "[a] sepia-colored woman—large, but shapely"; he considers her "a beautiful, full-faced woman with serious eyes and a mouth, I knew, that was always ready to laugh" (16). Easy is also enamored with her body: "The biceps of her right arm bulged, because EttaMae Harris was a powerful woman who, in her younger years, had done hand laundry nine hours a day, six days a week. She could knock a man into next Tuesday, or she could hold you so tight that you felt like a child again, in your mother's loving embrace" (16). Not only does EttaMae's strong body captivate him, but he adores her for possessing the kind of strength that translates into domestic peace and safety. She provides the detective with the kind of maternal nurturing that is the bedrock of conventional domesticity that Easy has yearned for since he was deprived of it as a little boy.

EttaMae's tumultuous marriage to Mouse and Easy's friendship with him complicate the relationship; Easy's interactions with her are often full of sexual tension. Easy describes EttaMae as his "first serious love" (*CK* 10); and, although he has been smitten with EttaMae since they all lived in Houston, Easy understands that he "had always been her second choice" (*CK* 177). In *A Red Death* Easy speaks of embracing EttaMae: "I buried my face in her neck and breathed in her natural, flat scent; like the smell of fresh-ground flour. I put my arms around EttaMae Harris and relaxed for the first time since I had last held her—fifteen years before" (18). He confesses that, "I looked into her eyes and thought about poetry and my father" (19). Both of these passages, tinged with nostalgia, suggest that EttaMae represents comfort, family, and love; for a man who desires middle-class domesticity, she symbolizes home.

In EttaMae, Mosley creates a character who carries the values of home for Easy and, thus, suggests how Easy's hunger for a material house may be transformed into a home. Easy feels great pride in owning a house and takes many

LISA B. THOMPSON

detective jobs in order to make his house payments. Given, as Clifford Edward Clark, Jr. suggests, that "ownership of the single-family dwelling has persisted as one of the major symbols of middle-class social status" (239), for a black man from the south to secure his own home in California takes on even more resonance. In *A Red Death*, when EttaMae and her young son LaMarque arrive on Easy's doorstep in California, he is elated with hopes that they may become more than friends. When Easy comes home and hears EttaMae humming, he confesses: "The timbre of her voice sent a thrill through me" (16). When he sees what she's prepared in his kitchen, Easy finds himself contemplating the possibility of a new life. Easy describes how EttaMae's seductive and enchanting down home presence has domesticated his house, transforming it into a version of home: "The smells of southern cooking filled the house. Etta had made white rice and pinto beans with fatback. She'd picked lemons from the neighbor's bush for lemonade. There was a mayonnaise jar in the center of the table with pink roses in it. That was the first time that there were ever cut flowers in my house" (18–19). EttaMae's appearance in Easy's kitchen is so significant because while quotidian pleasures are the hardest for Easy to attain and enjoy, they are the things that he values most. Throughout the series he has various, but fleeting, moments of successfully creating a family life, and EttaMae's presence suggests a way in which a bachelor's house can become a familial home. Despite her marriage to his best friend, EttaMae evokes home for Easy, and he considers the possibility of marriage for the first time.

While Easy finds himself drawn to EttaMae because of her sensual beauty, her power to create a comfortable home binds him to all that she represents. Although critics repeatedly mention the fair-skinned Daphne Monet's physical beauty, in *Cinnamon Kiss* Easy proclaims, "Etta's sepia hue and large frame, her lovely face and iron-willed gaze, would always be my standard for beauty" (177). In *A Red Death* Mosley describes EttaMae's attractiveness further: "The love that poetry espoused and my love for EttaMae and my father knotted in my chest so that I could hardly even breathe. And EttaMae wasn't something slight like a sonnet; behind her eyes was an epic, the whole history of me and mine" (19–20). EttaMae, a woman more substantial to Easy than a delicate sonnet, symbolizes the epic of African American history. Mosley's notion of black history that emerges through the Rawlins tales certainly encompasses triumph and survival. Importantly, though, this epic history is peppered with tragedy, sadness, and loss, it also contains Easy's love for EttaMae and for what she represents: African American beauty, motherhood, domesticity, and the African American community.

Mosley's sympathetic portrayal of black women who are simultaneously strong and vulnerable extends beyond EttaMae. In *Black Betty*, he also undercuts the conventional rendering of African American women as undeserving of defense and adoration with Elizabeth Eady, the eponymous Black Betty, a woman who lived to break men's hearts. As a young boy, Easy was nearly struck dumb by Black Betty whom he considered "'bout the prettiest woman I ever seen" (14). When

Easy is hired to look for Betty, he views an old photograph that evokes her danger-ous sexuality and power: "Her name struck a dark chord at the back of my mind. It fit with the humid September heat—and with my dreams. . . . Lynx handed me an old brittle photograph. Its colors were rose-brown and tan instead of black and white. . . . She was tall and big-boned and very dark, even the rose coloring [of the photograph] couldn't hide Betty's blackness. Her mouth was open as if she were smiling and flirting with the photographer. It brought a sense of intimacy that few amateur photographs have. Intimacy but not warmth. Black Betty wasn't your warm sort of home-making girl. . . . Betty was a great shark of a woman. Men died in her wake" (12–14). Easy finds this representation of Betty alluring and dangerous. Despite her size and strength, she does not exude the kind of domestic warmth customarily associated with large black women. And even though she is a mother, Betty is no mammy figure. She evokes intimacy, but little maternal tenderness.

However, later, Easy encounters Betty in the flesh and views her distress when she learns that her beloved daughter has been murdered. Meeting her in person evokes a conflicted response: " 'Noooo,' Betty beseeched with upturned eyes. She began to tear at her chest, ripping open the man's work shirt that she wore, reveal-ing a large breast that looked as if it had never suckled a child. I tried to cover her up but all I did was to keep grabbing her like some rough kind of lover. . . . Betty turned . . . in rage and terror. . . . We got Betty up and led her to the bedroom. Felix took off her clothes and dressed her in a nightgown. He surrounded her head with pillows and kept his body between the bed and me and Saul. All the while Betty was sighing and muttering to herself. I didn't understand the words but I know what she was saying" (241–42). In this scene, Mosley draws a complex por-trait of strength and weakness, courage and pain, beauty and vulgarity, maternity and raw sexuality. Easy's conflicting fear, empathy, and arousal reveal an apprecia-tion for Betty as a woman and as a mother. He recognizes her maternal suffering even while he simultaneously appraises her body. Betty's demonstration of incon-solable grief—overturning furniture, breaking dishes, shattering a mirror—and her nudity elicit an awkward response from Easy as he attempts to shield her body like "some rough kind of lover," and he acknowledges his failure to console her. Although Black Betty is a strong and dangerous woman, Mosley allows for her fragility by revealing the powerful connection with her daughter. At this climax of the novel when Easy meets the photographic image in the flesh, Mosley compli-cates his representation of the sexy and tough Betty by rendering her devastation in the face of loss. Despite Betty's promiscuous and risky lifestyle, she deeply loves her children. Her maternal aspect now balances the power and danger Easy felt viewing the photograph.

In *Little Scarlet*, set in 1965 four years after Betty's story, Easy finds himself immediately attracted to Juanda, a young woman he meets after the Watts ri-ots while investigating Nola Payne's murder. She is sexually alluring and also a reminder of Easy's down home roots and thus another emblem of his longing for domesticity: "Juanda was waiting out in front of her door on Grape Street. She had preened a bit too. She was wearing a white mini-skirt and a tight-fitting multicolored striped blouse. She wore no hose or socks and only simple leather-like sandals. She wore no jewelry and had nothing in her hair. Juanda's hair was not straightened, which was rare for Negro women in the ghettos of America at that time. Her hair was natural and only slightly trimmed. There was a wildness to it that was almost pubic" (138). Juanda's "natural" African American hair signifies a "wildness" that is provocative and sexual. While Easy considers Juanda a "poor man's dream" because of her simple ways and natural beauty, he also values Juanda because she willingly makes sacrifices in order to aid him in the case (68). As with his descriptions of EttaMae, Mosley once again evokes Easy's longing for traditional domesticity when he likens Juanda's conversation to "home cooking" (139). Although he is in a relationship with the cosmopolitan Bonnie Shay when he meets Juanda, much like EttaMae, she feeds some of Easy's hunger for his past and home in the South.

Like Mosley's other black women characters in the Easy Rawlins novels, Juanda contests unflattering notions about the beauty and value of black women. But for Mosley black beauty is more than skin deep and like many of his other black women, she also evokes traditional conventions of domesticity that essentialize black womanhood. In this way, black women characters often function as maternal figures or romantic blues-tinged symbols of the race. Throughout the series Easy particularly romanticizes southern black women. He appreciates the Ethelines, Rubys, Juanitas, Georgettes, and the EttaMaes who remind him of the rare sweetness in a painful Texas childhood that orphaned him by age eight. Although these women all live in Los Angeles, the southernness of their names reveals the southern culture transplanted to the black Los Angeles neighborhoods that Easy and his heroines now call home. When Juanda tells him a story using "the prattle that [I] hadn't heard since childhood," Easy confesses that he "could have listened to her for weeks without getting tired" because "she was from down home, Louisiana and Texas" (139). The rhythmic voices of these women populate Mosley's work and while the world devalues and neglects them, Easy recognizes their importance, meaning, and worth, especially in nurturing the African American sense of home and community.

That Mosley values black women for their beauty and centrality to community becomes clear in Easy's reactions in *Little Scarlet* to the serial murders of African American women that set him in motion. Easy agrees to aid the police who are slow to connect the murder of Nola Payne, dismissively labeled "victim number thirty-four," to thirty-three other African American women (13). Like the killing of black bar girls in *White Butterfly* (1992), which is set in 1956, this fictional crime spree is reminiscent of the murders of twenty-nine African American children killed in Atlanta between 1979 and 1981 when law enforcement officials were also accused of failing to see a pattern or connection among the murders.[7] Throughout *Little Scarlet* Easy comments on the value of black lives but is especially adamant about the worth of black women. When the Los Angeles Police Department calls on Rawlins just after the Watts riots because they require a stealth operation in order to avoid reigniting racial tensions, Easy complains about the police inattention to African American lives: "With the stack of dead black women on my desk now, I felt differently. Nobody cared about them. I had told the police about what I suspected about Jackie Jay's death. I'm sure there had been other complaints with so many women dead. But the denizens of Watts were under the law with no say. We were no different than pieces on a game board" (204). The slain black women trouble Rawlins because of the value he places on the victims and on the vulnerability of his community. He understands that his warnings went unheeded because of his race and because the bodies of the black female victims are disregarded by those sworn to protect and serve them.

Always mindful of the tragic loss of his own mother and the security of home that black women represent, Easy is haunted by the mistreatment of the dead black women and has a nightmare in which he is forced to confront one of his deepest fears: "I was walking through a full meat locker, wearing only a T-shirt and cotton pants. It was freezing in there. The carcasses were black women hanging from hooks. I recognized all of them but couldn't put a name to anyone. Women I had known from Texas to California as lovers and co-workers, neighbors and friends. They were naked and hard, beyond hope for any heaven or afterlife. They were hung in rows that went on forever and it came to me that I might be in hell. There wasn't much light but I could see" (188). Easy's notion of hell is a place where black women are slaughtered and discarded like animals. In this nightmare the horror does not derive from the danger that he might face, but from his inability to rescue innocent black women and by extension the African American community. When Easy awakens from his nightmare, he is overwhelmed with grief and explains: "[T]he despair I felt was beyond anything I had ever imagined except when I was a child and my mother died while I slept" (189). The nightmare returns him to the horror he experienced when he became a motherless child. The tragic loss of his mother and a secure home defines Easy and undoubtedly shapes his devotion to black women and also underscores their vulnerability and that of the community.

Little Scarlet frames Easy's quiet, powerful black masculinity against the beautiful, loyal, and passionate black women who inhabit his post–World War II Los Angeles. Shaken by his nightmares and the difficulty of the case, Easy explains his appreciation for black women to Mouse: "Black women, Ray. You know how they are. Tough as you ever wanna be. Go up against a whole gang to protect her man. Ready to walk away if you do her wrong the next day. But you know about her heart. You know when you talk that sweet shit, she gonna believe every word even if she knows it ain't true. And when you leave her alone it eats at her like acid" (229). Black women hold unparalleled significance for Easy; indeed, on occasion his life quite literally depends on them. Mosley's characterization of black womanhood vigorously contends literary and social stereotypes by representing their complexity, a complexity that is rarely afforded black women who have too long been depicted simply as strong matriarchs upon whose shoulders the survival of the black race depends.

As several critics have noted, Easy Rawlins is interested in "middle-class respectability;" nevertheless, he does not value it at the expense of the black women from his own class background (Mason 178).[8] Easy does not reserve his admiration for middle-class professional women who are often held up as role models for the African American community; instead, he considers working-class women one of African America's greatest cultural assets. At the end of *Little Scarlet*, Easy attends the funeral of Nola Payne and her aunt. Easy finds his reverence mirrored in the minister's eulogy that situates these working-class women as equals to people with more money, honor, and prestige: " 'These women were taken from us, Lord,' he said. 'They were good women who worked hard and who loved each other so much that they come to you in one chariot. They are the best we have to offer, Lord. You may see millionaires and kings and queens this week. There may be saints and hardworking clergy at your door. But no one of them will shine brighter in your heaven. Our own lives will be less for their absence' " (304).

The eulogy stands as a love letter to poor African American women. The minister's words allow Mosley to present working-class black women as worthy of appreciation. Nola and her aunt deserve the reverend's praise not because they were exceptionally strong, moral, or beautiful, but because like Easy, he recognizes their humanity. Easy's reverence for the beauty, power, bravery, and vulnerability of black women calls into question society's treatment of them and makes them central to the creation of an African American sense of home. Mosley's mystery series stands as a significant contribution to the representation of black women in African American literature and culture.

Notes

1. See Michael Fleming.

2. The coverage of the disappearances of Laci Peterson, Chandra Levy, and Natalee Holloway by television news anchors such as Nancy Grace, Rita Cosby, Greta Van Susteren, and Catherine Crier has been excessive. Those victims are typically young, attractive, middle-class and, more often than not, blonde. As others have noted, the disappearance or killing of African American women never garners the same amount of attention. See Alex Johnson and Memott.

3. The notion of the overbearing black matriarch made its formal appearance in *The Negro Family: The Case For National Action*, the United States Department of Labor report authored

by Daniel Patrick Moynihan (popularly regarded as the Moynihan Report). The study blamed the African American mother for a significant amount of the black family's problems.

4. For instance, black feminist critic Patricia Hill-Collins emphasizes the need to acknowledge the diversity of black women so that they are not governed by the image of the strong black woman. See Patricia Hill-Collins, *Black Feminist Thought: Knowledge, Consciousness, and the Politics of Empowerment* (2000). Also, in *Feminist Theory from Margin to Center* (1984), bell hooks argues that "racist stereotypes of the strong, superhuman black woman are operative myths in the minds of many . . . allowing them to ignore the extent to which black women are likely to be victimized in this society" (13).

5. See Wesley; Young; Helen Lock; and Berger.

6. See Mosley, *Six Easy Pieces.*

7. After more than a year and a dozen black children murdered, the Atlanta Police finally formed a task force to investigate the killings. Many criticized officials and remarked that it would be impossible to imagine that many missing and murdered white children without a concerted effort by police to link and solve the crimes.

8. For an extended discussion of class in Mosley's work see King.

The Visible Man

Moving Beyond False Visibility in
Ralph Ellison's Invisible Man *and*
Walter Mosley's Easy Rawlins Novels

—KELLY C. CONNELLY

"Why not give them a glimpse of the man who hid from them in plain sight?"
—MOSLEY, *Six Easy Pieces* (175)

"They see the hat, not me. There is a magic in it. It hides me right in front of their eyes."
—ELLISON, *Invisible Man* (366)

Both Ralph Ellison and Walter Mosley explore the predicament of the black man[1] struggling to define his identity, to find a home within his community, by making himself visible as an individual. In attempting to locate their own place in the world, the narrator of *Invisible Man* (1952) and Easy Rawlins, the protagonist in Mosley's most popular series of detective novels, try on various disguises that the black man has hidden behind in order to survive in America. These disguises have offered safety to the black man, by masking his individuality and rendering him nonthreatening to the white community. Both Ellison's narrator and Easy seek such safety by temporarily donning the guise of the trickster, or the hustler, the man who uses the white man's expectations to manipulate both the black and white communities for his own gain. Both men eventually come to realize, though, the incomplete and untenable nature of the visibility offered by such disguises. They seemingly allow the black man to become visible, or recognizable, to the community—at times even providing a temporary safety thereby—but this visibility is false because all the community can see is their own predetermined notions of the role. In the end, both men ultimately seek to find their identity, their home, in some middle ground between their own invisibility and the fraudulent hyper-visibility of folkloric character types like the trickster.

Throughout *Invisible Man*, Ellison's narrator struggles to become visible as an individual to a world that refuses to accept him as anything other than a stereotypical image. As James B. Lane suggests, "Ellison's fundamental assumption in *Invisible Man* was that black people became recognizable only when they suppressed their real self and conformed to emasculating parodies of the white man's self-contradictory image of them" (65). The black man can become visible to the white community by playing an expected role, but what the community sees is a devalued, inauthentic caricature rather than a whole person. Ellison's narrator is invisible, then, because people refuse to see him unless he conforms to one of the readily identifiable stereotypes they carry with them; they see instead his "surroundings, themselves, or figments of their imagination—indeed, everything and anything except" him (*Invisible Man* 3). The narrator attempts to force those around him to see him, by struggling to make himself heard by the crowd at the Battle Royal, by developing an identity through his education or employment, and by joining the Brotherhood. In each of these attempts, the narrator is unable to transcend the role he is expected to play and become visible as himself, rather than as a type, to the community at large.

Throughout much of the Easy Rawlins series, Easy suffers from an invisibility similar to that of Ellison's narrator. In fact, Mosley has argued that Easy is a direct descendent of Ellison's narrator; he is "a concretized invisible man" (Interview with Samuel Coale 204). If he plays his expected role in the community, the white community will assume that they see him, but what they will actually see is only their own preconceived notions played out in front of them. Easy is invisible as an individual because the white community "couldn't see the man standing in front of [them] but only the man [they] had been trained to see" (*CK* 99). Moreover, Easy is initially invisible even to his own black community: "Nobody knew what I was up to and that made me sort of invisible; people thought that they saw me but what they really saw was an illusion of me, something that wasn't real" (*Devil* 128). No one can see Easy as an individual because he is viewed instead as a projection of the viewer's own fears, concerns, obsessions, needs, and imaginings.

Easy's invisibility is not entirely particularized; it is the black community as a whole, in addition to the black individual, that remains invisible. The white community's refusal to acknowledge the presence of the black community is reflected in the absence of newspaper reports on black Americans of any kind, whether hero or victim: "Fallout in Alaska had increased three thousand percent and there wasn't a Negro in the world worthy of an article" (*BB* 175). Mosley's single overt reference to *Invisible Man* in the Rawlins series subtly emphasizes this refusal to acknowledge the individual accomplishments of black Americans. When Easy tells Civil War enthusiast Robert E. Lee that he has been reading *Invisible Man*, Lee assumes that Easy is referring to the novel by the white H.G. Wells, not Ellison's novel (50). This failure or refusal to see either black accomplishments or the black community as a whole is not only local; Africa is conspicuously absent from discussions of world affairs (*CK* 37). Black Americans could hope, at best, to be a part of the unrecorded history of the world.

At first, Easy takes comfort in the safety offered to him by his ability to remain hidden behind the expectations of others. His anonymity allows him "the safety of being homeless and nameless and not known, not really, to anyone" (*BB* 160). In fact, it is this very desire for anonymity, for invisibility, that has led Easy to Los Angeles in the first place (*GF* 237). He has been able to lose himself by becoming just another anonymous black man in the big city. Easy has not just encouraged but has actively sought out the kind of invisibility he now experiences.

Both Ellison and Mosley recognize that the individual has played a significant role in contributing to his own invisibility. In the introduction to a later edition of *Invisible Man*, Ellison recounts how in an early short-story version of the novel he attempted to depict the plight of a black pilot struggling to maintain his humanity while straddling the line between the black and white communities. The biggest obstacle to the pilot's visibility was his "difficulty in seeing *himself*" (xiii, italics in original). Because he could not accept his unique position as a member of two disparate communities, the pilot was unable to see himself as an individual. Ellison elaborated on this difficulty in *Invisible Man*, depicting a character who "had been looking for something" his entire life (13). What he has been looking for is his own identity; it is only through coming to some understanding of himself that he can begin to make himself truly visible to others.

Mosley similarly argues that the invisibility of the black man has come as a result of his inability to see himself. Mosley explains that "[o]ver hundreds of years, black people developed identities designed to deal with the tyranny of capitalism in its most naked state: slavery" (*Workin'* 42). Not even the black man himself can consistently recognize his true identity because of false identities he has been forced to adopt and multiple masks he has had to wear: "We have notions and hints of who we are, but we cover up quickly and close our eyes because our sense of survival relies on a certain code of behavior and a need to feel anonymous" (57).

Easy Rawlins, like the narrator of *Invisible Man* before him, makes multiple attempts to find a definable self amidst the masks he must wear within both the black and white communities. Both Easy and the narrator of *Invisible Man* attempt to move among white society, adapting their actions and appearance to fit each situation. Rawlins must move between two worlds, as he is an unofficial private investigator who often works for white institutions, such as the police, within a black community: "[H]e continually struggles with the duality of his life—working for a power structure that despises him and living in a community that trusts him with their personal secrets, the tools of his trade" (Lomax 32–33). Although Rawlins knows how to play his expected roles in both communities, his true self remains invisible in both of them.

Both Easy and the narrator of *Invisible Man* find themselves needing to alter or disguise their speech in order to blot out their individuality and remain hidden safely within a folklore stereotype. In *Invisible Man*, the narrator is invited to give his graduation speech on humility as the essence of progress before a gathering of the town's leading white men. Despite viewing himself as a "potential Booker T. Washington" (15), based on his dignity and intelligence, the narrator finds himself fulfilling a stereotypical role, fighting and grasping for coins at the Battle Royal with all the other black men who have been gathered for the enjoyment of the white audience. When he does step outside his expected role, using his articulateness to plead for social equality rather than the more palatable social responsibility, his life is quickly endangered. The narrator's language has the potential to empower him as an individual, and the community is quick to remind him that they are unwilling to allow him such empowerment. The narrator must either remain hidden in the shadows of a stereotype the community will accept or accept the danger that accompanies a black man's demand to be seen as a vocal individual in a hostile white world.

In the early Easy Rawlins novels, Rawlins explains that although he can use the language of both worlds, he is actually more comfortable hiding behind the popular language of the streets: "I always tried to speak proper English in my life, the kind of English they taught in school, but I found over the years that I could only truly express myself in the natural, 'uneducated' dialect of my upbringing" (*Devil* 10). Despite taking English courses at a community college, Easy continues to resist changing his language. When being questioned by black detective Quenten Naylor, Easy reflects: "I could have talked like him if I'd wanted to, but I never did like it when a man stopped using the language of his upbringing" (*RD* 143). Easy argues that in order to fit into white society, black children are taught by their white educators "to abandon their own language and stories to become a part of [their] educated world. They would have to forfeit Waller for Mozart and Remus for Puck" (*WB* 54). Rawlins can, like the narrator, use the expected language of the streets and continue to be seen only as a stereotype to the white community, or he can speak in his own language, blending both of his inherited cultures and suffering the potential consequences of becoming visible as an individual rather than as a type.

Rawlins's liminal position between two communities results in a certain uneasiness about where he belongs. In the early novels, Easy admits a sense of jealousy towards those in his community who have risen to the level of property owner. Unless he is a homeowner, he is visible to the white community only as a type, as an anonymous poor black man: "I felt that I was just as good as any white man, but if I didn't even own my front door then people would look at me like just another beggar, with his hand outstretched" (*Devil* 9). Easy realizes that one way to achieve his own identity, to "buy [his] own life back," is to make money (*Devil* 121). Once again, though, Easy's identity is split. When he actually finds enough money to become a property owner, he allows the black community to believe that he is merely a manager, working for Mofass (*RD* 3). He uses the illusion of his poverty to make himself more threatening and, therefore, more powerful: "Everybody knows that a poor man's got nothing to lose; a poor man will kill you over a dime" (*RD* 108). Easy will go so far as to deny ownership of his properties to his wife, Regina. However, he will admit that he owns properties when this admission will make him visible to the establishment (*LYD* 68). Because Easy refuses to allow either community to see him as he is, and instead chooses to be visible only in the roles expected of him, he cannot feel truly at home in any of the multiple communities within which he must exist.

The narrator of Ellison's *Invisible Man* can be viewed as a prototype for Easy, who is searching not only for solutions to criminal mysteries but also for an identity that will create a unique space for him, a home in the world. The narrator of *Invisible Man* is searching, at least superficially, for the meaning of his grandfather's cryptic advice from his deathbed: "Live with your head in the lion's mouth. I want you to overcome 'em with yeses, undermine 'em with grins, agree 'em to death and destruction, let 'em swoller you till they vomit or bust wide open" (13–14). He is convinced that the true meaning of this proverbial wisdom will reveal a new way to live and make a difference in the community around him.

Easy initially believes that he is seeking home in a different form, through the possession of property. At first, Easy seeks what his closest and most violent ally, Mouse, would describe as a "white" form of home. In *A Red Death* (1991), Easy explains that he is subject to the American view that it is the ability to buy and possess that makes one "a man of substance" (85). Easy will later replace this desire for real estate with a desire for family, collecting children and girlfriends in the process of his investigations. However, he ultimately comes to realize that home is more complicated for him than it may be for other men. For Easy to be at home, he must find a place that will accommodate both his love of family and his love of the streets, his desire to be a family man and his desire to be a detective (*LYD* 186). He will find a sense of home only if he figures out who he is, if he finds some way to be "at home in [his] own life in spite of everything" (*LS* 281). He must find a way to transcend expectations, to live as a unique individual, and to force the community to recognize him as such.

For both Ellison's narrator and Mosley's Easy, the road to visibility and home will not be a smooth progression. Along their paths, both men will adopt the role of the trickster figure, attempting to remain only partially visible by putting on the disguise of a traditional African American folk character.[2] Ellison has described Bliss Proteus (B. P.) Rinehart, whom the narrator will come to impersonate, as "the perfect example of [Stanley Edgar] Hyman's trickster figure" ("Change" 110).

For Ellison though, the trickster figure is actually a blend of Western and African tradition, representing the dual heritage of the literate black man. However, he also represents the false visibility that is available to the black man enacting the trickster role. Although the white community recognizes the trickster as a type of black character, they see only his type and not his individuality. The trickster is, therefore, "both America and the inheritance of illusion through which all men must fight to achieve reality" (Ellison, "Brave Words" 154).

The trickster is defined largely by his willingness and ability to play multiple roles in order to manipulate the community's expectations: "He is a figure in a country with no solid past or stable class lines; therefore he is able to move about easily from one to the other" (Ellison, "Art" 223). He is a uniquely American figure, "a type of leader that has seldom received national attention" (Fleming 430). He is the hustler, marked by his "zoot suits and wide-brimmed hats, his role as a lover, and his street-wise attitude toward life" (Fleming 430). He is also the "black confidence man in his protean guises . . . a dazzling parasite who feeds off the white folk while reinforcing their illusions" (Thomas 98).

Ellison's narrator does not initially choose to take on the protean role of Rinehart voluntarily; instead, he finds himself defined as Rinehart by the society around him. Fleeing from Ras the Destroyer, the narrator attempts to disguise himself in "the darkest lenses [he] could find. They were of a green glass so dark that it appeared black." Putting on the glasses, the narrator finds himself "plunging into blackness" (364). He is, for perhaps the first time, emphasizing rather than attempting to minimize his blackness. Upon adding "the widest hat" he can find, the narrator completes his journey to visibility: "With this, I thought, I should be seen even in a snowstorm—only they'd think I was someone else" (365). The narrator has achieved visibility, but it is a false visibility, as he is seen only as a familiar type, not as an individual.

In his disguise, the narrator is mistaken for Rinehart, a figure who has always been around but has been invisible to the narrator. The narrator comes to realize that although Rinehart has been invisible to him, he has become visible to his community by playing a number of significant roles: "Rine the runner and Rine the gambler and Rine the briber and Rine the lover and Rinehart the Reverend" (376). With these roles comes a power the narrator has never been able to attain. Rinehart is respectfully addressed as "Mr. Rinehart" (370); he has the ability to give other members of his community jobs; his sermons are sold even within the white community; and he has the apparent respect of the police. This respect is an illusion, based not on Rinehart's individual power or identity but on his willingness to play the roles expected of him by the white community and to do so in order to manipulate his own people.

Rinehart's world is one of possibility; it is a world that is fluid and "without boundaries" (376). However, it is also a world of "Rinehartism—cynicism" (381). Rinehart is, in Maceo's words, a "confidencing sonofabitch come in here bluffing"

(368). He offers hope, but it is a false hope, a hope founded on the techniques of the charlatan. Even worse, Rinehart's world is filled with the potential for violence. As the narrator slowly begins to see more of Rinehart's world, he is forced to choose whether to allow himself the possibility offered by his disguise or to continue his search for a new form of self-identification.

As a concerned member of the larger community, the narrator at first attempts to keep a distance between himself and the character of Rinehart, using the possibility offered by Rinehart without succumbing to its corresponding chaos and violence. When confronted by an old friend, the narrator "feints" with a broken bottle, not wanting to fully commit himself to violence (369). However, he feels anger rising in him: "Here I'd set out to test a disguise on a friend and now I was ready to beat him to his knees—not because I wanted to but because of place and circumstance" (369). Like Rinehart, he has allowed his environment to control him. He has given in momentarily to what is expected of him, to the chaos with which Rinehart is associated.

After narrowly avoiding a physical confrontation with his friend, the narrator becomes even more uncomfortable with his adopted role. He begins what will ultimately become his rejection of the possibility and chaos offered by Rinehart. In a handbill, Reverend B. P. Rinehart, Spiritual Technologist, promises that Rinehart will "DO WHAT YOU WANT DONE!" (374). The narrator has seen the potential that this promise holds; through the dark lenses of Rinehart, he has seen the world change and begin to see him. Yet, he will reject this promise of seeming visibility, "dropp[ing] the leaflet into the gutter" (374). The narrator is not willing to commit himself to being Rinehart full time or to following in his footsteps; rather, he wishes simply to don the disguise of Rinehart when it suits his purposes.

The narrator tests his resolve to resist the temptation to become Rinehart through his involvement with Sybil, a married, but lonely, white woman. Sybil cannot see the narrator as an individual; instead, she sees him only as a stereotype of the violent and sexually powerful black man. When Sybil suggests that the narrator pretend to rape her, he is faced with a decision: "What would Rinehart do about *this*, I thought, and knowing, determined not to let her provoke me to violence" (391, italics in original). He almost gives in to her demand that he do her some kind of violence, but he cannot act as Rinehart would because "[s]uch games were for Rinehart, not me" (395). In order to fully inhabit the world of Rinehart, "You got to have a smooth tongue, a heartless heart and be ready to do anything" (373). The narrator is not willing to sacrifice his own morals, or to sacrifice the needs of the community, in order to achieve the kind of personal gains available to a trickster like Rinehart. Rather than living as Rinehart, the narrator chooses to live with a new awareness of Rinehart, knowing that "somewhere between Rinehart and invisibility there were great potentialities" (386).

Ellison has described the freedom inherent in living like Rinehart, the freedom to live in a world "without boundaries" (376). Rinehart, by playing into the expectations of white society in order to manipulate both black and white for his own gain, refuses to acknowledge any limitations on his freedom. Marked by his zoot suit, his illegal activity, his potential for violence, his smooth tongue, his street-smarts, and his willingness to do anything, Rinehart represents one method of survival, and freedom, for the narrator. However, this freedom comes at a great cost. By playing his expected role and failing to define himself as an individual, Rinehart remains in a sense homeless; Rinehart's fluidity may suggest that he is at home in any situation but he is unknown as an individual to anyone. No one, perhaps not even Rinehart himself, can truly know the trickster.

Although Rinehart's freedom makes him seemingly visible to both the black and white communities, his visibility is actually false. To begin with, Rinehart never actually appears in the text of the novel. Although we hear a great deal about Rinehart, and about the type of character Rinehart represents, we never see Rinehart for himself. Even the narrator, whom the reader follows throughout the novel, never sees Rinehart. Despite his seeming importance within the community, he is at all times invisible as an individual character. As a result, Rinehart is never given a voice or a point of view. He is never allowed to speak for himself, to explain his actions, or to voice his own fears, hopes, and motivations. In addition, Rinehart is defined solely by his roles, not by his individual characteristics. Rinehart is the roles he plays; he is a gambler, a lover, a minister, or a violent criminal. He is not a flesh and blood character who can be identified as an individual. For all of his seeming visibility, Rinehart remains an invisible man.

The narrator will therefore reject the seeming visibility of Rinehart, settling for an acceptance of his own invisibility with a plan to make his situation visible by telling his story. He explains, "Being invisible and without substance, a disembodied voice, as it were, what else could I do?" (439). In his acceptance of his invisibility, "a preeminent and self-reliant self lifts out of its confusing history in a *parousia* of self-knowledge and resolves to act or write—conflated by this logic into the same thing—a declaration of coherent identity" (Neighbors 227). He will force the world to see him on his own terms, without adopting any of the stereotypical or folkloric roles by which his ancestors have made themselves visible.

In the Easy Rawlins novels, the folkloric Rinehart figure is recreated in the persona of Raymond "Mouse" Alexander. Mouse represents a step along the continuum from trickster to badman chronicled in John Roberts's *From Trickster to Badman: The Black Folk Hero in Slavery and Freedom* (1989). Rather than relying solely on trickery or manipulation to serve his own personal needs, Mouse, like the badman, is willing to resort to violence even more quickly than Rinehart. However, the badman, like the trickster, "violates social conventions and spaces, virtually at will, and thereby represents not just black disdain for American oppression (and, by extension, trouble of all sorts), but the ability to face hardship and to win" (O'Meally 44). Also, the badman, like the trickster, is admired primarily for this absolute rejection of the white man's laws and for his success in rejecting them (Roberts 214; O'Meally 44). Mouse maintains the trickster's manipulations but adds the badman's violence and solidity and, therefore, represents a blending of the roles of trickster and badman.

The trickster/badman hybrid Mouse and Rinehart have much in common. Most superficially, Mouse's clothing recalls the zoot-suited trickster of Ellison's *Invisible Man.* Within the internal chronology of the series, Mouse first appears wearing "a plaid zoot suit with Broadway suspenders and spats on his black bluchers. He wore a silk hat and when he smiled you could see the new gold rim and blue jewel on his front tooth" (*GF* 4). Mouse maintains his style of dress even while in jail, remaining "decked out in green suede shoes, drab green pants, and a loose bright pink shirt," rather than a prison uniform (*WB* 146). Mouse's attire is a reflection of his inner state of mind, his freedom from society's restrictions, even while under the heavy restriction of incarceration. Mouse's stylish appearance is a reminder that he, like the trickster Rinehart before him, refuses to be controlled by the established order. Mouse's "splendor" in the face of those who would control him through his clothing is also a reminder of his ability, as the badman, to utilize violence without being affected by it. Perhaps Mouse's most distinctive characteristic is his ability to engage in acts of violence without remorse. Mouse's wardrobe is a symbolic reflection of this ability. Junior Fornay, one of Mouse's early victims, is amazed by Mouse's immaculate appearance in the face of unrelenting violence: "I remember when he killed Joe T., you know the pimp? I mean Joe had blood comin' from everywhere an' Mouse had on this light blue suit. Not a spot on it!" (*Devil* 32). His spotless clothing acts as a cloaking device; the police do not arrest him for Joe T.'s murder because they "didn't even think he could'a done it 'cause he was too clean" (32). Mouse's clothing, which places him firmly within an expected stereotype, renders Mouse visible as a type but invisible as an individual.

Mouse and Rinehart are also similar in their ability to serve in multiple roles at once. Mouse never truly deviates from his role as the violent, sexually charged, aggressive criminal who inspires his community with his refusal to accept the white man's law. However, he fulfills other roles simultaneously. He is a master storyteller (*RD* 56–57), a savior bringing out the love and hope in people (*WB* 222), and a bashful man afraid of a powerful mother figure (*WB* 197). At times, even his closest friend Easy is surprised by the range of his associates and by his ability to relate to "normal" people and to think insightfully about his future. Mouse's crises of conscience are temporary and his amoral center always remains steady, but his willingness to consider a nonviolent life and his awareness of his role in the greater community suggest that he has the ability to achieve more than just the mindless violence of the badman or the mindless manipulation of the trickster.

Mouse follows the path to seeming visibility modeled by Rinehart in that his violence leads not to ostracism from the community, but to ascension to the role of local folk hero. From early on in their relationship, Easy has been awed by

Mouse's ability to stand up for what he believes (*GF* 51). Rather than giving in to the white man's rules, Mouse has created his own: "Raymond was proof that a black man could live by his own rules in America when everybody else denied it" (*Six* 201). To Easy, Mouse is "the only black man I'd ever known who had never been chained, in his mind, by the white man" (*WB* 145). By refusing to accept his slave heritage, by refusing to bow down to his enemy, Mouse has attained the only kind of freedom a man like Easy can imagine. It is Mouse's freedom that creates the community's vision of him as a hero: "Mouse had a way of bringing out the love in people. It was because there was no shame in him. For the desperate souls in us all, Mouse was the savior. He brought out the dreams you had as a baby. He made you believe in magic again. He was the kind of devil you'd sell your soul to and never regret the deal" (*WB* 222). Mouse's ability to cross boundaries by living as he chooses, in any role he chooses, marks him as a trickster but also elevates him to "the most perfect human being a black man could imagine" (*Bad Boy* 237).

Despite these glowing words of admiration, Mosley's depiction of Mouse recalls Ellison's ambiguity about the Rinehart figure. Ellison acknowledges that the trickster, or hustler, represented by Rinehart, has attained a certain aura of mystery and prestige within poor black communities. In "Ellison's Black Archetypes" (1989), Robert E. Fleming explains, "[T]he hustler is familiar to any ghetto child and is often the focus of envy or admiration" (430). In his introduction to *Shadow and Act* (1967), Ellison similarly explored this childhood admiration of even the most dangerous of figures: "Looking back through the shadows upon this absurd activity I realize now that we were projecting archetypes, recreating folk figures, legendary heroes, monsters even, most of which violated all ideas of social hierarchy and order and all accepted conceptions of the hero handed down by cultural, religious and racist tradition" (53). It is the ability of these heroic figures to step outside the boundaries of tradition and seemingly to reclaim their own identities that renders them admirable.

The path to visibility offered by the trickster is not without dangers. Mosley demonstrates his awareness of the potential danger in the adoption of Mouse's total resistance to established moral and legal codes through his depiction of Mouse's crisis of conscience, which comes to its climax in *A Little Yellow Dog* (1996). Mouse's temporary breakdown suggests that even the most hardened individual endangers himself in adopting the trickster tradition of Rinehart. Mouse has a reputation for being able to "kill a man and then go take a catnap without the slightest concern" (*CK* 6). However, in *A Little Yellow Dog*, Mouse experiences his first hints of remorse when he kills Sweet William Dokes, whom Mouse has suspected to be his own father. Mouse attempts to repent, but his uneasiness with a life within limits leads him to accept Easy's proposal that he join him on a mission with the potential for violence. Mouse reasons that violence is an inherent part of nature: " 'I'ont think it's wrong to kill somebody, Easy,' he said at last. 'I mean, that's what life is all about—killin', killin' to survive. You see it in bugs and animals—hell, even plants kill to survive'" (*LYD* 256). Shortly after proclaiming that violence is not a moral issue, Mouse is shot while saving Easy's life and presumed dead. Once Mouse has fully accepted violence and chaos as part of his life, he becomes unable to survive. He has given up his individual identity entirely to the type he has portrayed and has lost himself in the process. In his presumed death, Mouse becomes even more like Rinehart himself; Mouse's presence continues to be felt although he does not appear in the novel and short stories that immediately follow.

Easy's understanding of his relationship to Mouse has begun to change in *A Little Yellow Dog*. In the course of his investigation into the deaths of the Roman twins and Idabell Turner, Easy has begun to view himself as more like Mouse. His identification with Mouse becomes so strong that when Mouse takes a drink, the currently sober Easy recounts that "I had the strange feeling that it was me knocking back a drink" (56). Although Easy refuses to call on Mouse's reputation to protect him from Sallie, a vicious gangster, Mouse's presence is still there (91–92). Easy has attempted to distance himself from Mouse's violence in the past, but he now realizes that he is more like Mouse than he once thought. Once Easy begins to recognize Mouse in himself, the two figures switch roles; Mouse is now the logical voice arguing for peace, while Easy is struggling to contain his own murderous rage (260). Mouse has even taken on Easy's trademark desire to educate himself, learning to read *Treasure Island* with Etta Mae and LaMarque. Mouse has tried to become more like Easy, to become a more peaceful family man, but he will not achieve his goals. Easy brings Mouse to one last violent confrontation, watching as Mouse tries to rise, but fails (291).

Although *Gone Fishin'* (1997) was written before and chronologically predates the first five novels in the series, its publication at this point in the Easy Rawlins series is significant. Mosley moves from Mouse's apparent death to the origins of Easy's complicated relationship with Mouse. In *Gone Fishin'*, Mosley describes how Easy initially sought distance from Mouse after Mouse's murder of his stepfather. After Mouse's apparent death in *Little Yellow Dog*, Easy has again become separated from Mouse and can return to his "normal" life. When Easy returns in *Bad Boy Brawly Brown* (2002), he has been "safely hidden" in the bosom of his everyday worklife (137), "living in shadows in almost every part of his life" (266). He realizes, though, that to become someone, to become visible, he must step out of the shadows: "If you wanted to be an important black man, you had to take a risk and go your own way" (237). As a result of Mouse's death, Easy will begin his experiments with various manners of making himself visible.

Near the end of *Bad Boy Brawly Brown* and in *Six Easy Pieces* (2003), the collection of short stories that follows, Mosley depicts Easy's initial attempt to become visible by donning the disguise of Mouse. At first, Easy simply conjures up the image of Mouse in order to gain power over those whose help he needs. He now proactively uses the fact that no one ever saw a body or a funeral to convince unwilling witnesses to provide information (*Bad Boy* 242). In "Smoke," the opening story of *Six Easy Pieces*, Easy quickly realizes the power of Mouse's name and begins using it himself when he investigates the arson and corruption at Sojourner Truth Junior High School where he is head custodian. In this moment, Easy tries on the Rinehart role for himself.

In the role of Mouse/Rinehart, Easy knows no fear. He comes so close to inhabiting the persona of Mouse that he believes he is merely acting as the mouthpiece for his friend (*Six* 28). He tries on not just Mouse's clothing or actions, but his personal tastes as well; when Easy casually orders Mouse's favorite breakfast, he comes to discover a previously unknown pleasure in food (*Six* 31–32). Although Easy is respected, though feared, in his new role, he finds it confusing: "I was walking tall and flush with pride. But in spite of all that I wasn't even sure of my own name" (*Six* 34). Rather than temporarily taking Mouse's place, as Easy had done in the past when he became involved with EttaMae, Easy is now *becoming* Mouse. At this point, he has lost himself to the role he has decided to play: "After all, I wasn't the moderate custodian/landlord Easy Rawlins, I was the crazy killer Raymond Alexander. I was dangerous. I was bad. Nobody and nothing scared me" (*Six* 31). Easy has been unable to play a role; rather, he has become what he intended to only pretend to be.

Easy realizes his unsuitability for the role of Rinehart, in the person of Mouse, when he is called upon to square off against another figure with no fear and no compunction about using violence. Like Ellison's narrator refusing to rape Sybil, Easy finds himself disgusted by the possibilities offered by the trickster or badman's role: "Fear was working its way into my gut because I realized that even though I was using Raymond's name, I'd never be able to inflict the kind of pain that he dished out" (*Six* 36). Easy decides that it is foolish for a man like himself to try to play Rinehart's games. The selfish and violent actions of men like Mouse and Rinehart may be admirable in their resistance to authority but they are ultimately untenable within a community. When Easy is next mistaken for Mouse in the story "Lavender," he corrects the mistake (*Six* 141). Easy wants no mistake to be made; Mouse is dead, not Easy.

Easy will not become Rinehart; instead, he will continue to struggle towards finding himself, blending all of his multiple roles into his own individual identity. Easy has been only falsely visible to white society, which sees him as a type, the poor black man, the trickster, or the badman, rather than as an individual. He has been only partially visible to his own community, which sees him as a resource but lacks a full understanding of his complexity. As a result, Easy has seen himself as lacking a home within both of his assumed communities.

After rejecting his temporary masquerade as the trickster/badman, Easy begins to view himself differently. In a child's portrait of him, Easy briefly sees himself as others see him: "It wasn't the person I saw every morning in the mirror; not the hard-knocks black man from the Deep South. Not my jawline exactly. But it had my spirit and my style. She caught the pride in my eye from being able to help a young boy make it on his way. It was the Easy Rawlins they knew at Sojourner Truth" (*Six* 185). He is "a black man in charge at a black school," (*Six* 86), well read, well respected, and sought after for his ability to control students, teachers, and parents. When Easy is able to blend the paternal role he has adopted at Sojourner, at home, and with his friends, with the tough, street-wise role he must play as a detective, he has found his home. Easy no longer needs the disguise of Mouse in order to be visible; he has become visible through his own actions.

At this point, Mouse can be resurrected to resume the role of trickster/badman. However, there is a significant difference in how Easy and Mouse now relate. In *Little Scarlet* (2004), for example, Easy is confident enough to depend on his own reputation rather than that of Mouse in interrogating a witness and potential love interest (74). Later, the role reversal begun in *A Little Yellow Dog* continues, as it is now Easy who comes to Mouse's rescue by using a letter from the Los Angeles Police Department to allow Mouse to escape arrest for trafficking in stolen goods. However, Easy does not elevate Mouse simply within the white institution of the police force; he also raises Mouse's value within the criminal community. The tables have turned, and it is now Mouse rather than Easy who is awed by his friend's power and visibility.

Easy's visibility reaches its climax in *Cinnamon Kiss* (2005), when he demands to meet Robert E. Lee, the detective who will become his client on a particular case. Ending a long series of cases in which he has no idea who he is ultimately working for or what they are actually seeking, Easy demands to be seen, in person, by Lee, the very same Civil War enthusiast who mistakes the black Ellison's *Invisible Man* for the white Wells's novel. Easy has realized his own value, he has seen himself for the first time, and he is now willing to demand that those around him see him as well.

In *Cinnamon Kiss*, Mouse confirms what Easy has suspected—that the visibility allowed by the role of the trickster is fraudulent. Mouse's dream reveals his fear that despite his "high visibility," he too has been invisible as an individual. Recalling the Prologue of *Invisible Man*, Mouse describes a dream in which he was made of glass. Although people knew he was there, "they saw sumpin' but they didn't know what it was" (188). As Mouse struggles to make himself visible, he begins to bump into people and walls, shattering and turning into "dust blowin' in the air" (189). In this moment, he reveals his innermost fear, which has been hidden even from his closest friend: "An' I'm still there but cain't nobody see me or hear me. Ain't nobody care" (189). Even Mouse has realized the false visibility of his personification of the trickster/badman; while he has been seen, he has been seen only as a symbol and not as a human being. He has played into the stereotypes expected of a Rinehart and has been hidden in plain sight for the entire series of novels.

At last, Easy has embraced his own complex identity and has decided to live, like Mouse, by his own rules. However, his visibility will be more permanent and revelatory than Mouse's. He is still uncomfortable with his newly visible status; his instinctual response to knowing that the Mayor knows his name and that the Los Angeles police department is willing to vouch for him is discomfort. However, seeing himself as others, including EttaMae, see him leaves Easy with "hope out there in the void" (132). Despite his personal circumstances, including Feather's illness and Bonnie's betrayal, Easy has begun to find his way home.

Notes

1. In the Prologue to *Invisible Man*, Ralph Ellison's protagonist dreams of a sermon on the theme of the "Blackness of Blackness" (7). Although the preacher is unable to define what black is and is not, he warns, "Black will git you" (8). Later in the Prologue, the protagonist recalls the words of Louis Armstrong, "What did I do/To be so black/And blue?" (10). In the Easy Rawlins series, Walter Mosley similarly muses on the fate of the black individual in society. In *White Butterfly*, Easy explains, "Defeat goes down hard with black people" (3). In *Black Betty*, he uses the term "black" to describe both Betty, whom he has been hired to find, and Martin Luther King. Given the protagonists' purposeful use of "black" to describe themselves and those within their communities, I will similarly use the term "black" throughout this article.

2. Critics such as Mary Young and Elisabeth A. Ford have suggested that Easy's playing of various roles during his investigations reveal him to be a trickster throughout the course of the novels. However, Easy lacks what Young herself has identified as one of the key elements of the trickster—Easy's goal is not primarily to humiliate "the man" but to survive and to enable the survival of those around him (142). Nor does Easy, like Rinehart, represent "freedom without responsibility" (Schafer 42); at all times, Easy is burdened either by his home ownership, his family obligations, or his debts to his friends. Rather than being a trickster, whose main goal in life is to manipulate those around him, Easy is simply trying on various roles in an attempt to "define himself in spite of the world, to live by his own system of values" (Mosley, "The Black Dick" 133). Helen Lock also notes that Easy has the consciousness that is necessarily lacking in the trickster (85). Despite Easy's manipulation of the white establishment and his black community, he generally lacks the both the fluidity and amoral center associated with the trickster figure.

Fearless Ezekiel

Alterity in the Detective Fiction of Walter Mosley

—JERRILYN McGREGORY

In his work Walter Mosley has created a diverse cast of African American male characters that oppose a prevailing essentialist view of identity. Two of the most powerfully counteractive characters in this vein are Tristan "Fearless" Jones and Ezekiel "Easy" Rawlins.[1] Mosley reveals Fearless "out" in all his rage and fury, whereas Easy chiefly operates on the "downlow," protective of his home and hearth. Easy typifies the folkloric trickster archetype and Fearless functions as the quintessential "badman" vernacular hero. Although they represent different character types, Fearless and Easy each exist as examples of the Other from the perspective of mainstream society. Mosley's putative heroes operate as Others both because of their race and because of their necessarily transgressive actions, making them "criminals by color" (*LS* 235). Both returned as war heroes "old enough to kill men in a war" but are not yet deemed men back home (*Devil* 43). Such an implicitly exclusionary identification functions in direct opposition to the process of realizing a self, or desired personal identity.[2] There is a great deal of empowering potential in both the trickster and badman roles, but neither ultimately offers a fully liberating paradigm for the realization of an authentic self. As a result, both Fearless and Easy fulfill their roles with an additional dynamic twist. Despite being regarded as the Other and, thus, "less than themselves," by oppressive forces, Mosley's African American protagonists contest this status with an additional layer of intentional re-Othering. Through this self-initiated process they gain free agency, positioning themselves as sentient individuals deserving of recognition (i.e., being a part of the American "homeland" for which they fought), not just as figures defined exclusively by their relation to the dominant culture. Confronting internal colonialism by articulating a vast array of defensive mechanisms, Mosley's heroes struggle to reclaim and retain a Self when faced with conditions of imposed alienation.

My approach is ultimately a polycentric critique of Mosley's fiction.[3] Of course, African Americans are not monolithic. Literary critic Lawrence Hogue notes, however, that elitist African Americans "had to crush African American differences, particularly subaltern African America's cultures and belief systems" (39). Yet the vernacular aspect of the culture makes space for internal differences within the group by privileging dialectical utterances, such as "if the shoe fit wear it."[4] In this essay, I argue that Mosley's Easy Rawlins and Fearless Jones detective series position the so-called Other as being derived from (and helping, in turn, to shape) notions of self and identity, thereby disrupting preexisting binary oppositions between privileged and marginalized groups. Mosley constructs a number of extraordinary characters who, if the power structure insists on their alterity, reconstitute their identity as Other by questioning this construction via self-definition. In essence, they invert the existing system by relexively referencing these oppressive forces again as their own Other, or the Other's Other. Rather than simply imposing a double negative, though, these protagonists shift their gaze by constructing an awareness of their regarded otherness while conspiring to combat these exoteric factors by their refusal to internalize oppression.

First, Mosley's fiction contests Western constructions of manhood, offering a new, more complex identity as the "radical Other" through an emphasis on alterity.[5] The radical Other gives meaning to one's self within a collective sphere in which his or her identity is normally extremely proscribed. According to Richard Yarborough, "[Masculinity] contained the following crucial ingredients: nobility, intelligence, strength, articulateness, loyalty, virtue, rationality, courage, self-control, courtliness, honesty, and physical attractiveness as defined in white Western European terms" (168). Nathan Grant explains how these criteria tended to exclude African Americans because of a self-fulfilling presumption of their atavistic Otherness: "Black men, however, had at best a tenuous hold on these definitions. At every juncture was the specter of black male as beast, a kind of raging, drunken Caliban who deserved his end of finally being subdued by his white male betters" (3). Easy and Fearless simultaneously conform to and overturn these presumptions about masculine identities as they enact their own distinct drives for an autonomous self. Easy's friend, Raymond "Mouse" Alexander, exposes his own sense of limitation through his assessment of Easy: "You learn stuff and you be thinkin' like white men be thinkin'. You be thinkin' that what's right fo' them is right fo' you" (*Devil* 205). There are times in the series that Mouse's white "shoes" do, in fact, seem to fit Easy's behavior, such as Easy's sympathy with Chaim Wenzler and brief entanglement with Wenzler's daughter in *A Red Death* (1991). However, Easy's gradual rise to success in Los Angeles is not due to his assimilation into cultural whiteness—an option that his interaction with the federal agents in *A Red Death* tellingly demonstrate is ultimately not available to him—but rather to a complex series of impostures and misdirections regarding his identity—many of which Mouse himself is not aware.

Overt acts of racism against Easy and Fearless foreground one constant, shared experience that inevitably shapes both protagonists' processes of self-definition. Mosley positions the two on the streets of Los Angeles, on the cusp of African American Civil Rights activism. In these dark ghettos, internalized oppression represented the biggest threat. Yet African Americans still achieved entrepreneurship and entered the capitalist system as part of the working class. In this historical context, Mosley casts this pair as the perennial Other, except that they exude a strong sense of subjectivity. Easy subverts all vestiges of the detective archetypes as delineated by Gary Hoppenstand: "The classical detective safeguards cultural rituals with his skills of observation and ratiocination, the avenger-detective with his skills of violence, the hard-boiled detective with his code of personal honor" (94). Implicitly excluded from mainstream "cultural rituals" (and thus from being a classical detective) by his race, Easy instead functions as both an avenger-detective and a hard-boiled detective, working for justice within a generally oppressive, rather than supportive cultural milieu. He battles and is embattled chiefly by institutionalized avenging forces, victimized by racial profiling. While as hard-boiled as they come, Easy's personal honor sways him to resist capitulation not only to "civic corruption, decadence and dishonesty" (Hoppenstand 92) but also the kind of unproductive, overly proscribed racial politics that leave him seething.

On the other hand, Fearless fulfills exoteric stereotypes of the brute; but Mosley instills Fearless with a more nuanced subjectivity. He is no mere "avenging angel . . . upon whom one can rely in difficult times" (Schwartz 42).[6] It is Fearless who determines the clever outcome of the situations in which he and Paris become entagled, even as he exudes the appearance of performing a more ancillary, accompanying role. The proficiency with which Fearless manages not only to extricate them from trouble but to do so in a way that redounds to his financial advantage at the end of *Fearless Jones* (2001) leaves his ostensibly more cerebral sidekick, Paris, in awe: "Fearless drove along, chatting happily. He had bought his mother and sister houses, and he owned the Ford he was driving. I did the math on one-half of one percent. The solution made me sweat" (312). Fearless's machinations in effecting a similarly happy resolution to *Fear Itself* (2003) lead Paris to comment that "Fearless had always come through for me. He's always been a better man than I am and smarter than I am too" (316). Such variegated representations articulate ways in which the radical Other negotiates a *via media* between the Same (i.e., the acceptable and expected cultural norm) and the Other. In Easy's case above, Mouse equates rational, cognitive thought with whiteness, something inherently outside himself; however, by enacting another level of alterity, Easy disrupts such totalizing theories and carves out a space for himself without being assimilated. Similarly, although Fearless maintains a facade of conventional subordination coupled with brute power, Paris remains awestruck by his "peculiar kind of smarts" (*Fearless* 41) along with his communitarian outlook. Whatever the nature of the conflict and against certain odds, Mosley's protagonists achieve their just reward as well as the retention of a fully embodied Self (cf. Hoppenstand's "personal code of honor") through a doubled Othering process.

Neither of Mosley's WWII vets feels himself marginal to a white norm. In a self-reflexive mode when he meets Albright, the white man about to draw him into detection in *Devil in a Blue Dress* (1990), Easy asserts: "When he looked at me I felt a thrill of fear, but that went away quickly because I was used to white people by 1948" (*Devil* 1). In keeping with the postwar historical moment and the pulp fiction and film noir it wrought, Mosley centers his depiction of African American masculinity on characters returning from military action, socialized to kill or be killed. Therefore, they assimilated the construction of alterity required for membership in the armed forces, reversing it to include their homegrown white foes. For African American men, warfare influenced and affected them most into becoming the "tough guy" on which crime fiction thrives.[7] Nyman suggests one way in which this relates to the hardboiled subgenre: "Since only a tough shield or shell helps to save his life, the need for protection pervades [the hardboiled hero's] mind" (33). Nonetheless, Mosley disrupts binary oppositions that embroil the hardboiled detective within dichotomies of "self/other, safe/threat, us/them, white/black, and masculine/nonmasculine" (33). Instead, most whites and authority figures (including Mosley's African American and Chicano detectives Quinten Naylor and Sergeant Sanchez) reify such dualities and steadily lose credibility.

Moreover, Easy does not move to separate himself from the subaltern. Tropes of violence, racial oppression, and social death imbue all of Mosley's texts as a kind of *testimonio*, derived from a "realist theory" of identity politics.[8] Based on his epistemic status, homeownership signals the means to achieve a modicum of, not so much upward mobility, but personal freedom in a world bereft of empathy for the so-called Other. His finances function as a buffer against the ravages of life under oppression. Therefore, Easy declares: "But that house meant more to me than any woman I ever knew. I loved her and I was jealous of her and if the bank sent the county marshal to take her from me I might have come at him with a rifle rather than to give her up" (*Devil* 11). Mosley here instates a survival imperative that some critics have misread as a bourgeois value orientation.[9] However, this imperative also manifests itself on a folk cultural level as interdependency. In *A Red Death*, a novel whose central plot is set in motion by a direct threat to his house, Easy characterizes himself as being "in the business of favors" for people who "had serious trouble but couldn't go to the police" and correspondingly becomes seen as a defender of the subaltern with a "reputation for fairness and the strength of my convictions among the poor" (4).

Historian Robin Kelley notes the economic gap regarding working class African Americans, one that becomes relevant to Easy's situation the more financially stable he becomes. Kelley writes, "Of course, we hear of the successful black middle class, and, on occasion, the phrase 'stable black working class' appears in the texts of some left-leaning scholars—but the latter is generally used as a moral category to distinguish the people we like from the people we don't like, the good Negroes from the bad apples, the Amos's from the Andy's [sic]" (12). This tendency erases the working class principles on which urban laborers formed unions and generally to which they adhered. For instance, Easy's exploits in *A Red Death*, are predicated upon such notions of economic colonialism. The threat to his house due to tax evasion does not excite just because it threatens his quest to attain the American Dream. Critical slippage conflates the American Dream theme to equate middle class attainment with its more politicized adherence to life, liberty and property (land). Easy clearly associates his financial solvency with freedom (*RD* 40).[10] Additionally, communism figures into the plot structure via Easy's covert and coerced assignment from the FBI to determine whether Wenzler relies on his "left or right leg" to dress himself (49). Wenzler is a union organizer and communist, speaking to the blue-collar working class world many African Americans occupied during this historical moment. In spite of his considerable holdings (both in raw terms and in comparison with his peers), Easy positions himself among working class people, seeking a "blue-collar paradise" like that mentioned in *Fearless Jones* (63).[11] Later, his short-lived move to an upwardly mobile neighborhood signifies a desire for anonymity to protect both his two informally adopted children and his own psyche due to the abduction of his only biological child by her mother.[12] By *A Little Yellow Dog* (1996), which is set ten years after *A Red Death*, Easy has clearly come to set great store by living in the working world and supporting its rules of survival (78). He proffers a separate degree of spatialized alterity. Based on his epistemic status, real estate furnishes the means by which to achieve a modicum of freedom and respectability for his wards' sake.

Conventional detective fiction often engages existentialist philosophy, and Mosley's work is no exception in this regard.[13] With its emphasis on freedom, Mosley's fiction offers strategies for how one can be free to act while also remembering that one must act to be free. His strategies of resistance are posed within the context of the most insidious forms of antiblack racism. By intention and design, internal colonialism makes tangible a sense of real difference to produce a sense of real Otherness, something that Mosley depicts his protagonists resisting again and again in his work. *Devil in a Blue Dress* introduces Easy exiting graciously from his "good job" at Champion Aircraft having refused to kowtow to a racist foreman, Giacomo: "My bills were paid and it felt good to have stood up for myself. I had a notion of freedom when I walked out to my car" (67). While the freedom he seeks is not absolute, his self emerges unscathed without having to "save face and still kiss [Giacomo's] ass" (66). While existentialism is well recognized within the genre of detective fiction, via Easy it speaks directly to the absurd reality faced by African Americans, particularly after a second world war to make the planet safe for democracy once and for all. Easy locates the essence of his own freedom, supplying its own existence. Fearless is similarly exalted as the epitome of freedom and responsibility, even while he is physically imprisoned. Paris avers near the start of *Fearless Jones*: "Fearless was more free in that iron cage than I was, or would ever be, on the outside" (45).

The two Mosley detective series also historicize the process by which the existing system of internal colonialism maintained, adapted, and modified its hegemony. As examples of historical crime fiction, Mosley's work traces a shift in the case of the colonized African American quest for freedom with the decline of overt racism, the rise of institutional racism, and the emergence of more symbolic forms.[14] Mosley's texts claim partisanship, rejecting and seeking to dismantle institutionalized oppression. Alterity emerges as Mosley's chief rhetorical weapon to counteract discourse of hegemonic Othering. As a matter of fact, his characters subvert being Othered within a system determined to keep them oppressed powerless, dependent, subordinate, and mystified. Not only do his protagonists engage themselves in the subject position, they give voice to a mass of grievances, especially pertaining to their assumed sameness, based on an oversimplification of their realities, i.e., stereotyping.

Mosley intentionally creates two characters in Fearless and Easy who implode a pantheon of popular stereotypes generally attributed to African American men. While conventional Othering pigeonholes them as examples of the same type of African American criminal (or, at the very least, law-bending) figure, they both embody substantively different ways of being. Their paths in life diverge significantly, yet they occupy the same temporal and narrative space: post–World War II Los Angeles. Fearless earns the right to be the protagonist in a text in which Paris Minton plays the part of the detective hero. It turns out that Fearless possesses not just the badman's preternatural ability to "make the right choices when the chips were down" (*Fearless* 41), but also a moral center: "[He] thought with a pure heart" (*Fear of the Dark* 26). In keeping with his role as a badman, he functions as the status quo's greatest nightmare, an avenging free agent who exists due to his recognition that people are oppressed and his unwillingness to be shackled.

Early in *Fearless Jones*, Paris Minton's narrative first gives voice to his intrepid partner. After being mysteriously brutalized in his hard-won bookstore, Paris conjures up his friend prior to the audience encountering him, associating him with deadly weapons. Fearless is first presented as a figurative warrior: "I lifted my head, and a pain as sharp as Fearless Jones's bayonet traveled the length of my spine" (*Fearless* 11). Next, Fearless is objectified by mentioning his gun, which Paris keeps for him while Fearless is jailed and awaiting bond "for felony assault on three crooked mechanics" (13). Due to a breach in their friendship and both parties' refusal to compromise—a word Paris claims Fearless "didn't even know how to spell" (14)—Fearless languishes there until Paris's sense of respite from the trouble Fearless seems to attract evaporates with the appearance of the "picture-perfect damsel in distress" (20), Elana Love. At that point, his immediate thoughts dramatize his friend in action: "If I were Fearless Jones I would have run headlong into the fray, taking my blows and doing anything to protect her. But I didn't believe that even Fearless would have stood long against Leon Douglas" (20). The perilous encounter with Love and Douglas swiftly ushers in enough danger for Paris prompting him to negotiate Fearless's release, thereby facilitating his first physical appearance in the text. Paris needs the agency of a partner who lives up to his acquired appellation: "[T]he best thing about Fearless was the attribute he was named for; he didn't fear anything, not death or pain or any kind of passion" (41).

In addition to having a significant (and signifying) nickname, Fearless's given name also associatively augments his exalted qualities, a symbolic pattern that applies to Easy as well, albeit in a somewhat different fashion. Although Mosley's confers Westernized legendary and biblical given names on these two heroes, each name functions as a trope, recontextualizing its affiliated traits. For example, Fearless's Celtic moniker, Tristan literally means "tumult" (Stewart 245). Tumult operates as a signifier that produces fear in the midst of turmoil or riotous chaos. Regardless, Tristan Jones in effect reinscribes the meaning of what constitutes a hero: "Hero is just bein' brave when there's trouble. An' bein' brave means to face your fears and do it anyway. Shoot. You can't call me a hero 'cause I ain't scared'a nuthin' on God's blue Earth" (*Fearless* 248). The Arthurian knight Tristan was one of the most versatile heroes in the legendary history of the British Isles.[15] The name resounds with overtones of nobility, chivalry, and honor, qualities that hold true even when Fearless is presented in negative or ambiguous situations—e.g., his aforementioned incarceration for taking vengeance on "crooked mechanics." Echoing his mythic significance, Paris anoints his comrade thus: "[H]e was like some mythological deity that had come down to earth to learn about mortals. . . . [B]eing friends with him was like having one of God's second cousins as a pal" (*Fear Itself* 102). Through this connection, Paris bestows sacrosanct and moral attributes as well as a divine lineage upon Tristan. Even though the usage of Fearless's given name is a rarity in the novels, utilized only within formalized settings generally or involving the judicial system, its reverberations give a nobly heroic spin to his more immediately visible (and thus easier to categorize as the Other) Fearless-ness.

Rather than using allusion to draw meaning from the mythic past, Easy's biblical given name of Ezekiel actually decenters and reinterprets the sacred text from which it derives. Ezekiel translates from Hebrew to "God is strong," one possessing the power and strength of a deity. In scripture, he is considered to be the forerunner of the apocalyptic writer of Revelation. Furthermore, Ezekiel is called by God to be the watchman of Israel. In Ezekiel 3:17–21, God tells Ezekiel to take the words of God and use them to warn his people. It is not Ezekiel's responsibility to bring about repentance, only to communicate the words of God. While Ezekiel is a major, visionary prophet within Judeo-Christian scripture, the character who bears his name in Mosley's series is afflicted by visions that often amount to waking nightmares, the responses to which are generally guided by his own emergent sense of pragmatic communal ethics rather than divine inspiration. Dreamscapes populate Ezekiel's world, giving expression to far more than escapist fantasy: "I was awake but my thinking was like a dream. All I did was sit in darkness, trying to become the darkness and slip out between the eroded cracks of that cell. If it was nighttime nobody would find me; no one would even know I was missing" (*Devil* 74).[16] Although his biblical namesake openly challenged authority through words and action, Easy resorts to trickery as part of his survival imperative. As the narrator, he levels judgment against oppressive conditions in his American homeland, especially showcasing the system of injustice leading up to the Watts riot.

As a part of the African American post-WWII migration experience, the mature Ezekiel Rawlins finds himself, like his biblical namesake, in virtual exile in a present-day Babylon. Of course, the association with Babylon proffers a critique of dominant cultures—powers unconcerned about accountability for their acts of social and political injustice. While writing in Babylon as part of his divine calling, the biblical Ezekiel often addresses the plight of the Jews in Jerusalem. As a possible paean to the duality of his own ancestry as well as to his character's broadly humanistic ethics, Mosley's plot structures in the Easy Rawlins novels often support countertexts in opposition to anti-Semitism as well. Commencing with his first novel, Mosley condemns the fascism that produced the Holocaust: "I remembered the Jews. Nothing more than skeletons, bleeding from their rectums and begging for food. I remembered them waving their weak hands in front of themselves, trying to keep modest; then dropping dead right there before my eyes" (*Devil* 137). Both Ezekiels prophesy about the meaning of Diaspora. Of course, it is primarily within an urban context that the Jewish and African dispersions become most intertwined. Mosley's rendering of Ezekiel Rawlins, and other characters graphically documents this interaction. Within this series, Jewish American private investigator, Saul Lynx, is one of Easy's most enduring friends. In *A Red Death*, Easy is essentially blackmailed by the IRS and the FBI into helping them expose suspected Communist Chaim Wenzler. Despite the grave threat to his own sense of autonomy—"Just one letter from the government had ended my good life" (4)—and the government's attempt to use that threat to get him to act against another Other, Easy sympathizes with Wenzler and ultimately refuses, albeit tacitly in keeping with his role as a trickster, to cooperate in his persecution.

Relying on the advantageous adaptive behavior that folklorist John Roberts ascribes to the trickster figure, Easy basks in contentment performing the subservient role of a maintenance man at his own rental properties with Mofass fronting for him as the building manager for an alleged white landlord. In typical trickster fashion, he subordinates himself to manipulate those Other than himself: "I had the feeling that Craxton [the IRS agent] didn't see the man sitting before him, but I'd seen pictures of Leavenworth in *Life* magazine so I pretended to be the man he described" (48). While the trickster element appears obvious, many of Mosley's literary critics only scrape the surface in interpreting Easy's (and thus Mosley's) intent in employing it. For instance, Schwartz attributes Easy's behavior to "a shuck-and-jive stereotype" (43). However, as a verbal art, shucking-and-jiving is a misdirectional skill used in the presence of authority figures. Andrew Pepper wrestles more deeply with the potential problems of Easy's characterization: "Which is not to say that he is [not] morally bankrupt; just that as a black man subject to the injustices of living in a hostile white-controlled world, he is forced to compromise any kind of moral 'code' simply in order to remain alive" ("Black" 219). Foremost, Easy enacts the duplicity of a trickster figure by craftily toppling those more powerful with his agile wit and by sheer guile.

Operating out of a trickster survivalist modality, Easy gains a measure of safe anonymity in downplaying his entrepreneurship: " 'I'll ask 'im [Mofass]. But you know he don't work for me.' I lied. 'It's the other way around' " (*RD* 3). For boundary crossers, the trickster figure operates as a model of inventive and innovative deceit, thereby creating a form of power out of a position of inherent Otherness. Furthermore, mythographer Lewis Hyde indicates that lying grants the "trickster the chance to remake the truth on his own terms" (73). Echoing this function, Easy's narrative voice proclaims in *White Butterfly* (1992): "I had slipped into the role of a confidential agent who represented people when the law broke down" (9–10). Nevertheless, Easy's status as a trickster is ambiguous. As part of the plot of *White Butterfly*, a rapist and serial killer preys on prostitutes, functioning as a daunting semiotic indicator that mirrors Easy's own conjugal relationship. Although his marriage to Regina is threatened, he dreads disclosing the financial reality of his self, in the process straining his wedding vows. The evident sexual battery of his wife further complicates a simple positive interpretation of Easy. In cultural practice, the badman seldom deigns to play the trickster, and the trickster seldom relies on coercion. Thereby, Mosley infuses Easy's characterization as the trickster with more than a hint of the badman, a status which both speaks to the "forced . . . compromise" that Pepper mentions and Mosley's desire to transcend overly simple categorizations for his characters.

Similarly, Fearless functions at some level as the quintessential badman, yet like Easy he subverts this largely predetermined role by adding another dimension. Force—at times verging on brutality—is his *modus operandi*, but he possesses a dialectical strain. Mosley complicates his badman figure by reconstructing this so-called Other as the epitome of fear itself while humanizing him in relation to his antiracist counterparts. For instance, while assisting Paris in uncovering a deadly plot involving an adoring elderly couple, Fanny and Sol, he steadfastly refuses to break the promise he made to them about not accepting payment in exchange for his protection, despite their protestations. Here Fearless stands in sharp contrast to Paris who believes himself to be realistic. Desperate for money after Leon Douglas burns his bookstore down, Paris negotiates with Fanny for a fee, and laments that "Fearless thinks he can live on air, but we need that money. After what he told Sol, he won't let you pay us a dime" (72). On the other hand,

Fearless even washes the old couple's dishes (*Fearless* 68). But Mosley later contrasts this benevolent image of Fearless "play[ing] in the soapy water" (68) with a thick description of him as a badman: "Fearless was one of the kindest men I ever met, but the devil lived in him too. In a rage he was capable of murder" (146). Fearless, then, personifies the "hardboiled" leitmotif.[17] According to Jopi Nyman: "A hardboiled character is a curious mixture of surprisingly contradictory strains: detachment and compassion, humanity and inhumanity, reason and emotion, rationality and idealism—all these traits can be found in hard-boiled protagonists, though to different degrees, perhaps" (32). Although operating as a hard-boiled badman, Fearless ultimately constitutes a more complex sentient individual than Paris.

Mosley's portrayal of Fearless first conveys and then subverts the aura of a badman. As Paris describes him, he is a straightforward foil to Paris's more trickster-like character. As Paris tells us, "On my own I watched or lied or misrepresented. I never took danger head-on if there was a second choice. Fearless was the opposite of me; he moved ahead as a rule. He might use a back entrance or even surprise, but no matter what, he was always going forward" (*Fearless* 181). While Fearless seemingly conforms to the brutal aspects of the badman, his construction of self moves beyond simple retaliatory acts by privileging feeling. For instance, Paris reveals Fearless's philosophy about lying: "'*It's okay as long as you ain't hurtin' nobody,*' he told me one drunken night. '*Matter of fact a lotta times a lie is better'n the truth when the whole thing come out*'" (114, italics in original). Therefore, Fearless manages to transcend boundaries, but he also is governed by a clear, if unconventional, code of ethics, in the process affirming the very thing that Pepper notes is most complicated for African Americans. For example, when Paris locates his partner hovering over Sol's corpse, he finds Fearless praying for Sol's soul as once instructed by his mother so that Sol's spirit "knows to go for Heaven" (246). Given Western empiricism, his presumptive irrational behavior occurs at an inopportune time, at Sol's bedside dispensing what some might call "mumbo jumbo." As part of the ethical code of "the sporting life," however, his gesture speaks worlds, echoing Easy's contention in *A Little Yellow Dog* that "the street is such a wild place and compassion there is more dear than gold" (105). Fearless's bold moniker, thus, extends to reflecting his lack of fear at demonstrating both compassion and contrition.

The complexities of Mosley's protagonists end up bridging conventional boundaries among genres. For instance, in an interview, Mosley states: "I consider *Fearless Jones* to be in the genre of comic noir. Even though these terrible things happen, very often you end up laughing" (Mudge 1). The term "comic noir" fits quite well, as it deconstructs the loaded mode commonly known as black humor, which is associated with a mordantly pessimistic tone. Mosley's comic noir syncretizes the grim realism and bleakness located in detective fiction with wry humor. For instance, despite the predicament the femme fatale Elana Love presents, Paris

Minton allows his desire to mock him: "I didn't believe a word she said, but that didn't matter. I told her my mother raised me as a gentleman. 'A gentle man,' I said before launching another kiss. That one missed too" (*Fearless* 30). In a recursive pattern, such scenes immediately exact a descriptive passage that is strictly noir, such as Paris's violent "reverie" immediately after the above scene with Elana: "I was coming down a dark street dancing to the jazz I knew I'd be hearing soon. When the cops stopped me, I guess I must have been a little too cocky. They didn't like my attitude and were correcting it with their nightsticks when Fearless showed up to meet me. He jumped in the middle of the fracas as if he were still under Bradley fighting the Germans hand to hand. He disarmed both men and beat them to their knees" (31). The Easy Rawlins texts, on the other hand, tend to project the more singular objective of cinéma vérité, presenting authentic people in the world as it is, inscribed with a sociopolitical consciousness, but generally without any incisive humor.[18] As with film noir's two most basic archetypes—the pursued and pursuer—Mosley's fiction inverts such pursuits; his protagonists engage in a constant exchange of roles, being African Americans who are pursuers pursued and Othering Others.[19]

By centering the American internal colonialism, Mosley foreshadows the demise of the working class in today's postindustrial, global economy. Far from being halcyon days, in hindsight, Mosley's two detective series throw away the script of Chandler and other white crime fiction writers and chronicle a window of relative opportunity swiftly closing. It is within the context of racial politics that Mosley interrogates Los Angeles, a city noted for generations of racial disharmony omitted from white writers' texts. He bears witness to palpable expressions of institutionalized oppression fueled by Othering in which "The air we breathed was racist" (*WB* 50). Mosley speaks multivocally of racial matters that transcend the boundaries of time. While positioning his novels as historical crime fiction, his texts privilege "the changing same." Easy constitutes an unheralded freedom fighter, without being part of a social movement, who actively deconstructs the capitalist power system. Even when compelled to work in cahoots with the police establishment, Easy states, "I didn't want to be there but I'd be damned if I could question black people and not white ones" (*WB* 119).

Finally, given former president Bill Clinton's enthusiasm for Mosley's fiction, some critics question the substance of Mosley's racial politics. As Lee Horsley poses the question: "Is it perhaps a more 'comfortable' read for white readers than it ought to be?" (221).[20] From my perspective such readings promulgate the colonizing discourse of the Other. A cultural divide perpetuates a resistance to contexts and the time it takes to unpack the Other. Even to describe Easy as attaining a "growing black consciousness" (Soitos 234) exposes an interpellative gaze that underdetermines cultural politics. Mosley's protagonists are saturated in African American life, history, and culture, bespeaking an advanced, alternative epistemology. Mosley grants visibility to a cornucopia of dashing characters, with names to match. Whether Ezekiel "Easy" Porterhouse Rawlins or Tristan "Fearless" Jones, Mosley's heroes represent both alterity and similitude, magnifying a polycentric view of the so-called Other. The failure of white audiences to read with polycentricity rests with their failure to concede their own racialized agenda and the possible implications of being the Other's Other themselves.

Notes

1. These protagonists never physically meet, except intertextually speaking. Technically, Easy Rawlins interacts with Paris Minton after the Watts Riot in *Little Scarlet* (2004). Easy speaks knowledgeably of Fearless Jones; and given Mosley's proficiency as a writer, this reference point may be destined to change in future texts.

2. Robert Staples is a proponent of the internal colonialism model, as articulated in his *The Urban Plantation: Racism and Colonialism in the Post Civil Rights Era* (1987). Internal colonialism occurs vis-à-vis the inequitable circumstances and exploitation afforded those Othered. On occasions when I capitalize "Other," I endorse the Lacanian perspective that seeks to establish two modalities of otherness. The "big Other" is symbolic, constructed by the dominant discourse. The "little other" is a reflection of the desired Self.

3. For more details delineating this polycentric approach, see Hogue who proffers discourse historicizing the "African American as Other" (13–34). He writes, "Within classical European colonialism, the African/African American came to belong to the Other, to the non-European, to alterity" (22).

4. I find Thomas Kochman's *Black and White Styles in Conflict* (1981) still of great relevance as it speaks to vernacular practice that preceded Western postmodern discourse. Postmodernism insists there is no overall myth, no overall history, no meta-narrative, no religious belief that holds for everyone, centering an inclusivity that already existed within African American cultural praxis. Therefore, I concur with Russell Potter's assessment: "[B]lack cultures conceived postmodernism long before its 'time'" (6).

5. I rely here on Elias Kifron Bongmba's *African Witchcraft and Otherness: A Philosophical and Theological Critique of Intersubjective Relations* (2001). Bongmba appropriates the Levinasian perspective that articulates a human Other who challenges "totality" (72). Such radical Others endorse an ontological heterogeneity, allowing for a sense of individuality within a collective identity.

6. According to Schwartz, part of Mosley's subversive agenda involves reinscribing his "accompanying figure to the protagonist" (42). Not only are they of the same race but constitute (more than likely) dual protagonists.

7. See Crowther, 13–38. Furthermore, part of the African American "tough guy" image pertains to fear of whiteness. In her *Traces, Codes, and Clues: Reading Race in Crime Fiction* (2003), Maureen Reddy substantiates that "the depiction of whiteness as terror found in many black-authored texts may not seem relevant to understanding this novel [*Devil in a Blue Dress*]" (93).

8. Cf. Mohanty, Butler.

9. See Lee Horsley's *Twentieth Century Crime Fiction* (2005). Apparently considering only Mosley's earliest crime fiction rather than his entire oeuvre, critics have often formed a

consensus, situating Easy's homeownership as "draw[ing] him ever more inexorably into the whole white-dominated system of capitalist exchange" (Horsley 220).

10. Quite a few of Mosley's literary critics situate him outside of the American working class, aspiring chiefly to achieve the middle class American dream, which is a gross error. Such readings by Wilson and Bryant negate a social class that is no longer considered viable due to the nation's deindustrialization: the working class. This social class holds the most credence for Mosley's historical crime fiction, not the middle class he's being affiliated with. See Kelley.

11. Pepper is among the few that speak to the social order to recognize Easy's quest "to carve out a small slice of the good life" ("Black" 219). Unlike those who link him to a middle class value orientation, elsewhere, Pepper locates Easy squarely within working class America (*Contemporary* 132). Others associate success as identifying with "white society" (Forter 217).

12. A full explanation is forthcoming in *Black Betty* (1994) when Easy explains his financial straits and eventual move to a rental property (32).

13. Ralph Rodriguez discusses the presence of existential questions in detective fiction as follows: "With its emphasis on reason, order, justice, and alienation, the detective novel is better suited than other genres to identify the shifting terrain of post-nationalism and to address the existential concerns that change entails" (6).

14. Mosley's detective fiction fits into the subgenre of historical crime fiction, which takes two forms. According to John Scaggs, "The first is crime fiction that is set in some distinct historical period, but which was not written in that period" (145). Scaggs also relates, "It should be noted that such developments in the genre in the 1990s were not restricted to historical crime fiction, and the most illuminating fictions of recent years have been those that construct the detective as a hybrid between the amateur and the professional" (32).

15. Malory's *Morte D'Arthur* (1485) is the seminal English text for delineating the heroic figure of Tristan. From birth, this knight's life is plagued by sorrow and treachery—especially in relation to his romantic relationship with Isolde/Yseult—making him close kin to Fearless in terms of their embattled existences.

16. In *New Hard-Boiled Writers, 1970s–1990s* (2000), LeRoy Panek attributes Ezekiel's visions to mere "escapist fantasy" (188), a reading that underdetermines the mythopoeic associations of the his given name.

17. As Scragg states, "Walter Mosley's appropriation of hard-boiled fiction is one based on racial and historical issues, in which Marlowe's xenophobia is inverted and deconstructed to reconstruct the history of black migrant experience in Los Angeles that Chandler's fiction marginalises or omits" (79).

18. In this series, there is an almost complete absence of humor, dark or otherwise, until *A Little Yellow Dog*. This miniature mutt becomes the source of comic relief in this as well as later texts in the series.

19. Dickos supplies insights about these archetypes (65).

20. Maureen Reddy stipulates that reading Mosley should be a "disquieting experience for white readers." Yet she further posits that it "does not force the white reader into the position of the Other's Other," due to its temporality and white readers' failure to situate his texts within the current historical moment and their willingness to identify with Mosley's representation of an oppositional culture (96).

American Negroes Revisited

The Intellectual and The Badman in
Walter Mosley's Fearless Jones Novels

—Terrence Tucker

W hen asked by *Publishers Weekly* whether he sees the post-WWII moment as "a particularly seminal time for America or African Americans," Walter Mosley argued that the period is "an important time that hasn't gotten much play in the media. Back then, black people migrated in great droves out of the south, went north and tried to create a new life for themselves. And those migrations haven't been talked about very much in history, much less fiction" (Hahn 54). Much has been made of what is called "The Great Migration," which spans 1910 to 1930, as African Americans escaped the Jim Crow South for the urban North and West. However, the work on the period from the 1940s through the 1960s, called The Second Great Migration, remains sparse. Yet Nicholas Lemann reveals in *The Promised Land: The Great Black Migration and How It Changed America* (1991) that "Between 1910 and 1970, six and a half million black Americans moved from the South to the North; five million of them moved after 1940, during the time of the mechanization of cotton farming" (6). Recent histories have followed the fiction of Richard Wright's *Native Son* (1940) and Lorraine Hansberry's *A Raisin in the Sun* (1959), focusing on the problems of overcrowding, police brutality and segregated black neighborhoods that were merely a precursor to the urban riots of the 1960s. However, in romanticizing the political activism of the 1960s and 1970s, historical events and figures—John F. Kennedy, Martin Luther King, Jr., and Vietnam, for instance—become fixed in the public's memory of the time. Conversely, the 1950s remains a time of collective amnesia. Yet the decade was rife with contention, from McCarthyism to the Korean War to the *Brown* decision. This is the world that Walter Mosley's characters inhabit so brilliantly. His *Fearless Jones* series—which currently includes *Fearless Jones* (2001), *Fear Itself* (2003), and most recently *Fear of the Dark* (2006)—presents two black male characters navigating the time between the end of World War II and the full onset of the Civil Rights Movement.

On the surface, Mosley's *Fearless Jones* novels resemble his well-known Easy Rawlins stories. In particular, these novels fuse hard-boiled detective fiction, like Dashiell Hammett's *The Maltese Falcon* (1930) and Raymond Chandler's *The Big Sleep* (1939), with African American literary traditions. However, instead of the conflicted Easy and his murderous best friend Raymond "Mouse" Alexander, Mosley presents bookstore owner Paris Minton and his friend Tristan "Fearless" Jones as the intellectual and the badman, respectively. Paris is constructed as an African American intellectual outside of the mold of the "New Negro" of the Harlem Renaissance, which associates critical analysis exclusively with black elite status. While Paris's standing as a working class intellectual questions the class politics of W.E.B. Du Bois's "The Talented Tenth," Fearless is a prescient interrogator of the amoral badman represented in Mosley's Easy Rawlins novels through Mouse. Although Fearless is a badman in that he "was the white man's worst dream: the slave or (after Emancipation) the laborer who refused to knuckle under. . . . He was the out-of-control black man, surly slacker, the belligerent troublemaker, and occasionally the killer of whites" (Bryant 2), he separates himself from the badman's synonymous relationship to the "Bad Nigger" as defined by Jerry Bryant in *"Born in a Mighty Bad Land": The Violent Man in African American Folklore and Fiction* (2003). Fearless is a World War II veteran who, according to Peter Canon and Jeff Zalenski, "combines the principles of Easy with the deadliness of Ray 'Mouse' Alexander" (53). Mosley uses Paris and Fearless to explore his favorite topic, black male heroes, in a moment when black migrants sought to reconstruct their idea of "home," distinctly African American communities that reproduced the cultural and social traditions and behaviors forged among the black working and underclass in the rural South, as a way of resisting the challenges of institutionalized racism in the city. Part of that reconstruction is the acceptance of characters as divergent as the intellectual and the badman and the ensuing exploration of the complexity of a hero. In "The Black Man: Hero" (1995), Mosley argues, "The truth is that heroism isn't defined by male or female, good or bad, black or white. Heroism isn't even limited to humanity. Heroism, to my understanding, is simply survival" (235). This paper argues, then, that Mosley's interrogation of the intellectual and the badman recovers a time and culture, the American Negro of the 1950s, so that he can redefine heroism and highlight the efforts of African Americans in overcoming racist oppression. Instead of dramatizing the national activism of the 1960s, Mosley's novels move beyond the hard-boiled detective and black protest fiction to examine the creation of home by African Americans during the Second Great Migration and demonstrate their survival as an act of heroism.

To be sure, the *Fearless Jones* novels are classic hard-boiled detective fiction in the sense that their working class detective protagonists reveal a criminal underworld that involves numerous characters that cut across class lines. At times, however, Mosley seems to be mocking the form itself in order to highlight the racial analysis that his works add to the genre. So, in *Fearless Jones*, Mosley does not give the reader the "standard opening for the classic California noir mystery story"; instead, Richard Bernstein notes that when "the novel opens, it is not a beautiful woman but two cops who enter the scene, incredulous that a black man could have all those books without having stolen them" (8). Although tensions with the police are typical in detective novels, Mosley's work possesses an especial racial layer. For example, Paris brushes off the police harassment: "I felt not rancor toward them. Being challenged by the law was a rite of passage for any Negro who wanted to better himself or his situation" (*Fearless* 4). When the "beautiful woman," named Elana Love, finally does walk in the door, Paris's comment, "Love walked in the door" (6), elicits snickers as well as heat. Even when he confesses, "Her face is what scared me. It was too wide to be pretty and too flat to be handsome, but she was beautiful anyway," his humorous skepticism is not far behind: "The last time I'd felt like that about a woman I almost got killed. So the fast beating of my heart was a coin toss between love and fear" (6). However, the novel quickly establishes its hard-boiled detective credentials when, within twenty-four hours of helping Love escape the "study in blunt" Leon Douglas, Paris has been beaten up, shot at, made love to, and found his bookstore after it was burned down. This final act leads Paris to bail his friend Fearless out of jail. Paris's decision mirrors Easy's frequent involvement of Mouse in the "favors" he performs. Easy situates the ownership of his own home as the source of his developing self and, in *Devil in a Blue Dress* (1990), the threat of losing his home leads him into the underworld of the hard-boiled detective on which the Easy Rawlins series is based. The ownership of the house and bookstore represent the promise the Great Migration held for African Americans. Thus, the destruction of the bookstore, and its symbolic threat to Paris's selfhood, forces Paris to turn to Fearless. Additionally, Paris needs Fearless for exactly the same reason Easy often needs Mouse.

As Mosley states in "The Black Man: Hero," "Easy needs Mouse because when somebody's out after him, 911 just won't work" (234). Thus, heroism in Mosley's novels is rarely a singular achievement. Instead it requires the presence of a loyal friend who knows how to negotiate the streets. For Easy, it is Mouse's well-known ability to kill as easily as he breathes. For Paris, it is Fearless's unwavering morality and a set of hands capable of leveling any jaw.

As usual there are an array of characters and suspects. Love is the mysterious woman in hard-boiled crime novels who plays all sides, while William Grove, the pastor and con man Love is searching for, is shady yet informative. Like Chandler's *The Big Sleep*, the number of characters and plot lines can seem to overshadow the narrative. Yet as Lev Grossman argues about *Fear Itself*, "the result isn't frustrating, it's hypnotic" (59). More importantly, Mosley moves beyond genres into the larger field of African American literary tradition by using his main characters' interactions across cultural lines to make a larger comment about race. So Paris and Fearless eventually encounter a Jewish couple, Sol and Fanny Tannenbaum, who are connected to Leon Douglas. It is Sol's bond, promised to Douglas when the two were incarcerated, for which everyone is searching. The couple's presence allows Mosley to link the oppression of the Jews in Germany to that of African Americans in the United States. When being questioned by the police after the death of Fanny, Paris notes the tone the police use when referring to the couple as "Jews." For Paris, "*Jew* turned to *nigger* in my ears, and I started to dislike the cop" (*Fearless* 151, italics in original). So it should come as no surprise in the novel when, as Richard Bernstein notes, "Israeli spies come into the picture along with an unsavory accounting firm, a crooked cop, and a man named Zuckerman who, during the war, cooperated with the Nazis in stealing the art treasures of fellow European Jews, one of whom was Sol Tannenbaum" (8). Paris's linkage of the terms "Jews" and "niggers" foreshadows the important, if sometimes contentious, relationship between African Americans and Jews in their fight for equality in the latter half of the twentieth century. Fearless's protection of the Tannenbaums mirrors black participation in World War II in ending the Holocaust. African American participation in one of America's most heroic moments is complicated and diminished, however, because of the discrimination African American veterans faced from a country for which they fought. Fearless's heroic action, then, occurs away from the key historical moments and figures of the time and focuses on the unknown individuals he saves and protects. Similarly, Mosley's novels are interested in the local/individual acts of African American male heroism, even as the novels never lose sight of the large, complex issues of history, race, and home.

As a protagonist for Mosley's novels, Paris is initially mind-boggling. Paris contrasts limited visions of black men as violent, sexualized objects that have been the basis—from slavery to the present—of political, social, and literary ideas about blackness. Tony Lindsay notes, "Loyal, chivalrous, empathetic and romantic are traits not often used when creating African American male characters. Not true with Walter Mosley. In fact, these traits seem to be requirements for Mosley's lead characters" (28). Notoriously brainy, occasionally self-absorbed, and unapologetically cowardly, Paris spends most of his days tucked way in his bookstore reading. Michael Rogers notes in his review that Paris's character is "refreshing in that the dangers typically ignored by steely nerved investigators petrify him" (106). Strangely, the response to Paris is not a rejection of the character but an understanding of his vulnerability often played for comic effect. In the clutches of Douglas, Paris thinks, "in a back room in Watts, Paris Minton would show some backbone. *Fuck you asshole*, was on the tip of my tongue," but instead spouts,

"Please don't, brother." My trembling lips betrayed me. "I don't know nuthin'."

He slapped me again. My head turned around so far that I was sure my neck had broken. (10)

In truth, his primary connections to violence are through Fearless, who once saved Paris by killing three police officers that were attacking him. Given their dynamic, it seems logical that in reviewing *Fear Itself,* Keir Graff suggests, "there's a central paradox that's addressed but not solved: if Paris is such a scaredy-cat, why does he keep plunging further into danger?" (619). The simple answer is his loyalty to Fearless and concern for his own skin. However, in casting Paris as an intellectual opposite Fearless, the novel questions what makes a hero. As Mosley argues, "Heroism, as a rule, is not a studied thing—one does not risk his own life if he has other options. It's when we are cornered, like that mouse, that we stand up and try to do the impossible" ("Black Man" 235). Therefore, we can see Paris's heroism being manifested only when he feels cornered, which emerges only when his bookstore/home is threatened.

Romantic definitions of heroism might suggest that heroes often act for a greater good of a country, a community, or another individual. Yet Paris's actions are about his own survival. However, Paris's impulse for survival reflects the heroism of African Americans in maintaining selfhood during the 1950s. In Paris's mind, "that bookstore was what made me somebody rather than just anybody. Burning down my store was just the same as shooting me, and somebody would have to make restitution for that crime" (*Fearless* 41). The presence of the bookstore elevates the story beyond a tale of revenge to a narrative of reclaiming selfhood. Also, situating Paris as the primary voice contrasts traditional portraits of black life in migration-era America. Instead of figures in black protest fiction like Bigger Thomas, Paris comes closer to the protagonist in Ralph Ellison's *Invisible Man* (1952) and Grant Wiggins in Ernest Gaines's *A Lesson Before Dying* (1993) who reflect critical thought that dominates the novels' narration and resists self-destruction. Paris's critical articulation of the social forces that impact the African American community is a central part of his character as a black intellectual.

As Peter Cannon and Jeff Zaleski contend, "Paris possesses a narrative voice that's more literate and middle-class than the street-smart Easy" (54). Paris, nevertheless, remains a working-class black intellectual who sits at the intersection of theoretical racial analysis and the complex responses utilized by the black working and underclass. Like Grant Wiggins and the Invisible Man, Paris participates in the life of the community but also dissects it with critical and compassionate eyes. These characters are in constant negotiation with their sense of home. While they come to recognize the importance of home in production of black cultural traditions and art forms, they are often removed or alienated from it. Home for Paris both sustains and restrains him. Paris's feelings of home are reflected in the fictional and historical attempts to re-create "home" of the rural South in the urban North that many black migrants attempted. He reminisces about his time in the South, with happiness instead of dread. For instance, in describing the black community in his native Louisiana, Paris comments: "Everybody was poor, but nobody starved. We partied on Saturday nights and praised the Lord for our babies on Sundays. We worked hard when we had to and took it easy when there was a chance. A lot of colored people tell me they hate the South; Jim Crow and segregation made a heavy weight for their hearts. But I never felt like that. I mean, lynchings were a terrible thing, and some of those peckerwoods acted so stupid that they embarrassed the hell out of you sometimes. But I still loved the little shack I shared with my mother. I'd have still been there if it wasn't for one terrible event. . . . That event was learning to read" (*Fearless* 115).

In addition to painting a brilliant example of survival in the African American community, Paris recalls Frederick Douglass's dread after learning to read revealed to him the inhumanity of slavery. In his *Narrative* (1845), Douglass laments, "I would at times feel that learning to read had been a curse rather than a blessing. It had given me a view of my wretched condition, without the remedy. It opened my eyes to the horrible pit, but to no ladder upon which to get out. In moments of agony, I envied my fellow-slaves for their stupidity. . . . Any thing, no matter what, to get rid of thinking!" (35–36). For black intellectuals who see the continued impact of institutional racism, Du Bois's ideas of "double consciousness" are often most strongly felt. Reading, for Douglass and Paris, makes them acutely aware of their condition in racist America. Sitting outside the library that only whites could enter, Paris is told by a white librarian that he would never be allowed into the library to read all of the books, because "these books are not meant for you. These books were written by white people for white people. This is literature and art and the way the country is and should be" (*Fearless* 117). Crushed by the librarian's words, Paris confesses that he left for San Francisco at seventeen, "not because I wanted to vote or was afraid of being lynched. I left because a man told me one night that in California black folks could go into any library they wanted. They could get library cards and check out books from here to Sunday" (118). Here we see the limitations of home for Paris, specifically the overt oppression of the Jim Crow South and its impact on African Americans, and the hope that the urban North and West represented. Many African Americans who left the South did so not only because of economic benefits of the city, but because the imposition of white supremacist hegemony manifested itself in the psyche of African Americans by substituting self-hatred for selfhood. The limitations imposed on Paris's home, then, threaten to inhibit Paris because of the African American community's continued status as a target for white supremacy. Of course, Mosley's fiction, like his fellow contemporary black male writer August Wilson's, has frequently shown that migration was as much a threat to African American life, culture, and tradition as the South had been. However, the use of literacy in Mosley's Fearless Jones novels is reminiscent of slaves' recognition of reading and writing as a defiant act during slavery. Paris's voice controls the story, if nothing else, to present a cogent racial analysis of postwar America. In contrasting the black protest novels that saw no possibility for escape for its African American characters, literacy is used to save Paris from self-destruction.

For example, in relating a story in *Fear Itself* of how he is turned down for the loan despite being more qualified than another, presumably white, businessman, Paris reports, "Literature came to my aid even when I had to face the hard reality of racism. Like when the bank turned me down for a small improvement loan. . . . I went home and reread thirty of the Simple stories by Langston Hughes as they were chronicled in back issues of the *Chicago Defender.* . . . Simple's view of the world was just what I needed to laugh off the bile that banker filled me with" (103–04). Instead of acting violently, Paris neutralizes his anger. Here there are echoes of Ellison's description in "Richard Wright's Blues" of the impact of the blues on African American life: "The blues is an impulse to keep the painful details and episodes of a brutal experience alive in one's aching consciousness, to finger its jagged grain and to transcend it, not by the consolation of philosophy but by squeezing from it a near-tragic, near-comic lyricism" (129). Literacy, augmented by humor, contributes to Paris's rejection of the inevitability of violence and death in novels like *Native Son*, William Attaway's *Blood on the Forge* (1941), and Chester Himes's *The Primitive* (1955). In particular, by turning to Hughes's most famous post–Harlem Renaissance work—his Jesse B. Simple stories appeared in the *Chicago Defender* beginning in 1943—and by alluding to *Invisible Man*, *Fear Itself* references two important works during the Second Great Migration where alternative responses to racist oppression were employed. Thus, we see how Mosley's novels seek to demonstrate the ways in which African Americans both tried to re-create "home" and used the benefits of the urban North and West to transcend the limitations placed on those who inhabit that home.

Of course, Fearless's moral certainty anchors both novels, explicitly examines black heroism, and solidifies Paris's connection to home. Paris's initial description of Fearless provides the physical image of a classic black hero. Paris notes, "Fearless Jones. Tall and slender, darker than most Negroes in the American melting pot, he was stronger than tempered steel and an army-trained killing machine" (*Fearless* 31). He is a bad man, to be sure, having killed those police officers despite sustaining a knife wound that still forces him to limp. In fact, Paris notes in *Fearless Jones*, "Fearless considered himself and maybe three other people he'd ever met to be *full bad*: Jacob Trench, Doolen Waters and, of course, Raymond Alexander" (164, italics in original). Mosley references one of his most famous characters, Mouse—and by extension Easy—to reveal the "badness" with which we are to consider Fearless. By placing Fearless on par with Mouse, who turns violence and murder into joyous, entertaining art, Mosley legitimizes Fearless as a badman who, nonetheless, is a perfect sidekick to Paris. Yet Mosley subverts the traditional link of the badman to the bad nigger by differentiating Fearless from Mouse. As Mosley tells *Publishers Weekly*, "Mouse is a sociopath really. He's amoral. Fearless is the opposite; he's completely moral. But it brings them to just about to the same place. Neither of them are afraid of anything" (Hahn 54). That both Mouse and Fearless end up in the same place despite their radically different personalities and approaches speaks to the nature of the badman and the sociopolitical forces that surround that figure.

Yet the depiction of Fearless draws a distinct line between the badman in African American folk culture and the bad nigger frequently used in mainstream stereotypes of black men that justify racist oppression and make blackness virtually synonymous with criminality. Mouse resembles the badman/bad nigger that Bryant claims "may be the product of a suppressed collective rage, his violence a displacement of his anger from the white oppressor to the less dangerous targets of other blacks" (6). He necessitates the presence of Easy as Mosley's protagonist in their series. As Mosley states, "Easy is a richer character because people can identify with him at more levels. Mouse is loved because of his heroic qualities, but the central character of a book has to have a broader range of possibilities emotionally and intellectually" (Hahn 54). Similarly, Paris possesses a greater palette of emotional and intellectual possibilities than Fearless, though his "heroic qualities" still have an unmistakable impact on the reader and Paris. Mosley's construction of Fearless as a badman in opposition to the portrait of Mouse, suggests a desire to explore the complexity of violence—and by extension heroism—badmen enact. Paris himself notes in *Fear Itself,* "it was more than just a feeling of security. Fearless actually had the ability to make me feel as if I were more of a man when I was in his company" (141). Also, Fearless and Mouse serve significantly different purposes in Mosley's novels. While, as Mosley confesses, "when Mouse comes around everyone know that there's bound to be blood" ("Black Man" 238), Fearless propels the novel forward, acting as Paris's moral center and often willing Paris into actions he normally avoids. Nevertheless in the case of Fearless and Mouse, heroism manifests itself through an overt defiance of the social forces that impact African American life.

Fearless's presence highlights the importance of the moment in which he appears. His heroism, where the line between legal and illegal is not only blurred but irrelevant, occurs in a context that makes his sense of morality possible. In American popular culture, for example, Westerns are a space where outlaw violence—as opposed to jury trials and due process—is romanticized, while films like *The Godfather* (1972) provide a context where criminal activity is justified by loyalty to the "family," a desire to go "straight," and strategic violence. In Mosley's novels the 1950s become a moment when the African American presence in urban Northern/Western cities was largely ignored. The result was that African Americans established their own conceptions of success, home, and heroism. The badman, as a result, exists in Mosley's novels as a hero in a world where outright defiance was often met with certain death. Thus, Mosley's description of Mouse in "The Black Man: Hero" also applies to Fearless: "He's a man who will stand up against bone-cracking odds with absolute confidence. He's a man who won't accept even the smallest insult. And for a people for whom insult is as common as air, that's a man who will bring joy" (239). However, Fearless also brings a voice of compassion that Paris lacks. After comforting Gella, the niece of the Tannenbaums, Paris accuses Fearless of trying to steal the woman from her husband. In response, Fearless informs his friend, "Sometimes you got to give, Paris. Sometimes a man or a woman needs the opposite sex to say, hey it's okay. But she don't mean nuthin' t'me" (*Fearless* 156). Fearless's revelation forces Paris to admit, "Fearless had a smart heart. He had a brave heart too. When he talked to me like he did about Gella, I never understood, not really, a word" (156). Despite Fearless's noble actions, he remains outside a time when African Americans most famously thrust "respectable" images of blacks into the national imagination to highlight the unfairness of racism. In adopting (white) middle-class ideology, African Americans in the 1960s rejected stereotypical ideas of blackness that had been used to justify segregation. Fearless's actions, killing police officers and kissing white women, are antithetical to African Americans' image in the 1960s because, regardless of their intent, they confirm stereotypes of violent, oversexed black men in the public mind. By presenting Fearless and Paris against the backdrop of the 1950s, however, the novels examine the complexity of heroism in the African American working and underclass outside the consciously nonthreatening, decidedly middle-class, counter-representations of the Civil Rights Movement.

Thus, Fearless's principles and compassion infuse the overall narrative and allow Mosley to reverse the scenario of *Fearless Jones* in *Fear Itself.* In the latter novel, it is Fearless who comes to Paris seeking help in finding his boss Kit Mitchell for a woman named Leora Hartman. Of course, soon after agreeing to help his friend, Paris has been harassed by the police and almost killed within hours. The crossfire of bullets and blackmail leads Paris and Fearless across class lines and racial lines to the African American cosmetics queen Winifred Fine and white real estate mogul Maestro Wexler. In critiquing the African American elite in *Fear Itself,* Paris and Fearless visit Fine, whose nephew Bartholomew Perry is suspected of knowing where Mitchell is. Fine is the dominant force in her entire family, controlling her sister—who also is Leora's mentally ill mother—and Fine's own brother Oscar, who works as her servant. As Paris mentions to Leora, "She got you comin' and goin'. Use your own family's money to keep everybody in line" (*Fear Itself* 248). Fine's monetary success belies an obsessive need to maintain a specific image. In particular, Fine's attitudes reflect the black middle-class that E. Franklin Frazier famously exposed in the controversial *The Black Bourgeoisie* (1957). Frazier argued: "Lacking a cultural tradition and rejecting identification with the Negro masses on the one hand, and suffering from the contempt of the white world on the other, the black bourgeoisie has developed a deep-seated inferiority complex. In order to compensate for this feeling of inferiority, the black bourgeoisie has created in its isolation what might be described as a world of make-believe in which it attempts to escape the disdain of whites and fulfill its wish for status in American life" (24–25). Like them, Fine has created a world of "make believe" that has made her oblivious to the black lower classes. Unlike

Paris's negotiation of the complexity of the "home" that is the African American community, Fine rejects any connection to the cultural traditions and practices.

Her actions are not heroic like Paris's recovery of selfhood and Fearless's morality. When asked whether she has heard about the rash of murders in the paper, Fine responds, "I have Oscar read to me those stories that are salient to our concerns" (*Fear Itself* 212). Instead of seeking to create a distinct African American cultural space, like their working class counterparts, the Fines have chosen a world of "make believe" that allows them to exist in a vacuum outside the reach of an individual, community, or history itself. Paris and Fearless, by contrast, recognize the centrality of a connection to their community as necessary to their survival. As a result, Fine's failure to realize that the murders may be indirectly connected to her surprises Paris, who argues: "She was like a child. Completely cut off from the world, so that all that was important was her needs and her desires. In her world me and mine had never drawn breath. The drama and tragedy of everyday people was invisible to her. In a way she was like Maestro Wexler sitting on his throne. I could see where money affected both of them more than race. It was the first time I had actually witnessed the power of money and class in forming character" (212). Fine's comments disrupt Paris's previous ideas of race as the sole factor in constructing identity. Her actions reveal an intersection of race and class through the African American elite instead of the traditional viewing of race and poverty.

The intersection reveals a black elitism that the narrative condemns. So, in *Fear Itself*, Fine's imposition of bourgeois values becomes a major catalyst for the crime that fuels the novel's plot. Her objection to the gardener Brown, the father of Leora's son, results in her refusal to return the child after Brown's illness forces Leora to send their son to live with Fine. As a result, Leora asks for Bartholomew's help, initiating the events that drive the novel. Through Paris's response to Fine, Mosley separates the black intellectual from the African American elite, a distinction that challenges Du Bois's belief that the upper crust of African America would be responsible for lifting the race. While Paris is certainly more middle-class than Easy and other characters in Mosley's work, he does not seek to become disconnected from his community. So, when Paris comes to terms with himself as a killer in *Fear Itself*—disrupting any possibility of conflating intellectual prowess with black bourgeois isolation—his connection to Fearless prevents him from imploding. Similarly, Fearless rejects bourgeois literary constructions of the badmen who, according to Bryant, "mastered the violent methods of the conventional 'bad nigger' but who has graduated to bourgeois self-control and renounced violence for the rewards that middle-class conformity gives him" (7). Implicitly, this construction maintains a class hierarchy that consists of the "accepted" black bourgeoisie vs. the uncontrolled violent underclass.

The embodiment of Fine's elitist attitudes, however, is the theft—made during the kidnapping of Leora's child—of the first volume of the Fine family diary that dates back to the eighteenth century. The book could initially serve as an antidote to the elitism that Fine has forced on her family. Yet her ignorance of its absence highlights her oblivious attitude. Despite the significance of the book to the Fine family, I am persuaded that it has a lasting impact on Paris. As Peter Cannon and Jeff Zaleski note, the book changes Paris's focus in the novel: "A desire to aid his friend Fearless initially motivates Paris, but his journey becomes a voyage of self-discovery" (54). Paris's discovery of the book in *Fear Itself* continues his progression begun in the previous novel. In continuing with the reclamation of selfhood, *Fear Itself* recalls themes we find in African American literature from the slave narratives to Alex Haley's famous book *Roots* (1976). The diary's first words, "*I am Gheeza Manli daughter of Menzi Allatou born into slavery in the year of the devil seventeen hundred and two*" (164, italics in original), simultaneously embody and reject traditional slave narratives. It forgoes the usual beginnings of slave narratives, where a white abolitionist confirmed the work as fact, while maintaining the act of writing oneself into existence that slave narrative authors sought to achieve. Moreover, the book charts the names of slaves given by the slave community to maintain a connection to their African heritage. In doing so, the diary reveals a resistant slave community that actively seeks self-definition in opposition to the institution of slavery.

Also, the diary contributes to *Fear Itself* re-visioning hard-boiled detective fiction. The detective fiction form, in Mosley's hands, becomes an ideal space for the exploration of African American life and culture in one of the most transformative moments in 20th century. In that search, Mosley reveals to us what Ralph Ellison pointed out in "The Art of Fiction: An Interview": "The history of the American Negro is a most intimate part of American history. . . . Negro folklore, evolving within a larger culture which regarded it as inferior, was an especially courageous expression. It announced the Negro's willingness to trust his own experience, his own sensibilities as to the definition of reality, rather than allow his masters to define these crucial matters for him" (214). As Michael Rogers points out, the search for the book in *Fear Itself* becomes "a quest for a priceless heirloom that makes this Mosley's answer to *The Maltese Falcon*" (106). Replacing the black bird of Hammett's novel with stories of black survival, Mosley completes his fusion of detective fiction with African American literature's blues-tinged search for identity.

Ralph Ellison dedicates his unfinished novel *Juneteenth* (1999) to "That Vanished Tribe into Which I Was Born, The American Negroes" (n. pag.). Charles Johnson's preface to the 2000 edition of that novel suggests that the dedication "signals [Ellison's] project of honoring and exploring the lives of black Americans who, from the nation's founding to the 1950s, and despite the burden of racial oppression, embodied our Republic's loftiest ideals" (xv). Ellison's work, from the epic *Invisible Man* through his essays and even in *Juneteenth*, has vividly chronicled the culture, struggle, and impact of the American Negro. Situating the culture of American Negroes with the end of Reconstruction in 1876, Ellison sees the American Negro community as the site that simultaneously represents the ideals of America and its most destructive impulses. The latter obviously results from Jim Crow segregation and emerges in the intraracial discrimination, self-hatred, or "make-believe" we see at points in both novels. The former, however, demonstrates through the loyalty between characters as opposite as Paris and Fearless what Ellison notes in "Richard Wright's Blues," that a Negro American community where "everyone is 'related,' regardless of blood-ties" (140) is one in which individuals are not merely members but family. It is that sense of connectedness that African Americans attempted to transport as they migrated to the urban North and West during the Second Great Migration. According to Ellison, "by comparison with the coldly impersonal relationships of the urban industrial community, [the Negro American community's] relationships are personal and warm" (140). Their sense of home produced constructive, distinct definitions of selfhood, a powerful sense of community, and alternative ideas of heroism.

The 1950s was central to the two decades that, according to Lemann, "made race a national issue in the second half of the century—an integral part of the politics, social thought, and the organization of ordinary life in the United States" (7). We can see the American Negro, then, as essential to the Civil Rights Movement of the 1960s and 1970s in challenging mainstream policies and resisting stereotypical definition of blackness. Thus, the construction of home that African Americans forged—and that Paris and Fearless navigate in Mosley's novels—not only re-creates the black folk culture of the rural South but also adapts to the new challenges of race and place posed by the urban North and West. Ellison's vision permeates Mosley's work through his presentation of a diverse, sometimes contradictory, black community that remains tied together by a common goal. The survival and progression of Paris and Fearless lend voice to a community that actively formulates techniques and traditions to survive, resist, and transcend racist oppression. Against the backdrop of this underappreciated time, Mosley revisits the time of the American Negro and explores and challenges traditional ideas of heroism, history, and home.

At Home on
"These Mean Streets"

Collaboration and Community in Walter Mosley's
Easy Rawlins Mystery Series

—ALBERT U. TURNER, JR.

In the Easy Rawlins mystery series, Walter Mosley employs many devices common to conventional hard-boiled detective fiction. This nine-text series features trenchant autodiegetic narration, a forbidding and alienating cityscape, and a full complement of transgressive tough guys, femme fatales, crooked cops, and amoral elites. Furthermore, Mosley's construction of Ezekiel "Easy" Rawlins as a hard-boiled protagonist links detection and philosophical inquiry into the nature of human evil. At base, these elements of Mosley's detective fiction evoke the hard-boiled writing of Raymond Chandler, Dashiell Hammett, and John D. MacDonald—authors Mosley identifies as significant influences on his early artistic efforts (Wilson 26). W. Russel Gray observes that Easy Rawlins's interactions with members of marginalized social groups, his resistance to coercion by the authorities, and his contestatory use of extralegal tactics are consistent with hard-boiled convention (489–94). However, the presence of echoes of traditional hard-boiled narration, setting, characterization, and inquiry in the Easy Rawlins series is not a capitulation to convention, nor, as Roger Berger argues, an "uncritical use" of an ostensibly Chandlerian "L.A. detective fiction paradigm" (281). As much as Mosley references these generic elements, he also explodes the genre as the Easy Rawlins series is a site where epistemological inquiry emanates from Mosley's pointed reconsideration of the convention of the aloof hero common to the genre. Mosley classifies hard-boiled heroism as the culmination of collaborative acts. He constructs Easy Rawlins and Raymond "Mouse" Alexander as African American co-protagonists. Consequently, the Easy

Rawlins series is a direct challenge to the heroic loner prototype advanced by Raymond Chandler in his groundbreaking theoretical work, "The Simple Art of Murder" (1950).

In this essay, Chandler sharply calls for more realism in hard-boiled narrative, and provides a still influential delineation of the traits of the genre's ideal hero. Chandler locates this figure in a forbidding cityscape—"these mean streets"— marked by a paucity of law and order (Chandler 17–18). As Chandler's "mean streets" are an arena of façade, moral decay and contagion, they call for a specific type of hero. Chandler's hard-boiled detective is an aloof individual who is "neither tarnished [by] nor afraid" of the city (18). Because of his outsider status, this hero is able to reify chivalric codes of conduct, identify transgressive actions and individuals, and master metaphorically dark urban territories.[1] The method of this mastery is seen as Chandler avers that the ideal hard-boiled hero's autodiegetic narrative reveals that "[t]he [successful detective] story is this man's adventure in search of a hidden truth" (18). Chandler suggests that epistemological inquiry is an individual rather than collaborative act. The narrative authority of Chandler's ideal hero is the product of a textual valorization of alienation that places the "pure" autodiegetic narrator above his mainly "impure" narrative subjects and the dystopian urban worlds they inhabit.[2] This problematic authority is evident as this figure's relationally superior voice gives him the authority to define and promote a reality far removed from the discourses of the common people and, potentially, community.

Charles Wilson, too, suggests that Mosley's detective fiction addresses the problematic of the isolate hard-boiled hero. In particular, according to Wilson, Mosley's detective fiction is a corrective to common depiction of hard-boiled detectives as "alienated from many of life's humanizing elements in that they [have] no families, no friends, no stable home life or jobs" (26). Consequently, Easy's achievement of heroic status is made possible through his acknowledging and embracing community membership. The detective hero of the Easy Rawlins series "is no longer the lone wolf whose personal life remains outside and distant from the criminal world he investigates. The mean streets he travels are his own" (Fine 147). Fine's allusion to the Chandlerian hard-boiled detective hero is suggestive of the alternative Mosley provides to exclusionary, hard-boiled ideological discourses that bolster masculinist, bourgeois, white social order.[3] Easy's narrative discourse asserts the value of home, community, and collaboration. Accordingly, Easy functions as a detective because he "is implicated by everything he shares with his neighbors—race, language, poverty, a migrant history that began in the South, and the neighborhood itself" (Fine 147). Therefore, it is credible that Mosley's particular construction of hard-boiled narrative provides a site from which to consider a means through which the hard-boiled hero can sustain African American communities. At base, Mosley's hard-boiled hero protects the private sphere of home and the public discourses that comprise community.

At a glance, the imperative that compels Easy to engage in detective work in *Devil in a Blue Dress* (1990)—finding the funds to pay his mortgage after he was fired unjustly from a defense industry job—does not seem to portend consideration of the problematic of community in hard-boiled fiction; concern for maintaining the private sphere of the home is not necessarily commensurate with concern for maintaining the public spheres in which communities have their being. However, Easy's complex reading of the significance of home in *Devil in a Blue Dress* suggests an overlapping of these spheres: "The thought of paying my mortgage reminded me of my front yard and the shade of my fruit trees in the summer heat. I felt that I was just as good as any white man, but if I didn't even own my front door then people would look at me like just another poor beggar, with his hands outstretched" (9). This passage stresses the unfixity of the line between private and public. Easy's statement asserts that home is a private site of individual pleasure and protection from natural forces. It also asserts that home is a potential safe space for ontological development. However, Easy's construction of home also has political and, thus, public dimensions. Mosley constructs Easy as a character aware that the loss of home would identify him as an inferior member of society and of his Watts community. Without a home, Easy would be inferior to "any white man." Moreover, the loss of home would lessen his esteem in the eyes of community residents who regard property ownership as fundamental to the potential realization of dreams of individual authority and attendant community viability. This passage demonstrates that the certification of Easy's residence in an African American community dominated by prosthetic memories of an enslaved, metaphorically homeless past is central to Mosley's vision of hard-boiled narrative.

That Easy contests white gangster DeWitt Albright's assumption of African American inferiority in *Devil in a Blue Dress* demonstrates the importance of this residence. When Albright and two of his minions have broken into Easy's Los Angeles home, Albright, who is interrogating Easy about the whereabouts of femme fatale Daphne Monet, makes a demand:

> "Give me some whiskey, Easy," he said. . . .
> "Get it yourself," I said. "Bottle's in the cabinet." Dewitt Albright looked up at me, and a big grin slowly spread across his face. He laughed and slapped his knee and said, "Well I'll be damned." I just looked at him. I was ready to die but I was going to go down fighting." (103–4)

As Easy resists Albright's attempt to expropriate his home symbolically, this scene anticipates a pattern of action in Mosley's detective series where Easy contests the incursions of transgressive whites like Albright into African American private and public spaces. Although homeownership is not identified as the signal requirement of community membership in *Devil in a Blue Dress*, Easy's verbal defense of the integrity of the private sphere demonstrates Mosley's propensity to examine the connection between the claiming of personal space and the public claiming of African American dignity.

Despite his resistance, in *Devil in a Blue Dress* Easy is coded as black, poor, desperate and, therefore, on the verge of losing his dignity. Consequently, Easy can be viewed as an example of the community instability that Chandler's ideal hero combats. In later novels, however, Easy's gradual transformation into a "confidential agent who represented people when the law broke down" (*WB* 9–10) is indicative of a dignified counterpoint to the alienated Chandlerian hero's dim view of ritually impure common people and their communities. As Mosley's artful representation of the expansion of Easy's consciousness from *A Red Death* (1991) to *Cinnamon Kiss* (2005) implies, the engagement of a ritually impure male subject—one coded as black and dangerous—in community affairs contradicts the broad assignation of social impurity common to the hard-boiled genre. Because the novels collectively foreground various phases of the African American historical epoch—the migration of African Americans from the Southwest to California, the postwar experience of World War II African American servicemen, the Civil Rights Movement, the Black Power Movement, and its unfortunate demise— they reflect Easy's individual participation in community history and discourse. Consequently, Easy Rawlins is a dignified man of his community as he asserts a distinctive and insolent voice that reflects the larger African American questioning of the dearth of American social justice found in the latter half of the twentieth century.

While Easy is not the aloof, alienated detective, his familiarity with underworld Los Angeles, his violent capabilities, and his sometimes irreverent discourse suggest that Mosley depicts him as a type of hard-boiled hero. In light of the obvious tension between this positioning and that of Easy as community champion, how does Easy the protagonist come to contest conventional hard-boiled ideological narrative? A potential answer is found in the means through which Mosley explodes the notion of the solitary hero common to this genre. As seen in the majority of *Devil in a Blue Dress*, Easy seemingly prefers to work in isolation; and in *A Red Death*, Easy at times exemplifies the propensity of the hard-boiled detective to be a vigilante. Nevertheless, Easy's relationships with various members of the African American community of Los Angeles confirm that he does not consistently exemplify the isolated, relationally superior nature of the traditional hard-boiled detective. Mosley's mystery series details the progression of his hard-boiled detective to a place within the ranks of African American "heroic individualists," namely, personalities who "align themselves with a group or mass public, but only on . . . their own terms" (Watts 111). Again, because of the ambiguity of this type of hero within and without the bounds of community, Easy's progression is problematic.

However, Easy's functioning as a trickster-like agent of community in *Devil in a Blue Dress, A Red Death,* and *White Butterfly* (1992) resolves the potential contradiction posed by the collision of Easy's occupational and community concerns. On one hand, Easy is employed by whites or white public authorities to provide the "favor" of searching Los Angeles's African American spaces for clues. Easy's ability to find missing persons or to discover the identities of murderers for his white employers is a product of his familiarity with African American individuals, communities, and social spaces. As detailed in the first three novels of this series, these acts of detection are textbook examples of dissembling since Easy's work addresses personal and community interests. On the other hand, Easy is also in the habit of openly providing favors for members of his African American community. Engagement in discourse to which whites have little, if any, access makes these labors on the behalf of members of his African American community possible. At base, detection allows Easy participation in the community dialogues that function as counterpublic discourse.[4]

The importance of protagonist engagement in counterpublic discourse to establishing a bond between detective and community is further established by Mosley's construction of Easy and Mouse as co-protagonists. Mosley's co-protagonists, at the least, are identifiable as hybrids of hard-boiled and African American folk heroic discourses. This is the case as the arguably hard-boiled heroes of Mosley's detective fiction also function as types of the "badman" and the "bad nigger" of African American folklore.[5] In light of his residence on the mean streets of Watts and his employment of violence in defense of his interests and those of African American communities, Easy is a type of African American badman. Mouse unrepentantly employs violence to assert his reputation and rule Mosley's version of the mean streets. Therefore, he is a type of bad nigger. Originally, the folkloric bad nigger was an antebellum African American outlaw who, through defiance and criminal behavior, asserted a hypervisible masculinity contrary to the aims of community building. The folkloric African American badman was a Reconstruction Era solid citizen—often a working-class African American male—who was forced to defend his life, his masculine honor, and African American notions of individual dignity with justifiable violence because of the threats posed by agents of the law and white masculine authority. John Roberts also observes that many African Americans of the Reconstruction era envisioned the badman as a hero who counteracted the threats to African American communities posed by bad niggers (214–15). Consequently, Mosley's portrayal of his co-protagonists is dependent on cooperation between character types who represent alternative and often conflicting strategies to combat racialist authoritative discourses. This cooperation is the product of their intimacy and regard for one another. For example, Mouse defines Easy as "the only good man that he ever knew" (*LS* 297), while Easy states that "Mouse was the truest friend I ever had" (*RD* 57). Moreover, Mouse's propensity for decisive action provides guidance to Easy that is uncharacteristic of common portrayals of the bad nigger; as Easy states in *Devil in a Blue Dress*, "[w]ithout Mouse I didn't know what to do" (194).

Mosley's particular depiction of this collaborative form of African American masculinist heroism allows for examination of African American communal discourses. This quality of collaboration is seen in *Devil in a Blue Dress* as Mouse compares Daphne Monet's willing experience with passing to Easy's attempts to attain middle class status through education and property ownership:

> "You just like Ruby [Daphne Monet]," Mouse said.
> "What you say?"
> "She wanna be white. All them years people be tellin' her how she light-skinned and beautiful but all the time she knows that she can't have what white people have. . . ."
> "What's that gotta do with me?"
> "That's just like you, Easy. You learn stuff and you be thinkin' like white men be thinkin'. You be thinkin' that what's right fo' them is right fo' you. She look like she white and you think like you white. But brother you don't know that you both poor niggers. And a nigger ain't never gonna be happy 'less he accept what he is." (205)

Mouse criticizes Easy's attempts at self-improvement as being assimilative, thereby highlighting the importance of Mosley's depiction of Easy's personal struggles with Du Bois's concept of double-consciousness to the success of this series. Mouse's commentary also demonstrates that this liminal state is a common topic of African American community discussion. Mouse's philosophical treatise on assimilation, African American positionality, and identity is representative of African American debates about the possibility of achieving full membership in American society. At base, Mouse is represented as a perceptive thinker who engages in the deliberation crucial to the construction of counterpublic discourses. Through his embrace of dialogism, Mouse serves as a means to implicate Easy further in the discourses of home and community.

This movement towards the discourses of home and community is possible as Easy and Mouse are products and conveyances of African American counterpublic discourse. Easy and Mouse exemplify the degree to which a counterpublic's "awareness of its subordinate status" allows for the circulation of alternative, contestatory discourses within public spheres (Warner 119). This is the case as their respective public assumption of badman and bad nigger roles circulates collective African American concerns within a larger, previously exclusionary public. Accordingly, Mosley affords his co-protagonists a specific discursive function; they are representation and conveyance of an African American discourse that would otherwise be subordinated. The connection of Mosley's co-protagonists to counterpublic discourse is also demonstrated through their negotiation and protection of African American private and public spaces. For example, Easy's acts of detection are only possible as viable African American public spaces and their attendant social discourses and cultural practices exist. The speakeasies, the jazz clubs, and the bars that Easy and Mouse frequent in Mosley's imagined Los Angeles of the 1940s, 1950s, and 1960s are sites where counterpublic discourses are formed. They are also generally inviolable African American public spaces where African American bootleggers, hijackers, prostitutes, drunks, blues and jazz musicians, and "square" individuals like Odell, Easy's church-going friend, engage in discourse. What is affirmed here is the democratic nature of these spaces; they are not solely the domain of badmen and bad niggers. Rather, they are cultural spaces that "offer bases for critical action within broader public spheres against the privilege of dominant social groups" (Lowney 358–59).

Easy's contestation of this privilege is impossible without the assistance of his bad nigger co-protagonist Mouse. This is demonstrated as Easy comes to work primarily for himself and the African American community in *A Little Yellow Dog* (1996), *Bad Boy Brawly Brown* (2002), *Six Easy Pieces* (2003), and *Cinnamon Kiss*. Mouse's relationship with Easy changes in these texts; Mouse often serves as means for Easy to understand when violent action is necessary. Moreover, in *Bad Boy Brawly Brown*, Mouse's function, as is the case in the earlier novels in the series, is to protect Easy. Here Easy and Sam Houston, an African American diner owner and street-corner philosopher, converse about the reaction of the African American community to Easy's relationship with Mouse:

> "You know, Easy," Sam Houston said. "I was surprised to see you when you walked in the other day."
> "Yeah?" I asked. "How come?". . .
> " 'Cause I thought you'd be dead by now," Sam said.
> "Dead? Why dead?"
> "Because the only reason a lotta mothahfuckahs out there didn't come after you was because'a Raymond," Sam said. "They hated you but they were more scared of Mouse. Some'a the peoples come in my place called you all kindsa dog, but they knew better than to even say sumpin' to you. Shit. Easy Rawlins got a guardian angel from hell, that's what they said." (*Bad Boy* 236–37)

As much as Mouse serves as an ironic champion of African American community, he also inspires African American heroic discourses. Mouse is "the most perfect human being a black man could imagine . . . and one of the best storytellers you ever heard" (*Bad Boy* 237). Mouse is, therefore, a subject and a conveyance of the community discourses that dominate Mosley's series.

Nonetheless, this contemporary bad nigger is consistently identified as a nihilistic, problematic African American personality. Lawrence Levine suggests that the figure from which Mouse is drawn kills "not merely in self-defense but from sadistic need and sheer joy" (Levine 417–18). Easy observes that Mouse, true to the outlines of this folk antihero, "didn't feel guilt or remorse" for the violence that allows him to maintain a limited social authority (*RD* 58). Moreover, as Mouse is a participant in the activities of the underground economy of Los Angeles, he resists mainstream American social norms and contests the standards of middle class African American communities. In *Little Scarlet* (2004), this tendency is confirmed through Mosley's detailing of Mouse's engagement in profiteering activities during the 1965 Watts riot. Consequently, Mouse's potentially positive connection to community is compromised by an ethic of opportunism.

In addition, throughout the Easy Rawlins mystery series, Mouse exhibits the vanity, womanizing, and pride-influenced viciousness that Daryl Dance identifies as traits of the bad nigger (224–25). Ironically, the result of one of his instances of pride-influenced viciousness leads Mouse to reconsider the efficacy of violence as a means to assert his masculinity and compels Easy to acknowledge Mouse's importance as a community figure. In *A Little Yellow Dog*, Mouse has a failed sexual encounter with a woman because of impotence. Because of his wounded pride, Mouse murders Sweet Willie, an older bad nigger and a running buddy rumored to be his father. Mouse's uncharacteristically visible demonstration of sorrow is also suggestive of the degree to which Mouse is willingly vulnerable to Easy and relies upon him for moral guidance: "'I didn't mean to hit him,' Raymond said. 'You know that woman didn't mean a damn thing t'me. When William hit the ground I knew I was wrong. I was gonna say I was sorry. I was gonna buy him a drink—but he went for his gun, Easy. I swear he did'. . . . Raymond was crying. Not blubbering or shaking, but there were real tears in his eyes. I had never seen him sad over anything he'd done. Seeing him cry brought tears uncontrollably to my own eyes" (31). Mouse's reaction to this killing indicates a point of progression in Mosley's complex depiction of Mouse as a bad nigger. While the traditional bad nigger employed violence indiscriminately and without remorse, Mouse attempts to live according to a specific, honorable code of violence. This is seen during the following exchange in *A Little Yellow Dog* between Mouse and his son, LaMarque. This conversation is related to Easy by EttaMae, Mouse's sometimes wife.

"You know what he said?" Etta asked.
"What?"
"LaMarque, don't you never kill a man that don't deserve to die." (77)

As a consequence of his remorse, Mouse gives up his firearm in *A Little Yellow Dog* and considers entry into legitimate spaces of home, employment, and community. The following passage explains the genesis of this transformation: "'I 'ont think it's wrong to kill somebody, Easy,' he said at last. 'I mean that is what life is all about—killin', killin to survive. . . . I don't have a gun on me but that's just because I don't wanna kill nobody right now. I mean, if I had to do it I could get me a firearm. But right now I just wanna see what it's like to live wit' your family an' work a job. But I ain't scared. I'm lookin' for a new way—that's all'" (*LYD* 251–52). This transformation evidences Mouse's awareness of the problems that his bad nigger existence presents to African American communities. Yet the fact that the unarmed Mouse is shot in *A Little Yellow Dog* as he assists Easy with a case allows for further examination of the significance of Mouse to Mosley's discussion of the relationship of the bad nigger to African American communities.

After Mouse is shot, Easy comes to believe that Mouse has been killed. Therefore, a major theme in *Bad Boy Brawly Brown* and the first five short stories of *Six Easy Pieces* is Easy's remorse at the part that he believes he played in Mouse's death. The elegiac opening scene of *Bad Boy Brawly Brown* reveals Easy's remorse and is central to Mosley's particular depiction of the hard-boiled hero: "Mouse is dead. Those words had gone through my mind every morning for three months. *Mouse is dead because of me.* . . . I wandered into the living room and pulled the sash to open the drapes. Red sunlight glinted through the ragged palms at the end of our block. I had never wept over Raymond's demise, but that tattered light reflected a pain deep in my mind" (3–4, italics in original). As it is linked to Easy's consideration of Mouse's reaction to his murder of Sweet Willie Dokes in *A Little Yellow Dog*, this meditation on remorse is significant to Mosley's larger discussion of heroism. Easy's sorrow at witnessing Mouse's pain in *A Little Yellow Dog* is indicative of his understanding of Mouse as a particular type of African American hero. In *Bad Boy Brawly Brown*, Easy is remorseful at depriving the African American community of this complex champion. As Mosley's discussion of remorse in these two novels suggests, Easy's reading of Mouse contradicts the notion that bad niggers were "marginal men . . . who had to be sacrificed whenever the business of living needed to be pushed forward" (Genovese 630).

In fact, *Bad Boy Brawly Brown* demonstrates that Mouse is integral to allowing the business of African American communal survival to be "pushed forward." The remorseful Easy reminisces about Mouse using the threat of violence to help two African American men, Mercury and Chapman, who had stolen a local dockworkers' union payroll. Once their identities were discovered by the white mob-connected union hierarchy, Mercury and Chapman went into hiding. Mercury later asked for help from Easy, who, after retrieving the stolen payroll, requested that Mouse accompany him to the union hall to meet with a union official. In the following passage, Mouse's defense of Mercury and Chapman involves discourse and decisive action:

"They made a mistake, Bob," Mouse said to the man who had introduced himself as Mr. Robert. He wore a long coat and hat and stood over Mouse, who, already a smallish man, was seated.

"That's not enough—," Mr. Robert began in his guttural, East Coast snarl.

Before he could finish, Mouse leapt to his feet, pulled out his long-nosed .41-caliber pistol, and shot the hat right off of Robert's head. The two men who stood behind him gestured toward their guns but changed their minds when they looked down the barrel of Mouse's smoking piece. (15)

After firing his weapon, Mouse convinces the mobsters to leave Mercury and Chapman alone and provide him with a "finder's fee" of ten percent. After giving Mercury and Chapman $500 each, he splits the remainder with Easy. While, in typical bad nigger fashion, the potential for financial gain seems to be partial motivation for Mouse's actions, it is significant that Mouse verbally and physically menaces the white masculine authority embodied in Mr. Robert *and* chooses to share his spoils with other African American males. However faint the evidence here, Mouse's connection to community is clear.

Accordingly, Mouse is a type of hero to some African American males in the social world of Mosley's detective novels. This view is affirmed in *White Butterfly* as Easy, upon seeing an incarcerated Mouse, considers the potential heroic status of this bad nigger: "The door behind me opened and Mouse, manacled hand and foot, shuffled in, followed by the warder. It made me sick at heart to see Raymond like that. He was the only black man I'd ever known who had never been chained, in his mind, by the white man. Mouse was brash and wild and free. He might have been insane, but any Negro who dared to believe in his own freedom in America had to be mad. The sight of his incarceration made me shudder inside" (145). Easy's valuation of Mouse as community symbol explains his complicated attraction to Mouse, and suggests the means whereby Mouse provides Easy with the space to act and engage in community discourse. It is significant that a main theme of *Bad Boy Brawly Brown* and *Six Easy Pieces* is the influence of Mouse's ghostly presence on Easy's actions to preserve his home. In *Bad Boy Brawly Brown*, Detective Knorr, a white supremacist cop, visits Easy at home, threatens Easy's livelihood and, through implication, threatens to end Easy's relationship with his unofficially adopted children, Jesus and Feather. Detective Knorr's threats are a means to get Easy to comply with his request that Easy become a police informant to help solve murders that are allegedly connected to the activities of an African American political organization. After ushering Knorr out of his home, Easy is led to consider decisive action: " 'Why don't you leave?' [Knorr] gave me a one-eighth nod and frigid grin, then got to his feet and moved toward the door. As I watched him leave, my mind went back to Mouse. 'Kill him,' my friend whispered from the grave" (107). This passage signals a shift in Easy's voice and the methods that he employs to ensure his safety and that of his family; Mouse, the bad nigger, inspires Easy. Further evidence of this shift occurs in the short story "Smoke" when Easy impersonates Mouse to allow a successful meeting with a white gangster, Mr. Hass. While Hass is a fearsome character, as Easy relates, "I would have been afraid, but because I was using Mouse's name, there was no fear in me" (27).

This ghostly presence is suggestive of the inner voice that advises Easy. In *Devil in a Blue Dress*, as Easy observes, the inner voice "is hard. It never cares if I'm scared or in danger. It just looks at all the facts and tells me what I need to do" (97). The unity of Mouse's ghostly presence and Easy's inner voice exemplifies the strong connection of Mouse the bad nigger to Easy the badman. This connection is also seen as Easy considers his relationship with Mouse in "Smoke." As Easy observes, "Raymond Alexander had been the largest part of my history. . . . Raymond was the only one who respected me and cared for me and was willing to throw his lot in with mine, no matter the odds" (35). How does one interpret this statement given the problems that characterize their relationship and the fact that Mosley's mystery series is replete with textual references to Easy's concerns about Mouse's propensity for violence? What is Mosley suggesting here as he links the histories of two character types whose world views are, at times, diametrically opposed? A potential answer is provided in "Gray-Eyed Death," the penultimate entry in *Six Easy Pieces*.

In "Gray-Eyed Death" Mouse's resurrection through the agency of his godmother Mama Jo, a conjure woman first introduced in *Gone Fishin'* (1997), is revealed to Easy. Through his reaction to his encounter with the "resurrected" Mouse, Easy provides an example of the crucial relationship of the badman and bad nigger in Mosley's detective fiction: "As the moments ticked by I got used to seeing him. That was easy because Mouse had never really been dead for me. I took him with me everywhere I went. He was my barometer for evil, my advisor when no good man would have known what to say. Raymond was proof that a black man could live by his own rules in America when everybody else denied it. Why couldn't he crawl up out of the grave whenever he felt like it?" (200–201). As Mosley's reunion of his bad nigger and his badman in "Gray-Eyed Death" suggests, Easy and Mouse are two parts of an ever-present whole. Their different approaches to combating threats to African American communities reflect a necessary and ongoing conversation about how to sustain African American notions of home and dignity. Moreover, Easy's identification of Mouse's capacity as an advisor suggests that the Easy Rawlins series creates a semblance of order that contests the privileged narratives of dominant social groups by shaping seemingly disordered or, rather, culturally specific clues into a coherent narrative structure. In effect, Mosley's manipulation of folk discourse represents the opposition between African American and white forms of cultural knowledge as a contest over meaning. The fact that Easy is more a moral badman than he is a hard-boiled detective provides him partial access to this meaning. More significantly, the status of Raymond "Mouse" Alexander is an unlikely revision of the hard-boiled hero, a bad nigger. As Easy's co-protagonist, Mouse allows Easy to access meaning and function as a hard-boiled champion of community. However, the value of this unlikely collaboration extends to more than the functioning of these characters in their social world. Readers of the Easy Rawlins series are afforded access to the possibilities that Mosley's hard-boiled narratives have for encouraging inquiry into the nature of heroic construction, heroic collaboration, and the means by which even outlaw figures can support home and community.

Notes

1. For further discussion of the characteristics of Chandler's hero see Rzepka.

2. My use of "pure" and "impure" is gleaned from the purity/impurity schema anthropologist Mary Douglas advances in *Purity and Danger: An Analysis of Concepts of Pollution and Taboo* (1966). In this text, Douglas discusses the construction of rituals of impurity as a process whereby individuals are bracketed within or separated from a dominant modern society. At base, subjects identified with the social upheaval found in the transgression of social rituals and order are seen as a source of contagion.

3. For discussion of the connection of the traditional hard-boiled detective hero to the establishment of authoritative discourses, see Reddy.

4. The notion of the counterpublic as an oppositional public discourse community is the product of Nancy Frazer's reading of the Habermasian bourgeois public sphere as a site where truly inclusive public discourse and rational-critical debate is impossible because of social stratification. For further discussion see Habermas, *Structural Transformation*; Fraser.

5. For discussion of the bad nigger and badman see Bryant; Roberts, John W.; and Thomas, H. Nigel.

The Mouse Will Play

The Parodic in Walter Mosley's Fiction

—Laura Quinn

In "Parody and Detective Fiction" (1997), Janice MacDonald claims, "There are reasons to believe that parody is at work within the genre of detective fiction." Among the reasons are these: detective fiction "creates the context necessary for audience recognition of parody" since readership tends to be habitual, even addictive; additionally, the formulaic specificity of the genre, its repetitive conventionality, has inherent parodic potential (63). As an element of the formula itself, parody is "designed both to foster credibility and to generate new material within the highly mechanical formula" (68). According to MacDonald, it achieves both goals in the detective novel when "authors used it to situate their novels self-consciously above those of their predecessors and competitors" (71). Here we have what Linda Hutcheon in *The Politics of Postmodernism* (1989), her important work on postmodern parody, refers to as "uses and abuses" of literary predecessors (95). The delineations of parody for these critics and for my purposes here go well beyond dictionary definitions of parody as imitation aimed to ridicule; what Hutcheon calls postmodernist parody that "works to foreground the politics of representation" and comprises a "value-problematizing, denaturalizing form of acknowledging the history (and through irony, the politics) of representation" (94) is the critical arena in which Mosley's detective fiction can be productively confronted.

That theories of postmodernist parody converge deftly with Henry Louis Gates Jr.'s thick description of "Signifyin(g)" in *The Signifying Monkey* (1988) is crucial to an understanding of Mosley as parodist. Both Gates's signifying and Hutcheon's postmodernist parody are grounded in formal and rhetorical repetition with a critical or "signal" difference (Hutcheon, qtd in McDonald, 62; Gates xxiv). For Hutcheon, that difference consists of a self-conscious acknowledgment of and subversion of the authority of form and convention: "What postmodern parody does is to evoke what reception theorists call the horizon of expectation of the spectator, a horizon formed by recognizable conventions of genre, style, or form of representation. This is then destabilized and dismantled step by step" (114). The more specifically racialized purpose of Gates's repetition with a signal/ critical difference is "to turn away from, to step outside the white hermeneutical circle and into the black" (258). In other words Gates's *difference* is a racialized revision of discourses of blackness as these appear in both white and black-authored texts. I argue that Walter Mosley's Easy Rawlins series gets a lot of mileage out of parodic signifying on the premises of the (largely white and male) hard-boiled genre of detective fiction and that the "critical difference" in Mosley's repetition of the conventions of that genre lies in the ways in which Mosley vexes the relationship between hard-boiled detection and the formal institutions of the law and the police. Inasmuch as these institutions underwrite a national social order and, given the racial history of that social order, Mosley's vexings might well be seen as part of the project to secure a homeland for black Americans.

There is a consensus in critical work on detective fiction that, however unofficial and maverick the fictional detective may be, he (and increasingly, she) works toward and brings about lawful and orderly ends. Detective novels are kissing cousins of the police procedural genre and true crime fiction, both of which are grounded in a fundamentally conservative law and order ideology. Mosley's African American predecessors, writers like Rudolph Fisher and Chester Himes, feature police detectives as their sleuthing protagonists and, nonetheless, often manage to level a critical attack on racist practices within law enforcement. Mosley critics, most notably Theodore O. Mason, Jr. and John Cullen Gruesser, have argued convincingly that he goes well beyond his predecessors in raising serious questions about the "order" protected by the "law" that polices the world of Easy Rawlins's Los Angeles of the late forties through mid-sixties. That order is tenaciously racist; thus Easy Rawlins, as an unlicensed and unsanctioned detective, needs to work to subvert the racist injustices of "the law," to protect his black community from predatory whites, from police abuse, and sometimes from itself. This will often amount to enabling "criminals" to elude the long arm of the law. Ironically, when Easy does become a licensed private investigator in *Little Scarlet* (2004) after the LAPD rewards him for solving a murder that threatened the tenuous post-Watts social order, the license comes to signify his complicity with a racist criminal justice system. The license and the professional legitimacy that it bestows are subsequently held over his head by the "authorities" in the recent Easy Rawlins novel, *Cinnamon Kiss* (2005). Thus, though the official status it allots to him does facilitate his efforts to do justice according to his lights and to serve his beleaguered community, the license becomes one among many racialized compromises that Easy makes in "finding a home" within his profession.

Of course, even within the moral economy of the genre, classic hard-boiled detectives often play fast and loose with the limits and structures of formal law enforcement, but they are understood generally to do this to supplement and improve upon those structures, all in the interest of seeing justice done and social order restored. Mosley's erstwhile detective—Easy Rawlins, after all, has two other professions, that of custodial supervisor at a public school and that of landlord and rental property owner—often (but not always) needs to subvert rather than supplement the efforts of formal law enforcement in order to protect and serve his marginalized community. Another way to put this is that Easy, as the (mostly) extralegal, unofficial protector and enforcer of law and order within his alternative community cannot afford to be altogether "at home" in either the value nexus or social order that undergirds an American Dream ideology nor in the hard-boiled genre to which he is narratively consigned. To paraphrase Janice MacDonald, whom I quoted in my opening paragraph, Easy in the detective's role must be simultaneously credible and new, both thematically and generically, in order to activate the critical dimension of postmodern parody.

Here, then is the parodic, signifying critical revision: Mosley uses the hard-boiled genre—with all of its gritty, seamy realism, its mean streets, and, yes, its routine police brutality that, despite the potential for critique of "the system," always manages to recontain its disruptions to its social order—at once to reiterate and to destabilize the formula. He makes rich use of its conventions while striving to bring its chickens home to roost by denaturalizing those conventions through a process of unmasking the undemocratic interests that they serve. Roger A. Berger argues that such an undertaking on Mosley's part is largely doomed. In answer to his own question—"Can he make the genre black, or will the genre essentially whiten him?" (291)—Berger lands in the following place: "African-American authors, of course, are free to intervene in any discursive landscape, but Mosley's entry into hardboiled detective fiction, a (white-male) genre rather inimical to a progressive struggle for racial equality, justice, and freedom, carries with it a heavy price; and Mosley cannot fully disentangle himself from the reactionary politics that are embedded in the genre. At the same time, however, one might say that, just as there has always already been an Africanist presence in American literature, so there has also always already been a black presence in American hard-boiled fiction, and Mosley is actually making manifest what has previously been latent" (292). Berger's conviction that Mosley fails to avoid the genre's political trap interestingly equivocates toward the end of the passage above; the act of making manifest the latent presence of blackness in the hard-boiled genre begins to gesture toward the self-conscious denaturalizing work that postmodern parody does. Mosley's commercially successful appropriation of the hard-boiled genre might not wholly or coherently subvert the "reactionary" and mostly unacknowledged politics of the genre, especially for readers with entrenched horizons of expectation, but it does go a long way toward destabilizing those politics, a claim that can most compellingly be made through an analysis of the most highly stylized character in the series.

The primary engine and repository of postmodern signifying parody in the Easy Rawlins series is Mouse, aka Raymond Alexander, whose presence, absence, and reappearance in the eight novels (plus the short stories that appeared in 2003 as *Six Easy Pieces*) constitutes that "black presence" that Berger, drawing on Toni Morrison's *Playing in the Dark* (1992), implicitly posits as the antidote to the conservative (that is, anti-liberatory) straitjacket of the hard-boiled form. This essay seeks to examine the ways in which the figure of Mouse is parodic and the ways in which parodic figuration of Mouse works to "slip the yoke" of genre, as well as to destabilize ideologically conservative and reductively redemptive notions of "home" and "community" in the series.

More than one critic has written at length and with acuity about the figure of Mouse and his relationship with Easy as well as his ambiguous and evolving structural role in the series. John Cullen Gruesser calls Easy's relationship with Mouse "one of the most innovative features of Mosley's mystery series" (248). William R. Nash sees the sidekick relationship of Mouse and Easy as "the clearest manifestation of Easy's double consciousness" and, thus, central to the world of the works (306). Berger, who calls Mouse "a kind of amoral double for Rawlins," goes on to say that "Mosley has thus split the hard-boiled detective into two, reflecting or almost parodying Du Bois's notion of an African-American 'double consciousness'" (291). I would get rid of the "almost" in arguing that Mouse's relationship with Easy most certainly parodies Du Bois's double consciousness as well as the literary concepts of both the foil and doppelganger, and the popular culture convention of the sidekick. Mouse is parody multiplied in terms of both his representation and his relationship with Easy, the protagonist of the entire series. Mouse serves as a multipurpose trope or rhetorical device in the novels, contributing in crucial and ironic ways to the series' political edge.

The figure of Mouse is ubiquitous in the Easy Rawlins series. In all nine installments, from *Devil in a Blue Dress* (1990) to *Cinnamon Kiss* (2005), he is a looming presence or absence. This remains true even though Mouse ostensibly dies in *A Little Yellow Dog* (1996). *Bad Boy Brawly Brown* (2002), the next novel in the series, opens with the sentence "Mouse is dead," and, yet, Mouse appears on at least forty-five pages of the novel—in fact Easy, who has given up life on the street for a life of respectability and child-raising, goes back to the detective business in this novel to get his mind off of his sense of responsibility for Mouse's death. Moreover, uncertainty as to whether Mouse is really dead holds open the possibility of his narrative reappearance. In fact, throughout *Bad Boy Brawly Brown* Mouse is a catalytic absent presence, perhaps more consistently present in his absence than he is in the novels in which he is alive. Of course, even prior to his death, Mouse is as powerful in his absence as in his presence; Easy is frequently backed up by Mouse's deadly reputation in the street, even if the murderous sidekick is not around. Mouse's violent deadliness is the stuff of urban legend, and the excess in both the violence and the potency of the reputation are the stuff of parody.

Mouse is emphatically a parody of the buddy or sidekick figure, so ubiquitous in popular film and fiction. He is loyal—in a way—to Easy, has "got his back," and comes to Easy's rescue—often, seemingly out of nowhere—multiple times in the series. Even in his absence from an immediate dilemma into which Easy is placed, Mouse's reputation for violence provides Easy with "muscle." Mouse is, again, parodic in his excess; much of the time Easy can not control or predict Mouse's violence, Easy is often terrified of him and what he might do, and yet, Easy himself betrays Mouse by sleeping with Mouse's main woman EttaMae, thereby surely playing with fire, and being aroused by the danger of doing so. The convention of a sidekick who is a foil by virtue of being what MacDonald calls "the slow-witted partner of the Great Detective," or the Watson model (64), is adhered to on the surface; Mouse can not read anything but his own name throughout most of the series, which sharply contrasts with the well-developed reading habits of Easy, who is drawn to used bookstores and canonized African American literature. But both the conventional sidekick attributes of loyalty and mental limitation are excessively offset—undone, in effect—by his radical self-confidence: "Mouse was a small, rodent-featured man who believed in himself without question. He only cared about what was his. He'd go against a man bigger than I was with no fear because he knew that nobody was better than him. He might have been right" (*RD* 27). Clearly this representation and this particular sidekick relationship self-consciously signify on innumerable Sancho Panzas and Watsons and Tontos in both literary and pop cultural texts. In exceeding—by so much—conventional sidekick containment, the figure of Mouse works to critique the power relations inherent in that convention, deflating and destabilizing the predominance of the detective/protagonist. In other words, by refusing to be "at home" in any conventional auxiliary role, Mouse threatens to dislodge Easy from his protagonistic home base as the center of the novel's values, authority, and narrative ownership.

Additionally, Mouse is parodic by virtue of being a small man, not a burly black brute, a blaxploitation Superfly or a Shaft figure physically, however much his impact on those around him mirrors that of such figures. The nickname Mouse is playful; it points to his ratlike facial features but also to his diminutive status and to the glaring and over-the-top ways in which he is a man rather than a mouse according to the standards of the mean streets. He, above all men, can afford to be called Mouse. The nickname and the rat-face description also gesture toward signifying animal folktales in which smaller creatures outwit larger, seemingly deadlier ones. Of course, his caricatured diminutive stature is overcompensated by both the larger-than-life size of his signature .41-caliber weapon and the self-proclaimed size of his dick: "'Cause you know I got sumpin' give any man pause"

(*RD 56*). Here is the stuff of parodic hypermasculine cliché. In narratives that discursively mean to live in the world of gritty, hard-boiled urban realism, inflected by the kind of moral realism shaped by Easy's middle-class consciousness, we have a fabular, comic book-like character whom Easy describes as "the truest friend I ever had. And if there is such a thing as true evil, he was that too" (*RD* 57).

But Mouse is also a shape-shifter. He slips persistently throughout the series between "Mouse" the legend, and Raymond or Ray Alexander, the material man, especially in Easy's references to him, remembrances of him, dreams and nightmares about him. It is Raymond Alexander who settles down in *A Little Yellow Dog*, after killing Sweet William, his current running mate and probable biological father in a fight over a woman. It is Raymond Alexander who makes a home in that novel with EttaMae and his son Lamarque, who starts going to church, teaching himself to read, working under Easy's supervision at Sojourner Truth middle school as a janitor. Mouse seems to be following in Easy's footsteps in this effort to substitute "home" for the streets. However, it appears that this domestication and materialization of Mouse the Legend leads to the death of Raymond Alexander. Discursively, when the cartoon/comic book/animal fable figure slides down into realist (and domestic) narrative, he becomes vulnerable, post-invincible. The slippage from legend to mortal man is parodic in its temporal inversion—the legend both precedes and postdates the material man. When Mouse appears as an absent presence in *Bad Boy Brawly Brown*, it is mostly as Mouse the legend. Interestingly when he reappears in the short story "Gray-Eyed Death" in *Six Easy Pieces*, all prior melodramatic treatment of Easy's guilt and grief over his death gives way to a comic moment that highlights Mouse's diminutive stature: "The knocking was soft and unhurried. Whoever it was, he, or she, was in no rush. When I pulled the door open I was looking too high, above the man's head. And then I saw him" (198). This moment falls immediately after yet another confirmation that Mouse is, in fact, dead. Its self-consciously anticlimactic quality is further enhanced by a description of Mouse that, like most previous descriptions in earlier novels, concentrates on his clothes, as if he were indeed a disembodied figure, only given material shape and substance by what he wears: "He wore gray slacks and an ochre-colored jacket. His shirt was charcoal and there was gold edging on three of his teeth. On his baby finger he wore a thick gold ring sporting an onyx face studded with eight or nine diamond chips. His shoes were leather, honed to a high shine. He wore no hat. Kennedy killed hats by going bareheaded to his inauguration, any haberdasher will tell you that. And if Mouse was a slave to anything it was fashion" (198–99). The passage is richly playful. The ring has a face but Mouse's is not mentioned. He is dapper and gilded, but the colors are conservative for Mouse. Mouse's following the fashion of Kennedy who got killed the same day that Mouse was shot—seemingly fatally—shifts that monumental convergence of events onto the trivial plane of fashion where Kennedy "kills" hats instead of being killed by getting shot in the head. And in the short story just prior to "Gray-Eyed

Death" in *Six Easy Pieces*—entitled "Silver Lining"—we are told that Easy always loved Mouse because "he never accepted our slave heritage" (99). On his return from the dead, he is depicted as a slave to fashion. It is as if all the damage of that epic moment of November 22, 1963 has been undone. This is not the discursive world of gritty urban realism or moral, middle-class domestic realism; we are at "home" in the realm of the parodic.

Throughout the series, Mouse's signature dapperness is paradoxically paired with the messy spillage of his excessive and often gratuitous violence. For example, his killing of Joppy in *Devil in a Blue Dress*, in which Mouse shoots the bound and tied man first in the groin and then in the right eye, is not atypical. His acts are described by Easy as amoral, and Easy anguishes over them. Yet what marks Mouse and his violence in every novel is his effectiveness. With his violent acts or merely with the threat of action or even with his looming absent presence, Mouse gets the job done. In this regard Mouse—far more than Easy—is akin to pop culture figures with superhuman powers of the Batman, Superman, Blade ilk, to martial arts movie and TV figures such as Bruce Lee or Walker, Texas Ranger, to the Blaxploitation heroes, to Terminator-like fantasy figures. Mouse's intuitively timed appearances on the scene when Easy is in trouble are the equivalent of the cavalry arriving in the nick of time. To the extent that Easy partakes of the vulnerabilities of hard-boiled detectives like Phillip Marlowe, he is foiled by Mouse, who is invincible. Jerry H. Bryant claims that "Mosley clearly wants us to think of Mouse as part of the old-fashioned badman tradition" (147). And stylized as this figure might be historically and in Mosley's version, badman Mouse goes beyond the sidekick function of "having Easy's back," reaching toward a generically and thematically disruptive representation of the latent threat of deadly black retaliatory violence that has historically struck fear into white hearts, a latter day version of the Nat Turners of the world the planters made. The formidable efficacy of Mouse's excess, along with Easy's inability to control him, imperils the synthesis that Easy doggedly attempts to forge out of his own middle class domestic values and vigilante commitment to justice for his community. Mouse is incompletely contained by his stylization, threatening always to step out of the cartoon into historically recognizable political space.

Until he dies, that is. The domestication and the taming of Mouse in *A Little Yellow Dog* that culminates in his death could be read as a textual abandoning of the kind of deadly pop-cultural efficacy of Mouse the Legend. It might be seen as signaling a serious material turn in the series—a sort of growing up—and one that facilitates the gradual intertextual movement of Easy, the hero-narrator, toward middle-class respectability and normalcy—indeed, toward a "home"-based ideology. This new grounding is multiply manifested in Easy's dedication to his job as supervisor of a janitorial staff, his deep commitment to his children, Jesus and Feather, whom he has adopted illegally and unofficially after rescuing them from the mean streets, and his promising and largely monogamous relationship with Bonnie Shay, who will move in with him after Raymond's death. William R. Nash argues that Mouse's exit from the scene enables Easy to transcend a limiting double consciousness, thereby attaining "a positive self-understanding and an affirmation of [his] blackness that counters the destruction of the streets that both beckon and threaten" (322), suggesting that with Mouse gone, an empowered and self-integrated Easy will be more effective at negotiating the mean streets of South Central L.A. Such high-serious readings, while intriguing in the way they tie Mosley's work to an African American textual tradition with its evocation of double consciousness, risk losing the sense of play and parodic troping that is an integral and signature part of Mosley's work. Mouse's death, its aftermath, and his resurrection are ludically and parodically rendered in several key narrative moments.

Consider the strikingly rhetorical staging of Mouse's death on November 22, 1963. Immediately following the traumatic experience of watching Mouse take a bullet intended for him, Easy drops Mouse's dying body off at EttaMae's and, as he drives the streets, he sees people weeping. Not knowing yet that Kennedy had been shot, he thinks they are weeping for Mouse: "Did everybody feel it when a brave gangster died?" (*LYD* 293). This is both sad and very funny. It parodically inflates Mouse's death, pokes fun at Easy's grief at that death, and mocks the process of martyr production. Harking back to Linda Hutcheon's theorizing of parody as marked by "critical ironic distance, whose irony can cut both ways," (qtd. in MacDonald 62), it is tempting to claim that juxtaposing Mouse's death and Kennedy's also works to ironize the monumentalizing of the latter occasion in our national memory, particularly in light of the romanticizing of the martyred Kennedy's image, which occluded, for a long time, a judicious assessment of his record on and commitment to civil rights. This is not to suggest that the grief and shock over the presidential assassination, as represented in the novel, especially when Easy returns home to Feather, Jesus, and Bonnie, is not to be taken seriously. More than one thing can be true of the complex texts that Mosley crafts. But the critical ironic distance in the weeping-in-the-streets scene and in Easy's comic assumption that they are weeping for Mouse does resonate with other moments in the novels in which Easy, in his capacity as narrator, registers and rues the radical inequities in determinations of which deaths matter and which do not in a culture in which power relations are racially skewed.

A second key textual moment that supports a parodic reading of Mouse's life and death is narrated secondhand at the end of *A Little Yellow Dog* and repeated as secondhand narration in *Bad Boy Brawly Brown*. This is the story of EttaMae springing Mouse's body from the hospital. He is comatose and a nurse claims he is dead, that he has no pulse, but EttaMae invades the hospital with a brawny assistant and Mouse's signature .41 Magnum in order to make off with Mouse in her arms. She and Mouse, dead or alive, disappear. This colorful episode is interesting on several counts: it facilitates the suspicion/hope that Mouse is not dead, it puts his phallic weapon in the hands of the almost equally formidable EttaMae, and its secondhand story quality lends it urban legend status. The domesticated and rehabilitated Raymond Alexander, family man and working man, has been reclaimed by the realm of legend, and his domestic counterpart has joined him there. Much is being "sent up" here by means of this domestic couple foiling, particularly the redemptive middle-class valence of Easy's new commitment to domesticity and Bonnie Shay. To elaborate, the Raymond/Etta Mae "home-making" project is derailed by Mouse's sidekick sacrifice (he takes Easy's bullet) and, then, playfully put back on track, as it were, by the recruiting of EttaMae into Mouse's mean-streets world of tough guy efficacy. Clearly there is more than one way of keeping a home intact; more than that, though, the EttaMae/Mouse way of home maintenance parodies the domestic realism of the Easy/Bonnie Shay endeavor, threatening to denaturalize the class-based wholesomeness of the latter.

When Mouse is resurrected in "Gray-Eyed Death" and fully reactivated in the second-to-last novel to date, *Little Scarlet*, we hear more than once the story of Mouse's miraculous healing at the hands of conjure woman Mama Jo, who, like the other characters in Easy's circle, is a transplant from the Deep South. This reiteration combines with EttaMae's seizure of Mouse at the hospital to complicate any interpretation of Mouse reemerging by means of his own legendary hypermasculine invincibility. He has, instead, been resurrected via the actions of women, both of whose extra-realistic efficacy upstages Mouse. While a full consideration of the incremental empowering of women over the life of the Easy Rawlins series—and the implications of this trend for the trope of "home"—is beyond the scope of this essay, some projections can be sketched. In *Little Scarlet*, another seizing of the reins of power and efficacy by a female figure takes place. Easy seeks a black serial killer named Harold Ostenberg, who has been killing black women over the course of several novels. Easy feels Mouse-like and murderous toward Harold, who has eluded him in the past, and together with Mouse, who is now armed with two guns rather than one, sets out to kill Harold in what promises to be a seriously masculine and violently chivalric resolution of a longstanding threat to the safety of the women of Watts. The pair of enforcer/rescuers arrives at the home of Honey May, former nanny to the pathologized perpetrator, and it turns out she has done their work for them by shooting Harold, expressly to save the women of Watts from future victimization at the hands of the troubled man she raised. In a comically arduous scene, all that is left for Mouse and Easy to do is to get rid of the body so Honey May will not get in trouble for her vigilante act. The miraculous resurrection of Mouse has restored Mouse's presence, power, and efficacy to Easy; his sidekick is back, seemingly at double strength, with two oversized guns instead of one. But the work they set themselves to do in the interest of the women of Watts has already been done by a woman of Watts, and both the relevance and efficacy of the dynamic, reconstituted duo of Easy and Mouse have been diminished. The deflationary power of parody—of repetition with a critical difference—prevails, and what we get is a gendered inversion of the tasks of community policing and "home"-land security.

A further point can be made about the shifting shape of the Mouse figure who rejoins the series as an embodied presence in *Little Scarlet*. This novel is set in 1966 in the immediate aftermath of the Watts riots. In a wonderfully complex and nuanced treatment of the aftermath, Mosley demonstrates what Jerry Bryant calls "a strong middle class hand" when shaping his narrator's response to the "riots" (143). That is, Easy portrays ambivalence toward the rioting and looting that is predictable for a man who owns property. He empathizes with victimized small business owners who are not black but who have been neighbors and friends, demonstrating an integrationist, class-based loyalty. Nonetheless, as a politically astute thinker, Easy rues what he calls "the beginning of the breakup of our community" when he encounters a black soldier guarding the grounds of his school workplace: "It was the first time you could see that there was another side to be on. If you identified with the historically white point of view, you had a place where you were welcomed in" (*LS* 77). Easy himself has been press-ganged by the LAPD to solve the murder of a black woman who gave refuge to a white man during the riots. Positioned among the implicated and imbricated in this novel, Easy is not so very different from the black soldier sentry who tries to bar his entry to Sojourner Truth school. Mouse, on the other hand, has come to occupy a very different place in the aftermath of the eruption. He has joined with a white man, in his own parodic version of integrationism, to fence looted goods in what turns out to be a highly lucrative undertaking, a kind of informal economic efficacy that enables Mouse to buy a Continental and two guns which he does not end up needing. Mouse has certainly been depicted as engaged in extralegal economic activity before, but here he comes dangerously close to ordinary, exploitative criminalization, a discursive shift in status from that of murderous badman, avenging angel, effective backup for the more morally grounded Easy.

There is great risk in such a representational swerve, but Mosley is not averse to taking risks with stereotypes. What is powerful and yet not easily accessible in this representation of Mouse as a post-Watts looting entrepreneur is that his naked and unabashed opportunism in the aftermath of the tragedy of the Watts riot serves as a parodic inversion of the property ownership that inflects Easy's self-protective ambivalence toward the damage produced by rioting. Mouse continues to serve as the foil to Easy's incrementally middle-class consciousness. His relentless amorality throws a strong and potentially critical light on the middle class basis of more than one aspect of Easy's moral grounding, most pointedly vexing the property-rights base at the core of the American Dream ideology. And Easy appears to recognize the value of his sidekick's embodied political critique. At one point in the novel he describes Mouse as "a soldier who had been at war his entire life" (229). At another point he says, "I would have put Mouse in the White House if I could have" (205). The importance of the politically oppositional edge of Mouse's consistent and relentless repudiation of middle class respectability and values is not lost on the figure of Easy, as he straddles the dual role of narrator and hard-boiled protagonist in the series.

Despite this narrative insight into Mouse's political heft, Easy works to redirect and contain the centrifugal force of Mouse, whom he characterizes in another part of this novel as "a force of nature, the spawn of some nether god" (101). At the end of *Little Scarlet* Easy returns with relief to the privatized, respectable domesticity that he both longs for and is insistently drawn away from. At his most upright, he resists the temptation of Juanda, a young ghetto woman who has pursued him and sorely tempted him throughout the novel. Rather than sleeping with Juanda—who volunteers cheerfully to share him with Bonnie Shay—Easy opts for monogamy (very unlike Mouse who cheats on EttaMae serially) and, instead, pays for Juanda to go to college. He does this is by turning over to her looting money and a valuable ring given to him by Mouse as quid pro quo for Easy's having used his complicit "hall pass" from the LAPD to get Mouse's stolen goods through a police blockade. In a parodically utopian moment, the filthy lucre is re-routed, Easy's monogamy is preserved, Juanda's life is put on an upwardly mobile course, and Mouse has inadvertently provided the resources for this resolution. The ironies are palpable and self-conscious. What is signified upon are the many incidents—literary and historical—of dirty money underwriting clean outcomes and endings, a version of a Robin Hood-like distributive justice. Easy becomes a kind of money launderer here, Mouse becomes an unwitting benefactor and patron, and Juanda is sent to college instead of taken to bed, in a wholesome inversion of a hard-boiled sexual reward system. This novel in the series, in which the plot energies and momentum are focused on doing justice to and safeguarding marginalized young black women, ultimately puts the retributive gun in the hands of a black woman (Honey May) and uses blood money to send another black woman to college. The hard-boiled genre, in the hands of Walter Mosley, seems at this point to be wending its way toward a parodic expropriation that is liberatory in more than one way, as the hypermasculine agency of the genre is eclipsed by the incremental efficacy of the figure of the black woman.

This trend appears to take one step backward in the series' recent installment, *Cinnamon Kiss*. Here, Mouse appears at the start of the novel, trying to seduce Easy into joining a major armored car heist back in Texas in order to raise money to save the latter's adopted daughter, Feather, from a dangerous disease that can only be treated in Switzerland. The novel uses Mouse as a red herring; it appears as if Easy will sacrifice the respectability and stability he has attained out of paternal desperation—that he will join Mouse's world. Ironically, only his highly developed parental commitment has the power to lure Easy away from respectable domesticity. Curiously, Easy does give up both his custodial supervisor job and his relationship with Bonnie Shay in this novel—he does, in these ways, rejoin the street world—but he does it on his own terms, rendering Mouse more narratively peripheral as a corrupting force than he has been previously. The end of *Cinnamon Kiss* seems to point toward a new trajectory and less stability for Easy, while Mouse seems to be getting established as an entrepreneur in a criminal syndicate, rather than the lone wolf operator he has always been. The sidekick relation is shifting in the post-Watts L.A. of the series, but in a way that highlights the constrained economy of possibilities for black male agency. On *Cinnamon Kiss*'s last page, Easy expels Bonnie Shay from his domestic paradise because of the agency she has exercised in the rescue/cure of Feather. Bonnie enlisted the aid and resources of an African prince with whom she had earlier betrayed her fidelity to Easy. Middle class domestic values morph into self-punishing rigidity and a rather ugly double standard here. Earlier in this same novel, the same Easy who so righteously resisted the deeply tempting importunings of Juanda in *Little Scarlet* violates his commitment to monogamy under the Bonnie Shay regime in a raucous and extended scene of wild sex with Mouse and two hookers. By the end of *Cinnamon Kiss*, Mouse has returned to EttaMae and their version of domesticity, while Easy becomes morbidly single again. Such an inverted development—while no doubt preparing for future installments in the series—destabilizes conventional and redemptive notions of "home" and "family," importantly, perhaps, at a national moment in which both tropes have been consistently appropriated for conservative and repressive political purposes. That Mouse—the unabashed black badman—goes "home" to domesticity in this context asks to be read as a nose-thumbing gesture of ideological repudiation.

The parodic and racialized troubling of the hard-boiled genre at the hand of Walter Mosley continues to vex not only the form's conservative, law-and-order politics, but also the contemporary politics of a racially unreconciled nation. The liberatory, feminist thrust of *Little Scarlet* takes a detour in *Cinnamon Kiss*, but it is clear that Mosley continues to put pressure on the political unconscious of hard-boiled detective fiction and its relationship to national narrative. And Mouse, as the most polymorphous and perversely playful trope of blackness in the series, continues to be put to new and provocative uses.

Shadows of an Imminent Future

Walter Mosley's Dystopia and Science Fiction

—Juan F. Elices

Scholars and critics of Walter Mosley have tended to focus primarily on his detective fiction, the work for which he is most acclaimed. His Easy Rawlins and Fearless Jones series stand among the best mystery novels that have been published in recent decades, mostly because Mosley does not purport to write stereotypical hard-boiled narratives but to examine the deeply rooted racial components that underlie contemporary society. Race clearly informs and nurtures Mosley's writing, and his works are embedded in the longstanding traditions of African American history and literature. However, his science fiction (hereafter, SF) has passed comparatively unnoticed both among critics and general readers. In spite of its lower critical and commercial profile, Mosley's SF enables the author to anatomize the complexities of African American experience from substantially different perspectives than those of his detective novels. As the author himself points out: "Science fiction allows history to be rewritten or ignored. Science fiction promises a future full of possibility, alternative lives, and even regret. . . . Through science fiction you can have a black president, a black world, or simply a say in the way things are" ("Black to the Future" 405–6). With this goal in mind, Mosley departs from the relatively realistic scenarios of his mystery novels and engages in a new set of speculative milieus, a choice with unmistakable ideological undertones.

The aim of this essay is to study Mosley's complete SF production as of 2007—*Blue Light* (1998), *Futureland: Nine Stories of an Imminent Future* (2001), and *The Wave* (2006)—as examples of how the novelist draws and builds upon the foundations of both SF and dystopian literature in order to allegorize the search for a symbolic home in which African American sociocultural traditions are preserved and empowered. In classic dystopian fashion, most of Mosley's SF heroes—e.g., Chance and the Blues in *Blue Light*, Ptolemy Bent in *Futureland*, and Errol Porter in *The Wave*—face powerful external forces that vigorously oppose their search for a more egalitarian and inclusive society. For this purpose, I consider it essential to provide a succinct background on the evolution of dystopian narratives in order to grasp Mosley's approach in the abovementioned works and the way they both correspond to and diverge from other dystopian and SF narrative traditions.

The consolidation of the principles that governed the First and Second Industrial Revolutions—the progressive mechanization of labor and new scientific and technological discoveries—resulted in noticeable epistemological variations that affected both the social *modus operandi* and the literary and cultural foundations of Europe and the United States. The twentieth century started with a period of overt confidence in the beneficial effects of technological and cultural modernization. Nonetheless, the outbreak of the First World War and, later, the seemingly unstoppable growth of totalitarian regimes around Europe revealed the dark side of the optimism instilled by the new century. The harsh realization that these scientific and technological advances could become part of the war machinery or political mechanisms at a dictator's disposal promptly punctured the ambitions of those who sought to forge societies ruled exclusively by science and technology. This new reality was contested by a number of writers, philosophers, and freethinkers, who envisioned claustrophobic futures, compartmentalized societies, and brainwashed individuals. Their writings took them mainly in the opposite direction from that of utopians, uncovering the dangers and risks that the excessive idealization of the latter had generated.

Arthur O. Lewis was among the first to attempt a taxonomy of this new form of literary-philosophical expression, thereby also touching off an intense critical debate about the relationship of works such as Evgeny Zamyatin's *We* (1925), Aldous Huxley's *Brave New World* (1932), and George Orwell's *Nineteen Eighty-Four* (1949) to the utopian genre. Lewis focused on the concept of anti-utopia, designating primarily those works that emerge as a negation of utopia. In his catalogue there is no single allusion to dystopia as a genre, let alone as an expression that evinces key differences with respect to anti-utopia. Gary Saul Morson, however, considers dystopia a subtype of anti-utopia that debunks the predicted positive effects of the realization of a particular utopian scheme. Dystopias thus differ from anti-utopias, "which discredit the possibility of their realization or expose the folly and inadequacy of their proponents' assumptions or logic" (Morson 116). However, even agreeing with Morson's definition, it would be far too restrictive to simply categorize dystopia as a kind of anti-utopia. In my view, Alexandra Aldridge rightly points out that dystopia may be related to utopia or utopian thought, but it also has history of its own (16). Gorman Beauchamp, one of the most reputed scholars of dystopian literature, seems to circumvent this theoretical *cul de sac* when he says that "the dystopian novel . . . fuses two fears": technology and utopia

(53). Dystopias not only explore the extent to which exacerbated utopianism can give rise to disastrous consequences but also the way modern technological civilization has tended to precipitate nightmarish worlds. Therefore, most dystopias start out from clearly Swiftean assumptions regarding the condition of humankind to become more than just a refutation of or rebellion against the dictates of utopianism. *Gulliver's Travels* (1726) contains an essentially dystopian resolution, noticeable in the vision of Yahoos and Houyhnhnms projected in Lemuel's fourth voyage. In other words, dystopian authors do not simply aim to deconstruct the utopian project but, more importantly, to explore the excesses of technocracies, scientific abuse, and political oppression, thereby inherently placing it within the realm of science fiction (or its close cousin speculative fiction).[1]

Focusing particularly on the African American case, it is clear that the dystopian framework is a highly appropriate arena for the discussion of racial issues, although only a small number of African American writers produced explicitly dystopian works before the 1990s. In her incisive introduction to *Dark Matter: A Century of Speculative Fiction from the African Diaspora* (2000), Sheree R. Thomas explains the reasoning behind the collection's title, pointing to circumstances that might explain the apparent scarcity of African American SF or dystopian writers. She identifies the concept of "dark matter" with the sense of displacement and invisibility undergone by America's black population throughout history. In astrophysics, "dark matter" is assumed to exist although it has never been observed, something Thomas relates and applies to black writers, of whom she states: "Like dark matter, the contributions of black writers to the [SF] genre have not been directly observed or fully explored. For the most part, literary scholars and critics have limited their research largely to the examination of works by authors Samuel R. Delany or Octavia E. Butler, the two leading black writers in the genre" (xi).

Indeed, Delany and Butler emerge as the most direct predecessors of African American SF and dystopia. Their *ouevre* has encouraged many black writers to take advantage of new literary possibilities, a fact that has contributed to the emergence of a group of novelists who have chosen to write in these genres.[2] The relatively recent emergence of black SF writers has been spurred in large part by a desire to respond to all the clichés associated with African Americans that recur in "canonical" SF. In *Science Fiction*, Adam Roberts argues that black characters in SF have been repeatedly relegated to marginal positions and depicted in terms of derogatory stereotypes. Such a criticism is applicable to some of the best-known SF works, especially the *Star Wars* series of films. Here, the association of blackness with evil is best exemplified by Darth Vader, who is characterized in threateningly black attire and whose voice is that of African American actor James Earl Jones. Vader's despotic tyranny finds its antagonist in the infinite benevolence of the almost entirely white rebels. It is easy to remember Luke Skywalker or Princess Leia dressed in immaculate white garments or Jedi master Obi Wan Kenobi putting forward visibly essentialist messages about the dangers of the "dark" side. To this,

Mosley adds the following: "Watch the beginning of *Star Wars*, and you see all these blond, blue-eyed, white-skinned soldiers. You think, 'God, so *this* is what the future's like! The white people killed all the black people and Asian people and native peoples, and it's all Europeans in the future.' Of course they tried to fix it, but they never really did. Either you're white or you're an alien or you wear a mask ('cause you might be black under there, with that deep voice)" (qtd. in Brown 6).[3] Each of Mosley's three SF works attempts to nullify this kind of exclusionary SF discourse by representing the efforts of a character or a group of characters to transcend a dystopian—or at least highly marginalized—existence.

Mosley's first SF project, *Blue Light*, was published right after the immensely successful *Always Outnumbered, Always Outgunned* (1997). Narrated in a conspicuously transcendental philosophical manner, the novel examines the connotations of identity not only as experienced in the African American context, but, generally speaking, in any minority group. The novel's title already provides symbolic hints that reveal Mosley's new attempt to explore racial questions from the point of view of SF. *Blue Light* tells the story of a series of characters whose life is dramatically changed after they are irradiated with a light that enhances their sensory and physical capacities, albeit in an amoral fashion (i.e., it enhances whatever traits already are present in the affected individuals at the time of their "illumination"). Not surprisingly, the color of this light is blue, a signifier of African American consciousness and a connection with one of the most representative manifestations of African American culture: the blues. As David L. Smith notes, "the identity issues that blue light creates when it enters the world of twentieth-century America closely parallel the issues of black Americans coming to consciousness there" (10). The characters affected by the light fit perfectly into what Daniel Stein rightfully denominates a "blutopian community," that is, a realm, either real or imaginary, in which the African American consciousness is no longer a marginal concept but a visibly central one and in which African American identity can be experienced in multifarious ways.

Chance, both the narrator of the story and its protagonist, functions as an exponent of the racial crossroads many citizens face in the United States and which indelibly marks their daily existence. Born to a black father and white mother (like Mosley himself) and relatively detached from any sense of black identity as a result of his predominantly white upbringing, Chance is one of the first to experience the effects of the light, for which he is soon summoned by Ordé, a kind of prophet-like, quasi-divine figure who claims to be the keeper of the light. The initial interaction of these two characters unveils a number of typical power relations that have characterized the evolution of the African American community. Ordé's main project is to mix his blood with that of Chance, who is deemed partially "white" due to his mother's racial traits: "He was right. The darker blood and the lighter had formed into longish clumps like fat worms. They twisted and turned against each other, sometimes slowly, sometimes fast. Every now and then two worms would collapse and fall together and then fall apart—another color completely now, almost white" (47). According to Ordé, his mixed racial characteristics seem to prevent Chance from fully experiencing the effects of the blue light—i.e., feeling the blue(s)—and explain why Ordé wishes to help Chance become more attuned instead of remaining a "half-light." David L. Smith refers to Chance's inherent doubleness as the source of his identity conflict, something of which even his subconscious mind reminds him: "[I]n one crucial scene, Chance's father appears to him in a dream to remind him who he is. 'You still a black son to Africa.' The white blood Chance has from his mother is presented as something likely to distract him from his own better nature. . . . Here, then, Chance's black blood is paralleled with the 'blue blood' of truth he imbibed from Ordé. It is the thing that makes him 'better,' the inheritance that reveals his birthright" (19–20). Chance's journey through the novel thus becomes a journey of self-introspection into the nature of the internalized racial boundary that paradoxically seems both to limit and to presage his potential for transcendent development.

Similar to the XTs in his more recent SF novel *The Wave*, Mosley introduces a character—Gray Man—who undergoes a mystical transformation as a result of being touched by the blue light just prior to death. As a consequence, he becomes a creature that wanders mysteriously in a limbo-like space and whose only goal is to take over the world of the living, represented primarily by the Blues (i.e., those fully affected by the "Blue Light"). This takes him into an indefatigable search for all these characters so as to exterminate them and to impose the dictates of death, which he represents. The sudden presence of Gray Man and the threat he becomes to the Blues in turn bring about the appearance of Juan Thrombone, a visionary Mexican who devotes himself to safeguarding the Blues and leading them to escape from Gray Man into a safe haven known as Treaty. Thrombone emerges as a figure who reunites the Blues, endowing them with the possibility of sharing a realm of mutual communication. Thrombone's Hispanic background proves essential in the first stages of the Blues' stay in Treaty, since he embodies the utopian aspiration of racial intermingling (and concomitant deracination). Treaty represents the last bastion of life and peace as opposed to death and war epitomized by Gray Man. As Smith argues, "In *Blue Light*, that possibility is represented by Treaty, the deep-woods colony created by Juan Thrombone. Here Blues, half-lights, and their ordinary companions are temporarily reconciled in an uneasy alliance. . . . They provide a space for life to thrive momentarily in the face of death and social decay" (21). Furthermore, Treaty, as a genuinely natural environment, allows Mosley to giver free rein to his most ecological side, something that he later evinces in *The Wave* as well. Curiously enough, this ideal context and bearer of human, animal and vegetal life is exposed to the brutal intrusion of Gray Man—the embodiment, even in color, of urban degeneration—after which a confrontation between the forces of life and death takes place. *Blue Light* ends with Chance in a mental institution, having been diagnosed as a paranoid schizophrenic, which would seem to suggest a complete victory by the reactionary forces of the Gray Man. Nevertheless, this conclusion retains some kind of Swiftean dystopian overtones, for Chance can no longer reintegrate into his society simply because he is emotionally drawn by the Blues.[4]

Mosley's extrapolation of the African American experience in *Futureland* is suffused by the realization that the achievement of equality—whether like that of Treaty or that of post–Civil Rights America—is ultimately more *de jure* than *de facto*. The acceptance of this failure is what pushes Mosley to create a world in which racial injustice is pervasive—despite myriad legal mechanisms ostensibly rendering it impossible—from the first story onwards thereby establishing its dystopian tenor. Dystopias can be usefully classified into predominantly political and scientific varieties, in the manner of Orwell's *Nineteen Eighty-Four* and Huxley's *Brave New World*, respectively. While the former focuses primarily on the nature of dictatorships and its mechanisms (such as the manipulation of the media, propaganda, or the distortion or falsification of history), the latter aims to demythologize science's presumed infallibility, creating a world in which machines end up annihilating any vestige of human conscience. Mosley's *Futureland* succeeds in interweaving political and scientific elements, since one of his main objectives is to reveal the ideological components that operate (often clandestinely and nefariously) within technocracies.

The collection's first story, "Whispers in the Dark," establishes one of the fundamental aspects of dystopian literature in that it presents a scenario dominated by a suffocating discourse (and in this case, an importantly white one), whose authority is exerted through the control of education and the exploitation of the African American population. This recalls one of the central concerns of a totalitarian regime: to restrict and even forbid access to knowledge to people or institutions that might be considered dangerous to the state. Therefore, any sources of information—namely books, schools, or newspapers—have to be coerced and manipulated so that only a one-sided, partial vision of reality is transmitted. Consequently, all those who attempt to deviate from this imposition to foster their own access to knowledge must necessarily be controlled. Winston Smith, the longsuffering protagonist of Orwell's *Nineteen Eighty-Four*, is imprisoned and tortured precisely due to his clandestine diary-writing and his subversive *liaisons*. Similarly, in Robert Harris's *Fatherland* (1992), Detective March takes for granted that the victorious Third Reich proscribes books by Grass, Orwell, Salinger and other polemical writers who may instigate the popular conscience against the dictates of the ruling power. Mosley picks up this distinctly dystopian theme by examining the way Ptolemy "Popo" Bent, a precociously visionary genius, is nearly forced to join a white-oriented school that is only interested in putting his talent at the service of mainstream society. His uncle Chill's response is to cut Popo off from any such influence and turn him into a self-taught scientist, which he eventually becomes. As Chill himself points out: "'I love that boy more than I love anything. . . . I will not let them take him. I will not let them white people and them people wanna be white turn him into some cash cow or bomb builder or prison maker. He will find his own way an' make up his own mind, god dammit'" (17–18). Chill's sole, and final, purpose is to be able to finance Popo's education at the so-called "Jesse Jackson Gymnasium," where the boy can understand the essence of his race. However, as history has repeatedly demonstrated, many of the social, political and economic gains made by the African American community have been accompanied by deeply unfair consequences. The price African Americans have been forced to pay for escaping the "system" is metonymically epitomized by Chill who, in his desire to protect his nephew, ends up selling parts of his body, including his genitalia, to support Popo's education: " 'That was one million seven hundred an' fi'ty thousand,' Chill said. 'My eyes were a perfect fit for a Swiss banker's son who lost his in a ski accident. But when I was there they had a emergency. It was a Russian general needed the nerve in the spine where he could use his legs. They offered two million for that. I figgered that if I cain't see then I really don't need to walk. One thing led to another and I got outta there wit' six million. They transferred the whole thing into my name 'fore I went under the knife'" (20–21). By means of Chill's self-sacrifice, Mosley foregrounds the assumption that an African American citizen necessarily depends on white mediation—especially that of the power elites (e.g., a Swiss banker and a Russian general) to be socially fit and accepted.

Picking up on this same theme, "Dr. Kismet" emerges as the most purely dystopian story in the collection. "Dr. Kismet" draws on a series of motifs that strengthen its dystopian associations, not the least of which are the character of Kismet himself and the artificial microcosm—significantly entitled "Home"—in which he is the supreme and uncontested authority. As the title of the collection suggests, the stories of *Futureland* are set in a relatively near future, which enables Mosley to problematize contemporary racial questions by imagining one potential version of their impending repercussions. M. Keith Booker argues that one of dystopia's recurrent strategies is what Viktor Shklovsky and other Russian formalists defined as defamiliarization, that is, the fictionalization and estrangement of reality by means of introducing "imaginatively distant settings," either temporal or spatial (*Dystopian Literature* 3–4). Dr. Kismet's "Home" is conceived as a simulacral representation of the world in which he controls all its resources and supervises all sites of production and commerce. Apparently a realm of endless pleasures and hedonistic overindulgence, "Home" suggests any number of classical utopias due to the seeming infallibility of its sociopolitical and economic structures. Kismet himself gives an idea of how he understands his own creation: "The view has that effect. . . . High above the world, looking at the mother of all life, feeling her power and her indifference. Here we stand as near as possible to understanding the truth of our mortal predicament" (61). This superior position, intentionally isolated from any contact with the lower classes and social underdogs, also determines Kismet's adoption of a godlike dimension. Kismet rules his empire ostentatiously if distantly, and the social differences between himself and those not invited to live in "Home" end up being unbridgeable since exclusion from power and privilege in dystopian societies is not only complete but also generally permanent.

The gap between Kismet's extravagant luxury and the marginalized individuals banished to the anonymous and empty existence known as "Common Ground" allows Mosley to uncover the flaws and dangers of capitalism, which he sees as both a cause and a consequence of the preeminence of white values: "The weight of poverty, the failure of justice, came down on the heads of dark people around the globe. Capitalism along with technology had assured a perpetual white upper class" (73).[5] Through the figure of Kismet, Mosley explores the idea that capitalistic excesses inevitably lead to the implementation of ill-conceived globalizing assumptions and eventually of a totalitarian imperialistic consciousness.

Such attitudes are certainly present in Kismet's world-view and are openly challenged by Fayez Akwande, an activist summoned to "Home" for an interview with Kismet. Akwande's main aim is to recuperate the African ancestry of the African American population, and his conversation with Kismet reflects on questions that have historically undermined African American identity and contributed to the black population's sociohistorical alienation. The conversation between Akwande, representative of the so-called RadCon6 (Sixth Radical Congress), and Kismet, epitome of the white authority, is articulated within the same power structure that has defined the relationships between the black and the white populations in the collection as a whole to this point. Furthermore, Akwande is even tempted to join Kismet's project and partake of the privileges and opportunities it affords, an offer that sets Akwande at the crossroads of choosing between a simple, uneventful and comfortable pseudo-white existence and his committed, nonconformist and rebellious spirit. Although Akwande eventually prevents Kismet from continuing with his off-planet colonization scheme, the story's concluding image of the activist abandoning his endeavor to accept a peaceful retirement on Mars manifests, once again, the triumph of the values of the *status quo*. In a conversation with a more radical fellow-activist, Akwande defends his decision with a dim hope of a better future in *de facto* exile:

"But even if it's true, even if they turn their backs on us, what the hell do you accomplish by flying off to Mars?"

"On Mars there will be fewer people. There will be a new world. Maybe we can have something there. Maybe."

"You just runnin' away." (83)

In exploring power relations, dystopian authors tend to focus on the range of mechanisms, physical and psychological, that are employed in manipulating both individuals and societies as a whole. Thus, it comes as no surprise to find scenes of torture, extortion, and brainwashing as the circumstances that characters have to negotiate in these accounts. The famous "two-plus-two-equals-five" formula Winston Smith is forced to accept at the end of *Nineteen Eighty-Four* exemplifies quite accurately the Machiavellian principle of "the end justifies the means" underlying most dystopias. In this vein, Renata Galtseva and Irina Rodnyanskaya assert that: "Tortures and executions are the dystopian world's inevitable fellow travelers. If they are unnoticeable at the surface of life there, that is because they had been experienced in the past" (317).

These instruments of repression and surveillance, along the lines of what Michel Foucault would define as "panopticism," are recurrent in *Futureland*, especially in "Angel's Island" and "Voices." The former story depicts a high-security corporate prison outside the borders of any nation-state to which the most dangerous convicts are sent. Mosley's Angel's Island emerges as an illustration of Foucault's theories on discipline and punishment which are best evinced in the dystopian tradition by Orwell's all-vigilant Big Brother. The prison's policies mainly seek to do away with any feeling among convicts, which is why they are injected with an intravenous chemical "snake pack" that warns wardens about any emotional disturbance or sexual arousal. The inhibition of anything that might give free rein to outbursts of unrestrained passions or energy turns out to be the central concern of dystopian powers, which consider such feelings the most likely source of rebellion and insurrection. Booker notes that Freud's postulates upon the repression of sexuality are broadly applicable to dystopian literature, since "for both Freud and dystopian governments, sexuality functions as a central focus for repressive energies largely because it is also a potential source of powerful *subversive* energies" (*Dystopian Impulse* 12). Angel's Island pursues the annihilation of all these powerful subversive energies, as the prison's medical assistant assures: "You are the property of Angel's Island now, convict. No sex or violence or insubordination will be tolerated. The ChemSys snake pack on your arm can identify almost any antisocial behavior that you might exhibit. . . . If a question is asked of you and the truth monitor has been activated you will be punished for lying. If you have an erection in your sleep it will be inhibited. If you have an erection when you're awake it will be inhibited and two or more pain doses will be administered" (93). Mental regimentation and physical coercion, thus, determine the ordinary existence of the convicts, constantly under observation and threatened with painful punishment for any transgression of the rules.

"Voices," on the other hand, deals with such current technological issues as neuronal manipulation, clone technology, and artificial life extension, which Mosley satirizes as potential mechanisms to keep populations under suffocating control. "Voices" narrates the schizophrenic delirium of Leon Jones, who is being treated for his addiction to Pulse, a highly addictive and debilitating drug whose distribution is state-controlled. Jones is restored to life by Dr. Bel-Nan, a futuristic analogue of Mary Shelley's Dr. Frankenstein, who also believes himself to be capable of both creating life and preventing death. Mosley denounces modern science's arbitrary abuse and victimization of the weakest social sectors, once again represented by a moribund black man. As Chill was dismembered in exchange for money to finance his nephew's education in "Whispers in the Dark," Jones undergoes an experimental operation that on the surface appears to undo the damage Pulse has inflicted on his brain, but it also secretly transplants the personality of Bel-Nan's recently deceased daughter into Jones's brain. Bel-Nan plans to retransplant his daughter's personality into a clone at a later date, but he needs Jones for temporary storage until he perfects the transfer technique, at which point Jones will become superfluous as an individual. "Voices," in this sense, is very Shelleyan in its warning about how the excessive dependence on scientific advances can distort the value we place on ourselves and on others. Bel-Nan, who is affiliated with Dr. Kismet (and thus power) in several ways, sees Jones as little more than a convenient but ultimately disposable commodity who should be grateful for whatever he is given, as shown in the following passage: "You were dead when they brought you to me. . . . Confined to a gravity chair, having to undergo shock treatments eighteen hours a day. Hardly able to speak more than a sentence before you went into spasm. There was no cure. There was no hope but me. I gave you life. And now I'm asking for repayment. Your few months of grace for the life of my daughter" (202). Although Jones is ultimately rescued before Bel-Nan's plan can be carried out, his manipulation expresses the fear and lack of faith that dystopias have traditionally displayed towards the utopian scientific project, something that is confirmed by Krishan Kumar: "The whole of western development since the time of More was re-interpreted and re-counted as a disaster, in so far as it represented the dominance of utopian principles. Science and democracy were no doubt noble ideals, good in themselves, but the attempt to institutionalize them in society had produced the exact opposite of utopian hopes" (111). In *Futureland*, science no longer supports all human existence but rather is an all-powerful mechanism used to enslave the population, especially its most marginal and vulnerable sectors.

In addition to lamenting the destructive effects of science, Mosley also demythologizes technology, which is even more perniciously influential than science in *Futureland*. The world Mosley creates is strongly dominated by the stifling presence of electronic artifacts that are intended to enhance social observation and vigilance. Furthermore, Mosley reveals that this mechanical tyranny is closely associated with capitalism, provoking, in the long run, a "Catch-22" spiral in which economic and technological dictatorship inevitably go hand in hand. The story that best exemplifies this interconnection is "En Masse," which presents a futuristic New York where unemployment is severely penalized and jobless citizens are compartmentalized in underground cubicles—the aforementioned "Common Ground"—and barely allowed any contact with the outer world. "En Masse" revolves around motifs such as the dehumanizing effects of mindless, unfulfilling labor and the extent to which one's life is determined, molded, and potentially even sent into oblivion by coldly monetary dictates and Western capitalism.

Simply by looking at the work environments in which this story is set illustrates Mosley's focus on the threat this system poses to any meaningful sense of individualism: "Every chip-prod office was dominated by a GT workstation. Every GT was composed of twenty quarter-circle tables that formed five concentric circles around a center table where two or three unit coordinators worked. These electronic tables were wired to the fully computerized floor. The smaller inner tables were equipped with three clear monitors embedded in the tabletop; the next tier of tables had four monitors each; the number of monitors per table increased until the final tier, with seven workstations per table" (234–35).[6] This regimented mentality fosters and, in fact, relies upon the suppression of individualism to such a degree that any expression of emotional freedom is, as was the case in the prison system to a greater degree, admonished and even penalized. The reappearance near the end of the story of the visionary genius Ptolemy Bent—now grown up and leading a subversive underground movement—enables Mosley to condemn the effects of contemporary technocracies, which Ptolemy summarizes as follows: "The world is going in the wrong direction. Our judges are machines, our prisons and military and mental institutions and workplaces are planning to mechanize their human components with computerized chemical bags. The spirit is being squashed for the sake of production and profit. If we don't do something the race itself will become a mindless machine" (311).

The reality Mosley explores in "En Masse" does not, in general terms, differ much from what is actually happening in most Western societies where the use of machinery for many kinds of labor is progressively substituting for that "human component" and relegating it to minor and secondary positions. The world of unemployment the author describes in this story appears, thus, as a direct consequence of this overwhelming mechanization, curiously promoted and endorsed by human beings, and Mosley is unequivocal in his attitude regarding the uncontrolled use of technology in Western societies: "I think all throughout history, the greater the power, the more centralized the use of that power. I don't think there is any time where somebody got greater technology, greater power, greater ability to bring people together, to make their lives better. The more power you get, the more it trickles up, as Ronald Reagan forgot to say. I think that the idea that technology is going to liberate us is false" (qtd. in Perez).

Less embedded in the formal conventions of dystopian literature than *Futureland*, *The Wave* nevertheless serves as another attempt to reconfigure African American reality by situating the novel at a crossroads between SF and magical realism. *The Wave* intermingles quite successfully the worlds of the dead and the living, diffusing the boundaries that have conventionally separated them in Western culture and constructing a realm in which difference is celebrated and penalized in almost equal terms. The novel narrates the story of Errol Porter, a brilliant computer programmer who is unexpectedly fired from the company for which he works. The financial collapse he endures is aggravated by what he believes are a series of prank calls from someone claiming to be his father, who has been dead nine years. These calls trigger a profound emotional outburst in Errol, leading him to seek out the company of this caller despite his doubts as to his identity. From the moment they meet each other, Errol and his seemingly resurrected father begin a process of self-reconciliation and discovery which leads them to explore metaphysical notions that are deeply rooted in our consciousness and which have been very rarely challenged. GT ("Good Times" as Errol calls this fatherly figure) affirms that he has returned from the dead, together with other resurrected people, to accomplish a mission, for which he needs the help of his son. GT maintains that he is the keeper of a secret that may change the course of civilization and which might dismantle the pillars that sustain contemporary societies as we know them. He repeatedly refers to "The Wave" as a philosophical and spiritual concept that embodies a radically different way of understanding life, a fact that triggers a ruthless pursuit led by Dr. Wheeler—this novel's representative of the established power structure—and his acolytes to put an end to the Porters' efforts to unleash the wave.

The narration, thus, is framed within very typical Mosleyan parameters of a seeker, a somewhat mystical guide, and an oppositional force, although his intention is not so primarily focused on the African American case in *The Wave* but rather on denouncing power structures and relations that are clearly unfair for the oppressed *perforce*. Through the figure of Arthur Bontemps Porter (aka GT), Mosley's critique of exclusion in this novel is directed at the marginalization suffered by the XTs, individuals resurrected via the wave. Dr. Wheeler and his ilk believe that the XTs have to be ostracized and sent into oblivion because they are different and, thus, menacing to more long-established value systems. *The Wave*, like Mosley's other SF works, contains sympathetic characters who express views that might be called utopian (or at least mythic-heroic, in Joseph Campbell's sense), for they seek the complete reunification of the human species, disregarding any racial or social barrier. The voyage that Errol and his father undertake in search of the ideal home represented by "The Wave" enables them to anatomize the miseries that lie beneath the superficial state of apparent normalcy found in contemporary societies and to show how this normalcy relies on the suppression of potentially liberating knowledge by the extant powers. It is precisely against this façade of democratization that Mosley addresses his most mordant critique, for the novel demonstrates that, as in the workplace of "En Masse," difference and unconventionality are no longer welcome in the world of *The Wave*. Dr. Wheeler represents, in this sense, the figure of the paranoid authoritarian who struggles to suppress anything that might weaken the purity of his species.

If the XTs represent "otherness," Dr. Wheeler seems to capture the most insidious side of Hitlerian ideology in his attempt to annihilate any remnant of non-Aryan population, epitomized, in that case, by the Jewish people. The way he addresses the XTs puts him in line with Nazi eugenic discourse, as the following words accurately demonstrate: "Wheeler waited for her to depart again before he went on. 'The men and women who have risen from those graves are puppets. They're an infestation that will drive us into extinction. You and I cannot allow that to happen'" (129). To achieve his ultimate aim of sweeping away all these expressions of divergence and deviation, Wheeler sets up a prisonlike building in which to torture and exterminate the XTs. It is at this very moment that Mosley's novel attains its most dystopian tenor, for like Angel's Island this house is equipped with state-of-the-art technology for the control, supervision and punishment of its hostages. What Errol encounters in Wheeler's house turns out to be a macabre recreation of Nazi extermination camps, in which prisoners were brutally killed in gas chambers and incinerated in massive crematoria. Echoes of Auschwitz, a quintessentially dystopian paradigm given its status as an obsessively efficient mechanism of death, reverberate throughout *The Wave*: "GT's meaning came clear within the next few minutes. Wheeler returned to the cell block with two men wearing nylon protective suits and carrying a metal canister connected to a corrugated plastic hose. They attached the hose's nozzle to a conduit in my cell. When one of them turned a knob, I could hear the hissing of gas, and I detected a slight sweet odor" (204–5). Mosley's characterizes Wheeler in a manner that channels the contemporary atmosphere of extremism and intolerance toward difference, in the process suggesting that racism or xenophobia are not so far removed from genocide.

Wheeler's pathological need to impose a one-sided and partial vision of reality clashes with the all-embracing and multi-ethnic spirit of the XTs, whose purpose is to live communally so as to discover the real essence of the human being. From their quasi-ethereal state of existence, they tackle questions that uncover the shortcomings of human life and demythologize the longstanding belief in its superiority. Throughout his entire work, one of Mosley's distinctive literary features is the way he reverses assumptions that have long remained unquestioned. For instance, in his detective fiction, especially in *Devil in a Blue Dress* (1990), the author challenges the connotations that seem to be inextricably attached to the very notions of whiteness and blackness: good and bad, integrity and dishonesty, purity and chicanery. He subverts these clichés and uplifts blackness as a realm of celebration and joy, intruded upon and assaulted by the presence of white characters. In this case, *The Wave* takes this process further to question even our fundamental notions of death and life in a manner that is also potentially quite subversive. While hiding out in a cave the XTs use to protect themselves from Dr. Wheeler, Errol tells GT that: "Humans believe that they're the most important creatures in the universe. . . . It's hard for us to think that you [i.e., the XTs] wouldn't want what

we have." GT's response suggests a continued diminishment of the cosmic significance of humanity in language that echoes the end of white colonial hegemony:
"Or maybe they know that the Wave is superior to man. Maybe we present an end
to the dream of humankind as the rulers of all they see" (191–92). The reemergence
of the XTs, which essentially discredits the foundations of life and death, also
becomes a clear and present threat to many underlying political and economic
interests that go hand in hand with that "dream of humankind" Errol refers to
above. Mosley thus suggests that hidebound adherence to the latter prevents any
greater understanding of the former.

To conclude, my aim has been to demonstrate that the spirit that underlies
Blue Light, *Futureland*, and *The Wave* sets the three works as noteworthy examples of African American SF and dystopia. Despite the relatively rare presence of
African American authors within these traditions, the use of these frameworks can
be enormously fruitful for exploring racial and identity conflicts from new, defa-
miliarized perspectives. Walter Mosley's SF is an example of how African American
writers might engage in discourses from which they have been traditionally marginalized. In other words, SF does not merely represent another literary genre
but, more importantly, an arena of debate and contestation where durable clichés
associated with African Americans can be dismantled. In this respect, Mosley's SF
and dystopian works emerge as powerful indictments of the hardships endured by
African Americans, which he sees as the result of the excesses of capitalism and
uncontrollable technological and scientific development.

Notes

1. Aldridge refers to both Swift's and Butler's reaction to science and technology in their
respective times: "Though allusions to science and technology are absurd and extravagant in
all these satires, Swift is the first to actually satirize the uses of science in his day, and Butler's
novel mocks the technological obsessions and progressivist-evolutionary fervor of Victorian
England" (7).

2. Saunders suggests that the increasing presence of black writers within the scope of science fiction and dystopia is mostly due to the fact that black people have made their "mark in
the Western world's popular culture" (404).

3. In "The African American Science Fiction Character," Ben Davis Jr. observes that black
characters are rarely found in twentieth-century science fiction, and when they are, they
mostly respond to bland archetypes.

4. Gulliver goes through the same rejection after he abandons the land of Houyhnhms.
His inability to readapt himself into a human context again is quite similar to Chance's response when he is sent back from Treaty: "My hope now is that they'll release me, that they'll
find me sane, so I can go looking for my friends. . . . I know too much. That's why I'm trying
to close my eyes to the history of light and matter. Because if I stop seeing things the way the
Blues do, I'll become less like them and more like regular people" (296).

5. This is not the first time Mosley has dealt openly with the effects of capitalism on contemporary societies. *A Red Death* is especially prolific in the inclusion of references to communism as an ideological positioning that was embraced by a large number of black intellectuals and public figures who observed many parallels between the communist postulates and the claims put forward by the Civil Rights movement.

6. Kumar notes: "But there were always those who pushed their anxiety about the uses of technology further, and who came to see, in the very fact of large-scale industrial technology, the essential obstacle to their hopes. Technology, in whatever hands, seemed to have the same results. . . . Large-scale technology, wherever it appeared, produced the same effects: alienation, de-humanization and domination" (402–3).

Cyberfunk

Walter Mosley Takes Black to the Future

—DEREK C. MAUS

Walter Mosley is not a writer whose career has found him predominantly working in the genre of speculative fiction. With his collection of stories entitled *Futureland* (2001), however, Mosley returned to the genre in which he previously found critical and commercial success with his novel *Blue Light* (1998). Numerous reviewers compared Mosley's speculative stories of the near future with the "cyberpunk" novels of such writers as William Gibson or Bruce Sterling, and, to be certain, parallels of characterization, theme, and aesthetics do abound. Folio Johnson, Mosley's streetwise, technologically enhanced private eye—cleverly refashioned as "the Electric Eye"—is a descendant not only of Mosley's own hard-boiled gumshoe Easy Rawlins, but also of Rick Deckard, Philip K. Dick's cop-turned-bounty hunter from *Do Androids Dream of Electric Sheep?* (1968)[1] Likewise, Mosley's revolutionary hackers Vortex "Bits" Arnold and Ptolemy "Popo" Bent are closely related to Gibson's marginalized "console cowboy" Henry Case from *Neuromancer* (1984).

Despite their aesthetic overlap, though, Mosley's stories move beyond the realm of what has become definitive cyberpunk fiction—assuming, as critics such as Darko Suvin repeatedly have, that such a thing can genuinely be said to exist in a genre still so young. In *The Dystopian Impulse in Modern Literature* (1994), M. Keith Booker summarizes the milieu of Gibson's cyberpunk narratives as a balance of utopian and dystopian attitudes toward technology: "In Gibson's future, advanced technology (especially computer technology) makes possible the realization of a number of traditional human dreams, even including immortality. At the same time, these dreams are realized at a price: immortality achieved via computer may be bought at the price of a process of dehumanization that converts the empowered and even immortalized humans into computer artifacts themselves" (148–49). *Futureland* certainly follows this formula as far as the overall social structure in which the stories take place is concerned, thereby corresponding to Charles Scruggs's observation of a tendency in twentieth-century African American literature to "describe relations between black people and urban life and mediate, balance, or swing radically between utopian and dystopian vision" (2). Technology pervades every facet of life in Mosley's future, and the primary beneficiaries (and often creators) of this technology are a very privileged few, most of them associated in some way with the ubiquitous Dr. Ivan Kismet. Nearly everyone else is consigned to an existence of clockwork drudgery not dissimilar to that of the workers in Fritz Lang's classic dystopian film *Metropolis* (1927), right down to the grim underground ghetto ("Common Ground") in which the least valuable members of society ("White Noise") are forced to pass time meaninglessly: "The biggest problem with being White Noise is perpetual and unremitting boredom. Day in and day out you sit hunched over in your octagon tube or against the wall in the halls that always smell of urine and mold. . . . There's no books made from paper because trees have more rights than we do. There's no movies because that costs money and we aren't real so there's no credits to our names. Singing is illegal, who the hell knows why? Breaking a wall down so you can share a bed with a friend is against the law too. . . . There's no way upside unless you die" (218).

Nevertheless, Mosley differentiates himself by foregrounding racial and socioeconomic politics much more explicitly, thus creating a level of social allegory that is rarely present in cyberpunk as a whole.[2] The grim lives that his characters endure as a result of technology are not simply the result of a oligarchy run amok (as with the giant *zaibatsu* conglomerates that dominate the world of *Neuromancer*), but also of an inherently racist and classist system[3] of oppression becoming entrenched via technology. Mosley made the purpose of *Futureland* clear in a November 2001 discussion with Nnedi Okorafor, a journalist and emerging author of speculative fiction: "I created a world where blacks are a very motivational force. . . . In *Star Wars*, you have that opening scene with the tiny ship fighting the big ship. On both sides, all the people are white. To Spielberg, and I mean no disrespect, it was a white world. I don't attack that. Instead, I say we should also make up our own worlds. The future is very important. If we [black people] aren't careful, we won't be in it" (n. pag.).[4] This desire to carve out and maintain a niche for the excluded—in Mosley's case the racially excluded—echoes that of the dystopian social satires of Ray Bradbury or Yevgeny Zamyatin, both of whom Mosley has named as formative influences. As a result, the realms that Mosley's black characters carve out for themselves in the nine interrelated stories that make up *Futureland* bear more than a passing resemblance to the underground society of book-memorizers with whom Montag associates himself at the end of Bradbury's *Fahrenheit 451* (1953) or the exiled atavistic Mephi of Zamyatin's *We* (1924). They constitute an alternate order whose goal is not simply revolution (i.e., the overthrow and replacement of the *status quo*), but rather liberation, which will be accomplished only when the system recognizes their right and need to exist autonomously.

Mosley extensively discusses the racial and socioeconomic inequities that he sees pervading contemporary America in his book-length philosophical essay *Workin' on the Chain Gang: Shaking Off the Dead Hand of History* (2000). My argument is that Mosley adapts the premises that he sets forth in *Workin' on the Chain Gang*[5] to extrapolate a not-so-distant fictional *Futureland* in which African Americans have become even more "homeless" (i.e., marginalized from organized political and economic power by the unquenchable thirst for profit that Mosley identifies as "the enemy" in his essay). For example, in *Chain Gang*, Mosley writes that "[w]hen you add the selling of prison labor to private business you have pushed America back to a consciousness that predates the Civil War. The warden is the master and his profits rely on the labor of his inmates" (83). Mosley fictionalizes this phenomenon in the ironically named story "Angel's Island," which describes the dehumanizing abuse suffered by the inmates—the vast majority of whom are nonwhites—in an international, corporatized, high-tech prison located in the middle of the Indian Ocean. Not only are the prisoners deprived of their physical liberty to the point of near-complete sensory deprivation by chemical restraints known as "snake packs" and forced to harvest a noxious tobacco-like plant called "choke," but their national citizenship is also suspended to facilitate their unwilling participation in medical experiments.[6] The prisoners—many of whom, like the story's protagonist "Bits" Arnold, are incarcerated for acts of dissent and political subversion—are effectively "disappeared" without realistic hope of repatriation and used as raw materials for commercial research on everything from behavior control technology to drugs that treat especially toxic new strains of cancer with which the prisoners are deliberately infected. Mosley's fiction takes a condition he observes (and decries) in the present and posits what it might look like if allowed to metastasize in the future. The theme of imprisonment, which Mosley discusses both literally and figuratively in *Chain Gang*, suffuses the lives of the working class in *Futureland*, whether in the form of actual incarceration or the metaphorical confinement of the unyielding employment cycle.

The moralizing potential of Mosley's intertwined themes of imprisonment and displacement is heightened by both the name and description of the realm of privilege that serves as a foil to the condition of everyday life in Mosley's world. In the story entitled "Doctor Kismet" Mosley's narrator introduces the character whose influence seems to extend into every corner of the world. Dr. Kismet himself, though, has physically isolated himself on a "large island off the western coast of Mexico" in an artificial paradise tellingly called "Home" that "serves as both residence and sovereign nation" (59). A visitor to the island notes that "Home is beautiful beyond compare" (59), a comment that Mosley uses both as an introductory descriptor of Kismet's artificial utopia and as a poignant reminder of what is denied to others in order for Kismet to have his beautiful Home. After all, no one would describe Common Ground as either beautiful or a meaningful home. The detailed description of the Edenic island that follows is no less fantastic: "To the left and right were magnificent elevated views of Kismet's heaven on earth. Imported oak and eucalyptus forests, miles-long abstract mosaics achieved by flowers and multicolored leaves. The reproduction of an ancient Phoenician fishing fleet docked in the world renowned Harbor of Gold. There was even a small desert" (60). Kismet makes it clear that Home is not merely a physical paradise, though, but an intellectual one as well: "The finest art and relics of the pinnacles of history grace my lower halls. Atlantis [the main city of Home] is populated with the greatest scientists, artists, and artisans of our times" (67–68). When challenged that his "collection" of intellectual talent is a form of slavery, Kismet avers "We are very civilized about it. We supply a domicile, and a stipend, all stipulated in a mutually agreed upon contract. They are free to travel and seek profit through personal endeavors. All I ask is to be able to request their labor at various times" (68). The remainder of the book illustrates the dehumanizingly amoral (and, at times, immoral) nature of this final sentence, in the process collapsing the patina of "civilization" that Kismet imparts to his Home, which turns out to be more akin to Toni Morrison's "Sweet Home" plantation from *Beloved* (1987) for those whose labor Kismet "requests." The localized utopian Home thus comes at the cost of a near-universal dystopian homelessness for the nonprivileged classes.

Of course, dire dystopian prophecies are far from uncommon, either in cyberpunk or in science fiction as a whole. One may thus be tempted—as was Nikki Dillon, who reviewed *Futureland* for the *New York Times Review of Books*—to interpret the book as an African American *Nineteen Eighty-Four* or *Brave New World*. I would suggest, however, that this is an oversimplification that overlooks both Mosley's stated intentions and, perhaps more importantly, the presence of *successfully* subversive forces that pervade the stories. Unlike Zamyatin's D-503, or John the Savage in Huxley's *Brave New World* (1932), or Winston Smith in Orwell's *Nineteen Eighty-Four* (1949)—all of whose attempts at rebellion are ultimately defeated and utterly effaced—most, if not all, of Mosley's protagonists in *Futureland* achieve a meaningful, albeit unconventional, degree of freedom from the metaphorical (and, in some cases, literal) shackles of the system.

This measured sense of hope within a predominantly gloomy context is indicative of Mosley's reasons for temporarily departing from his "usual" genre in writing *Futureland*. When asked by a fan during an online chat[7] whether the book was an attempt at cautionary prognostication, Mosley answered as follows: "I never look at science fiction as being predictive. The best thing that science fiction can do is to break you out of ruts in the way you see the world and to shatter one's illusions about progress. . . . *Futureland* imagines black people in the future. Not only black people but even black culture, something that most other American science fiction has failed to do" ("SciFi.com" n. pag.). In this contention, Mosley both echoes and responds to a set of African American cultural critics who attack "science fiction and its futurism [as] expressions of an American popular culture dominated by the willful blindness of white racism" and claim that "the genre has failed to imagine any [futures] that contain a complex, affirmative portrait of the black community" (Kilgore 12–13). In an interview with Hugo Perez of *Science Fiction Weekly*, Mosley remarked about the intrinsic value to African Americans of writing speculatively about the future, despite any past shortcomings: "For black people in particular, the future is all we have because the past has been taken away from us and the present is defined in certain ways. You can't write today about *our* president, or *our* senator, or *our* multi-billionaire industrialist. Black people tend to get pushed into certain cubbyholes that at least white people in the culture don't, and so what you can do with science fiction is you can make a whole different world. You could say, for instance, that in the year 2060 there are only black people. You don't even have to say why. In that way, you can begin to create worlds which become interesting and also become yours in a certain way" (n. pag.).

By the end of *Futureland*, Mosley *does* in fact depict a society in which there are only black people, or, more accurately, people who once would have been identified at least as "octoroons." Only those with at least one black grandparent—or, as the novel clinically (if also somewhat biologically dubiously) puts it, "people with at least 12.5 percent African Negro DNA" (351)—survive the outbreak of a disease, ironically initiated by a white supremacist group's malfunctioning and accidentally triggered biological weapon. *Futureland* refrains from positing an idyllic black-dominated world; the world that remains after the epidemic at the novel's close is classically post-apocalyptic in its anarchy: "Two Spanish-black armies, a white—or so-called—group, and . . . the American blacks [are f]ightin' over groceries, guns, and women. Fightin' over control of the utilities and right-of-way in the streets" (355). Nevertheless, the motley cast of characters who populate the nine stories injects an alternate, nondichotomous, and unmistakably *black* parallel cultural presence into this future, much as the W.A.S.T.E. system in Thomas Pynchon's *The Crying of Lot 49* (1966) represented a wholly self-contained means of communication, not simply a competitor aspiring to overthrow (and thereby become) the current system.

The society created and dominated by oligarchs like Dr. Kismet—the megalomaniac genius behind the omnipresent MacroCode corporation and its techno-religious offshoot, the Infochurch—offers little to blacks and other economically marginalized groups except unadorned subsistence in return for a life of labor. Mosley pictures such a world in *Chain Gang*: "Beyond the veil, we are told, there awaits a paradise. But we know that there will be an admission ticket and a closing time tacked on to that utopia. We will have to pay for our future every day. We'll pay in sweat and blood and sacrifice. The future may be bright, but we fear the majority of its citizens will be beasts of burden hauling around the fuel necessary to maintain the brilliance" (7). Understandably, Mosley's assortment of heroes in *Futureland* heeds the advice that he gives his readers in *Chain Gang*, namely to "free ourselves from those cold chains anchored in the crimes and ignorance of the past hundred and more years." His heroes then do not aspire to master this fools' paradise, but rather to find ways to subvert the system from within (much like a computer virus) or transcend it entirely, thereby completing the cycle Mosley envisions in *Chain Gang*: "Once freed, we might enter this new era realizing that the dreams we once had for a bright future were just dim hopes compared to the possibilities that lay dormant within us" (7).

For instance, in the story "The Greatest," Amazon-like boxing champion Fera Jones is approached by both the established power structure and the established opposition. The former is represented by the simultaneously Disney-like and RAND-like Randac Corporation that pays her exorbitantly to promote LunaLand, their theme park on the island of Madagascar. The latter is represented by the FemLeague, a radical feminist political party that controls Massachusetts and wants Fera as their "pinup girl . . . [to] make the difference for the future of womanhood" (44–45). Despite being similarly trapped between rival groups attempting to use her cynically for their own designs, Fera avoids the self-negating fate of Ralph Ellison's narrator/protagonist from *Invisible Man* when she ends up playing the two groups against each other for her own purposes—which include helping her terminally ill father receive expensive treatment for his addiction to a powerful government-subsidized psychotropic drug known simply as Pulse. Fera declares that she wants to abandon boxing—a sport that Mosley explicitly labels as a distracting spectacle that is "the best remedy for rebellion" (*Workin'* 25)—in order to "get out there and fight for real, . . . to go against the people usin' me to keep people sufferin'" (*Futureland* 56). We learn in a later story entitled "Voices" that she has cleverly used Randac's money and the FemLeague's political clout to become a maverick congresswoman from the Bronx, beholden to neither group's agenda. Mosley's African American characters actualize his creative urge to "make up [their] own worlds" in order to ensure that the Siamese twins of government and the super-corporations can't entirely write them out of existence. While they may not accomplish the ouster or even drastic reform of the powers-that-be, their victories reaffirm the value and validity of life—specifically their own—in a society that is increasingly dismissive of it.

On numerous occasions in *Futureland*, Mosley reminds the reader of *Chain Gang*'s other guiding metaphor of enslavement, and as in his nonfiction, the enslavement to which he refers is principally economic and secondarily racial in nature. In *Chain Gang* he writes, "Regardless of the poignancy of the crimes against black Americans our oppression is, after all, only part of a much larger malignancy. The American structure of slavery was a consequence of the economy of the New World, its roots in Europe, not Africa. Mass oppression for mass production is a part of the Western psyche. Therefore the problems experienced by blacks in America have to be seen as part of that larger malady" (9–10). For

Mosley this malady results in a situation where "[w]e are all part of an economic machine. Some of us are cogs, others ghosts, but it is the machine, not race or gender or even nationality, that drives us" (12). Thus, in the novella-length story "En Masse," when Folio Johnson angrily exclaims "Can you beat that shit? . . . Bought his whole life, just like he was an old-time slave" (*Futureland* 276) in response to being told that a worker named Blue Nile had indentured himself to MacroCode for more than twenty years, we are meant to hear Folio's indignation at Blue Nile's economic maltreatment, rather than the racial iniquity associated with "old-time" slavery. In this instance, at least, Folio is appalled at the low value placed on Blue Nile's labor, as he makes clear with his wry comment at the end of their conversation: "Life is worth almost any price you have to pay. But that doesn't mean they have to charge you for it" (277). Fayez Akwande, a black politician who unsuccessfully attempts to oppose the *status quo*—and Kismet specifically—through conventional means by his leadership of the Sixth Radical Congress,[8] more explicitly laments the indelibly racial effects of slavery when he justifies his own exile to Mars by saying, "This world was set when they dragged the first African into a slave ship. . . . Like the child who sees his mother and father slain by devils wearing white faces. Like the girl raped by her imbecile brother in the playhouse next to her dolls. The heart . . . the heart is rotten" (81).

In *Chain Gang*, Mosley writes that "[t]here are only two ways for the slave to deal with his master. The first is to deny the so-called master's right to own another human being. . . . The second, and more common, way for the slave to deal with his master is to love him. . . . This is what makes freedom so difficult. Freedom threatens this false love" (32–33). *Futureland* is filled with examples of characters who choose the former path, although like Akwande, they very often do so by *appearing to* take the latter, more expected route of becoming content in their enslavement. As a result, many of Mosley's stories resolve themselves with clever endings in which the metaphorical slave gains his or her freedom from metaphorical bondage. These Chekhov-meets-Asimov twists almost always involve a marginalized character surreptitiously using his command of technology to achieve a transcendent state of existence beyond the reach of the technocratic power structure.

For example, "Whispers in the Dark," the story that opens the collection, features the technological apotheosis of two characters, Misty and Chill Bent. They have devoted their lives (and in Chill's case, his eyes, spinal cord, and penis, as well) to protecting their young relative Ptolemy, a budding computer genius, from exploitation by the state. In return, Ptolemy, still in his early teens, constructs a computer that is capable of transmigrating their existence to a form beyond that of their disfigured physical bodies. Ptolemy is sentenced to twelve years in prison on Madagascar for violating the laws against euthanasia, a sentence that requires him to use his prodigious technological knowledge in the service of the mega-corporation—the same Randac that will attempt to appropriate Fera

Jones's feral power for themselves—that runs the prison. However, the narration makes it clear that Misty and Chill continue to exist in a blissful, hyper-sentient afterlife thanks to Ptolemy's actions: "*God*, Chill thought. But there was no answer to his assertion. A halo of winking lights radiated next to him, mingled with him, and he knew in some new language that this was his mother [i.e., Misty]. The word *freedom* occurred to Chill, but the meaning faded with the clarity of his light. So much he knew that he was unaware of. So much beyond him even then" (24, italics in original).

"Angel's Island" ends with what initially seems a more Pyrrhic victory for its protagonist "Bits" Arnold in that his successful prison revolt is diminished somewhat by the fact that he nevertheless dies within the prison's walls because of the disease with which he was infected by his captors. However, a computer virus that he manages to unleash prior to his death not only brings an end to Angel's Island as a prison but also threatens the whole system that supported the prison's practices to begin with. In the epilogue to the story, a recording of Bits in his dying moments appears on a screen three years after his death and provides "detailed explanations of this prison and its inhuman practices, with special emphasis on the snake packs that they used on prisoners and guards alike" (125). Although restatement of this information seems somewhat insignificant at this point—given the fact that the reader has already been told that the prison was closed due to an "international outcry about the medical practices on Angel's Island" (123)—Bits's final words reveal the lasting importance of his message from beyond the grave: "I have done further study. The ChemSys Corporation has signed contracts with the federal government to supply over three million snake packs to the military and mental services by the year 2053. Snake packs used to make soldiers into drones, our mental divergents into brainwashed zombies. Read these reports and ask yourselves how long it will be before schoolchildren will be snaked" (125). Thus, although Bits himself has been killed, the bytes (of data) that he left behind continue to offer hope for reforming a system (by shining light on the practices it would rather keep hidden) in which schoolchildren will be treated like criminals.

Two of the book's most unabashedly didactic stories, "Little Brother" and "En Masse," conclude with characters entering into a cybernetic/metaphysical state of being, in each case escaping the forces that have controlled and/or ended their physical lives. "Little Brother" returns to the criminal justice system first depicted in "Angel's Island," though this time the focus is not on the incarceration aspect of the system but the judicial. The story depicts the trial of a man named Frendon Ibrahim Blythe, who stands accused of murdering a police officer and assaulting another. His trial is presided over by a cybernetic judge that is part of "Sacramento's newly instituted, and almost fully automated, Sac'm Justice System" (205). The overseer of his trial is a composite intelligence consisting of an "amalgam of various magistrates, lawyers, and legislators created by the biological linkage and compression system to be the ablest of judges" (210), and Frendon initially seems to stand little chance of winning his case, given his apparent powerlessness: "Frendon was White Noise. The only homes he had ever known were governmental institutions and the octangular sleep tubes of Common Ground. . . . By his sixteenth birthday he had been convicted in juvenile courts of more than a dozen violent and felonious crimes. This criminal history kept him from entering the cycles of employment. . . . He never had a chance to rise to street level" (211–12). However, Frendon's status as a near nonperson gives him an unforeseen advantage, which is that powers greater than the local governmental authorities (i.e., MacroCode) have taken a covert interest in him: "But he was no fool either. In the state prisons and detention centers he learned, via monitor, about the law and its vagaries. He studied tirelessly at Infochurch how to circumvent legal condundrums and maintain his freedom. As a matter of fact he had become so well versed in the legal wiles of automatic justice that for some time now he had been in direct contact with Tristan the First, Dominar of the Blue Zone located on Dr. Kismet's private island nation, Home. Together they had come up with a plan to use in one of the first fully automated cases" (212). The bulk of the story consists of Frendon's attempt to confound his computerized judge's efforts to convict him, an effort based as much on his own "street-smarts" as on the preparation he received from Dr. Kismet's lieutenant, who is simultaneously the leader of the Infochurch and the head of operations for Dr. Kismet's research center.

By the end of his trial, Frendon succeeds in planting doubt in the composite juridical mind, causing it not only to founder in rendering the seemingly inevitable guilty verdict but also to begin to question the ontology of its own existence: "There is doubt among us. . . . We have convened for long moments. New circuits were inhabited and long-ago memories stirred. We are sure you are guilty but the law is not certain. Some have asked, therefore, Who are we?" (224). Such a conundrum—as legions of science fiction writers have understood—is unsustainable for a logical system and an "error retrieval program" appears on the screen to reboot the system and delete the "emotional response" that Frendon has succeeded in evoking in the judicial machine. Once the artificial image of the composite judge ("the bearded image of a man whose color and features defied racial identification" [225][9]) returns and immediately condemns Frendon to death, a sentence carried out brutally and nearly instantaneously upon its utterance. The story picks up five years later as a disembodied voice speaks to Frendon's erstwhile patron, Tristan, asking, "Why did you set me up to die?" (226). Despite his initial doubts, Tristan recognizes the voice as Frendon's and informs him that Frendon's trial was part of a bet with Dr. Kismet: "[H]e designed the Prime Justice System. I bet him that he did it too well, that the compassion quotient in the wetware would soften the court" (226). Frendon responds with understandable fury, which Tristan dismisses, believing himself to still be unquestioned master of the electronic world, as befits "the man whom many called the Electronic Pope" (227). His confidence is shattered, though, when Frendon informs him—using the now-familiar metaphors of dehumanizing slavery and rehumanizing emancipation—that the system has been simultaneously subverted and transcended as a result of this experiment and that he now exists in a state beyond MacroCode's power and even knowledge: "You and your master are monsters. . . . The people who volunteered for this justice system, as you call it, never knew that you'd blend their identities until they were slaves to the system. It wasn't until your stupid game that they were able to circumvent the programming. They see me as a liberator and hate you more than I do" (227). Frendon leaves the Dominar in a state of "cold fear" before returning to his refuge "out here somewhere you'll never know" along with the other "ten thousand singers celebrating their single mind—and their revenge" (227).

"En Masse" similarly depicts a transcendence of the system, both by individuals and by collectives. The story centers around Neil Hawthorne, an ordinary worker at a MacroCode subsidiary named General Specifix, who arrives at work one morning to find he has been transferred to a mysterious new division entitled GEE-PRO-9. Already prone to fits of worry, Neil fears that this upheaval of his routine will result in "*Labor Nervosa*, [which] was cured by a prescription of permanent unemployment" (230, italics in original) and the attendant banishment to the slums of Common Ground. Contrary to his anxieties, though, GEE-PRO-9 turns out to be one of several rogue cells of marginalized workers who have managed to remove themselves from the oppressive slavery of the employment cycle that Folio Johnson bemoans. The work atmosphere they create in their autonomous environment is truly utopian, thanks in large part to the unnoticed computer wizardry of the still-imprisoned Ptolemy Bent. His most important contribution is Un Fitt, a sentient, self-aware, and almost Godlike[10] computer that Ptolemy had begun assembling in the collection's opening story, where it played a role in Chill and Misty's continued existence beyond death. Un Fitt provides cover for the dissident groups by masking any trace of them in the labyrinthine computer systems of the company, but also provides the members of the group with intellectually stimulating and personally rewarding work, rather than the drudgery their previous assignments entailed. In this way, Un Fitt genuinely aids GEE-PRO-9's members in becoming free, rather than becoming merely a kind of Augustine St. Clare-like "good master" in place of MacroCode's Simon Legree.

The subversive power of GEE-PRO-9 appears to be short-lived, however, when the group is discovered by MacroCode's accounting software, which discovers financial discrepancies in the company's books that are linked to GEE-PRO-9's activities. At the end of "En Masse," Neil lies in a hospital bed on a fully computerized life support system. He has suffered grievous injuries in a partially successful effort to foil a plot by a white supremacist group to release a virus into the environment that will kill all black people (in the process apparently mutating the virus so that it kills everyone *except* its intended target). Neil's brain is completely connected to Un Fitt, a situation that understandably causes him a great deal of existential discomfort at first:

"[T]he part of you that is consciousness resides in my matrix. It is a limbo of sorts. You can read the data of your life but you cannot alter it."

"Then how can I live?"

"You can talk to me, Neil."

"So that's it? It's you and me forever?" The hysterical shudder of claustrophobia went through the ex-prod's mind. (319)

Un Fitt reassures Neil, both with the promise that his lover, Nina, will be able to visit him as soon as the programming is worked out as well as with an idyllic vision of the Pacific Ocean that Neil had used earlier in the story to distract himself from his woes. The matrices into which each of these characters—symbolically enslaved like almost all of Mosley's characters in *Futureland*—are delivered represent a kind of cybernetic Beulah-land (note Chill's sensation of "freedom" in his new state), a home that offers release from suffering and servitude.

The emancipatory cyberspaces of *Futureland* are very different from Gibson's in their capacity to liberate more lastingly those who inhabit them. Suvin summarizes the transient escapism of Gibson's cyberspace as follows: "Cyberspace is a utopia out of video-arcades or pachinko parlors, a mathematized love-philtre of computer hacker lore; and . . . Gibson is on the side of his petty juvenile criminals trying to penetrate the corporate 'blue ice.' The cowboy-samurai love affairs [conducted within cyberspace] usually end badly, but at least they (and only they—not the rulers obscenely devoted to money or power) are capable of it" (Suvin 44). Had Mosley left off with Neil Hawthorne connected to Un Fitt dreaming of Nina and the Pacific, his vision of cyberspace would be very much Gibson's land of sex and diversionary virtual reality. The final line of "En Masse" reveals its more grandiose philanthropic purpose: " 'Here you may roam until there is a body for you to inhabit again,' Un Fitt whispered between the thundering waves. 'And a world worth living in' " (319). The cybernetic realm that Ptolemy Bent creates represents a genuine alternative to the prisonlike confinement of the physical world, which offers few spaces, real or metaphorical, in which disempowered individuals like Blue Nile, Neil, Frendon, or Ptolemy can thrive or even exist.[11] Mosley takes pains to demonstrate that his extraphysical realms are not merely a domain of respite and leisure like Gibson's, but also a place in which his heroes can recover their strength, gain valuable knowledge, bide their time, and await a better world. Metaphorically, these cyberspaces serve much the same role for the characters as Mosley's speculative fictions do for his readers.

The resolute idealism that Mosley displays in *Chain Gang* is clearly expressed in the *denouement* of most of the other stories, even though the collection as a whole ends somewhat ambiguously with the aforementioned bioweapon-induced apocalypse of "The Nig in Me." Mosley's use of almost exclusively black protagonists in *Futureland* may seem to undermine the claim he makes in *Chain Gang* that class, not race, is the predominant chain that binds, unless one hearkens back to his oft-stated desire to depict more African American characters in popular fiction in the first place. In an essay entitled "Black to the Future" (1999), Mosley called on more African Americans to write science fiction because "it can tear down the walls and windows, the artifice and laws by changing the logic, empowering the disenfranchised, or simply asking, What if?" (407). This passage almost precisely echoes the prescription for change that Mosley puts forth near the end of *Chain Gang*: "The only way out is to be crazy, to imagine the impossible and the ridiculous, to say what it is that you want in spite of everyone else's embarrassed laughs. This is a little easier for me because I am a fiction writer. Pushing ideas to their limits is what I'm expected to do—*in fiction*. But it's a small skip from fiction to nonfiction in this world of technology and change" (102–3, italics in original).

Thus, *Futureland* blends together two ambitious goals, one literary-political and one sociopolitical, both of which correspond to De Witt Douglas Kilgore's earnest defense of African Americans' interest in science fiction from the introduction of his *Astrofuturism: Science, Race, and Visions of Utopia in Space* (2003): "From my point of view, science fiction is not an alien subculture. . . . I believe that African Americans must participate in and contest those parts of American culture to which we are not supposed to belong. It is of critical importance to problematize the cultural essentialism, which would have us believe that some scholarly projects and aspects of the general culture are proper to black people and others are not" (16). The collection carves out an explicitly racialized imaginative space for black readers and writers to inhabit, but it also demonstrates to a broader, more inclusive audience the pressing need for liberation from the system that both literally and figuratively enslaves and imprisons the economically marginalized segments.

Notes

1. In *Blade Runner*, director Ridley Scott's loose 1982 adaptation of Dick's novel, the resemblance between Folio Johnson and Rick Deckard extends even to their common predilection for out-of-the-way Asian eateries.

2. In fact, Gibson and other cyberpunk writers have occasionally been chastised for fetishizing Asian culture (especially Asian women), though such critiques have usually implied inattention to the racial dimension of cyberpunk's orientalized aesthetic, rather than outright bigotry.

3. The system furthermore compounds its dystopian qualities by trying to mask its racism and classism beneath a veneer of putative impartiality, as evidenced by occasional statements such as "Racial image profiling had been a broadcast offense for more than two decades" (322) and "It's a punishable offense to slander race" (349).

4. In this regard, *Neuromancer* does perhaps present more of a positive literary model, via the presence of the Zionites and especially the character of Maelcum, pilot of the tellingly named spacecraft *Marcus Garvey*. Gibson's narrator describes their colony as follows: "Zion had been founded by five workers who'd refused to return [to Earth], who'd turned their backs on the well and started building. . . . Seen from the bubble of the taxi, Zion's makeshift

hull reminded Case of the patchwork tenements of Istanbul, the irregular, discolored plates laser-scrawled with Rastafarian symbols and the initials of welders" (103). Although far from ideal, especially compared with the luxurious Freeside satellite to which it is attached, Zion does represent an alternative, autonomous "home" for a black population in which their cultural tradition—in this case, an occasionally somewhat stereotyped version of Jamaican Rastafarianism—can continue.

5. In the interest of brevity, this work will hereafter be referred to simply as *Chain Gang*.

6. Lacking a nation, they also lack any legal status, since the very corporation that imprisons them seems to be the only international authority that remains.

7. Obviously, Mosley's comments in this forum represent an attempt to explain himself to fans of his work, not necessarily scholarly critics. Nevertheless, Mosley's message about the social and racial agenda underlying *Futureland* has been consistent regardless of the nature of his audience at any given moment.

8. The narrator explains this intention as follows: "And now, as the co-chair of RadCon6, he meant to engage the most powerful man in the world, to force him to bend his will for the good of Africa, Africans, and the African diaspora around the world. He felt that if he could turn Ivan Kismet toward his own goals, the rest of the world must surely follow" (65).

9. Mosley's language here evokes the composite of photographs of many of the twentieth century's totalitarian leaders that was used to depict Big Brother in the film version of Orwell's *Nineteen Eighty-Four*.

10. Ptolemy somewhat cryptically explains that the internal logic of his homemade computer is guided by "a spirit" he discovered as a child (i.e., during "Whispers in the Dark"): "Years ago . . . I discovered that the atmosphere of Earth was enveloped by an intelligent ether. It's a vast store of knowledge that exists in an area between five hundred and two thousand miles above the surface. . . . Over the next ten years I was able to use a transmitter to communicate with the entity. Back then I thought it was God; now I'm not so sure" (308–9).

11. Fera is an obvious exception to this rule, since her empowerment takes place in the traditional realm of politics, albeit not in the ordinary manner.

Epilogue

Whither Walter? A Brief Overview
of Mosley's Recent Work

—OWEN E. BRADY AND DEREK C. MAUS

Time and Walter Mosley wait for no critics, a fact that greatly complicates the task of presenting a thorough overview of his work. During the three years in which we were assembling this volume, Mosley continued his published exploration of the myriad meanings of home at a rate that makes the seemingly brisk pace of his early career seem almost slothful. Between May 2005 and May 2008, he published an astonishing eleven book-length works: the young-adult novel *47* in May 2005; *Cinnamon Kiss*, the ninth installment of the Easy Rawlins series, in September 2005; a memoir/ political essay entitled *Life Out of Context* in November 2005; his third book of science fiction, *The Wave*, in January 2006; *Fortunate Son*, a socioeconomic fable, in April 2006; *Fear of the Dark* , the third novel in the "Fearless Jones" series, in September 2006; a foray into erotica entitled *Killing Johnny Fry: A Sexistentialist Novel* in January 2007; a book of advice for aspiring writers entitled *This Year You Write Your Novel* in April 2007; *Blonde Faith*, the tenth and reportedly final Easy Rawlins novel, in October 2007; a noir-thriller entitled *Diablerie* in January 2008; and a collection of moralistic satires akin to Langston Hughes's "Simple" stories entitled *Tempest Tales* in April 2008. Thanks to the diligence and agile intellects of our contributors,[1] substantial critical discussion of several of these works has been incorporated into this collection in an effort to make it as contemporary as possible upon publication. Given Mosley's prodigious and wide-ranging output, this is no mean feat, so as part of this endeavor we thought it appropriate to append a brief critical glance at the recent past in an effort to keep the gap as small as possible.

In surveying Mosley's recent work, we find both continuity and change. As he has done throughout his career, he continues to experiment with a number of new (for him) genres, while also returning to familiar ground both in his chosen themes and occasionally in his milieus.[2] For example, *47* represents an ambitious foray into fiction designed to reach a younger audience. Marketed as a young adult novel, *47* is a sort of slave narrative combining elements of historical narrative, science fiction, and African American folklore to explore the potential of both fiction and history to serve the cause of human freedom. Thematically similar to adult-oriented works such as *Futureland* and *The Man in My Basement* (among others), *47* finds Mosley attempting to express some of the complexities of African American history in a form that retains most of the formal and philosophical complexity of his previous works, but in a language that is appropriate for adolescent readers.

Picking up where his previous works of nonfictional social commentary left off, *Life Out of Context* fuses meditation on the problematic past with speculation about a different future. Initially a memoir detailing Mosley's personal sense of dislocation from what he describes as the narrowminded and self-interested institutions of American politics, the book gradually develops into a series of conjectures about how and why African Americans and other individuals excluded from these institutions can push back against the global hegemony of the traditional elites, including the possibility of establishing a third major political party to represent African American interests directly.

Fortunate Son, while ostensibly a realistic novel, has the feel of a parable; in fact, Mosley uses that very word to describe the book in an interview included in the "Reader's Guide" at the back of the paperback edition. Its plot traces the diverging and intertwining fates of two American native sons, one white, one black, from childhood through early adulthood. In a number of ways (discussed in greater detail below), *Fortunate Son* fictionally instantiates the ideas about the significance of African American historical experience and its redemptive possibilities for all Americans that Mosley expressed six years earlier in *Workin' on the Chain Gang: Shaking Off the Dead Hand of History*.

Killing Johnny Fry is an excursion into literary pornography, a sort of prolonged and at times graphic meditation on the possible significance of sexual experience in the process of self-definition. The novels in the Easy Rawlins and Fearless Jones series and *Fortunate Son* all contain sex scenes for thematic purposes as well as to stoke popular (and perhaps even prurient) interest. Although critical reactions to *Killing Johnny Fry* ran the gamut from heated disdain to unhesitating admiration, one must acknowledge Mosley's audacity in delving into existential questions via the blunt (and potentially hackneyed) argot of literary pornography.

Returning to nonfiction, his *This Year You Write Your Novel* seems at first glance an attempt by Mosley to cash in on his celebrity and several reviewers dismissed it as little more than a collection of clichés. However, when considered in the context of his increasingly public agenda to encourage the marginalized to find ways to be heard, this short how-to guide becomes part of a larger effort to encourage ordinary people (not merely a writerly elite) to enter the public sphere, to articulate visions of possible worlds, and to use language creatively for self-empowerment and social transformation. This theme recurs throughout Mosley's nonfiction, from *Workin' on the Chain Gang* and *What Next: A Memoir for World Peace* through *Life Out of Context* (whose subtitle—*Which Includes a Proposal for the Non-violent Takeover of the House of Representatives*—reveals the unmistakable political intentions of his rhetoric) as well as in his fiction (cf. Paris Minton's efforts at self-definition as a bookseller in the Fearless Jones series, or the panoply of active dissenters and revolutionaries in *Futureland*).

Blonde Faith is arguably the most important of these recent books, chiefly because it serves as a capstone to the commercially and critically successful Easy Rawlins series that marked the beginning of Mosley's career. In this novel, Mosley brings his detective hero into the transformative period of the late 1960s and reflects through him the nuances of African American consciousness at a moment of both disillusionment and possibility when America, its Dream, and its racial relations were being renegotiated and refashioned. As the artistic culmination of an epic cycle of African American consciousness in search of identity and home, *Blonde Faith* is obliged to provide a satisfying resolution for Easy's ten-volume quest that stretches from the immediate aftermath of World War II through the difficult years following the peak of the Civil Rights movement.

Diablerie covers some of the same territory in terms of theme and style as *Killing Johnny Fry* in that it undertakes a frank examination of some of the darker aspects of human existence, especially those intertwined among issues of self-knowledge, memory, and sexual (in)fidelity. The book centers on Ben Dibbuk, a middle-aged computer programmer with a seemingly comfortable—if also somewhat duplicitous—existence that he has carved out for himself after a lengthy and largely repressed period of dissolution. When Dibbuk encounters a woman who claims to have known him and to have knowledge of bad deeds he committed during this time, he is forced to confront the repercussions of the former life he believes he has left behind (or at least effaced). Ultimately, the book ponders whether the dangers inherent in a genuine acknowledgment of his mottled past are preferable to the benumbed and deceitful life that Dibbuk has constructed in its place.

Finally, *Tempest Tales* is a series of stories about a morally ambiguous black man from Harlem named Tempest Landry who is unjustly gunned down by a New York policeman and subsequently denied admission into Heaven by St. Peter. When Landry refuses to go to Hell (literally and figuratively), contending that the "sins" for which he is being judged are being misinterpreted out of a lack of understanding of the realities of life in Harlem, St. Peter strikes a bargain with him, sending him back to Harlem in a different body along with a guardian angel. A classic battle ensues between the angel and the emissaries of the devil to win Landry's soul (metonymously that of "black folk" in general) for their side, marking the first time in which Mosley has explicitly framed the moral struggle of contemporary African American life in the overarching metaphors of Judeo-Christian mythic cosmology.[3] With *Tempest Tales*, the quest for home in Mosley's work is expanded to determine whether Heaven (or Hell) is open to people like Landry and, by extension, the similarly morally ambiguous protagonists who populate his complete *oeuvre*.

Although all of the texts mentioned above in some fashion continue Mosley's quest to find a way home for African Americans, *Fortunate Son, Killing Johnny Fry*, and *Blonde Faith* do so in ways that are most in harmony with the critical ideas expressed within this volume. Each of these novels depicts the ironies and ambiguities of America and African American identity in a different genre, yet each is also marked by Mosley's signature thematic structure of a quest for a home. Each features a black, male protagonist who is lonely and longing, although he is not often clear about precisely what it is for which he is longing. Each protagonist's heroism resides to some extent in his resilient survival in an American homeland that is often made harsh and unaccommodating by issues related to race and/or economic status. Furthermore, each of these protagonists pursues a sense of home embodied by a domesticating feminine presence, a figuration of the lost mother. Finally, each novel ends with its hero (flawed, yet resilient in Mosley's trademark manner) somehow creating a sense of home—tenuous and constantly threatened though it may be—rooted in nostalgia and loss that has been transformed in a "blutopian" fashion into a site of transcendence and affirmation.[4]

Fortunate Son depicts the parallel, though far from equivalent lives of two biologically unrelated boys who are unconventionally raised for several years as brothers. It opens with the image of an African American male who is already threatened at the moment of his birth: "Thomas Beerman was born with a hole in his lung. . . . The doctors told his mother, Branwyn, that most likely he would not survive" (3). With this stark statement, Mosley sets his tale of survival and maternal love in motion. While Branwyn Beerman is a single African American woman, her warm, loving, and comforting maternal presence is capacious enough to serve two boys: her own fragile introspective son, Tommy, as well as Eric Nolan, a blonde, blue-eyed all-American golden boy, the son of a successful, recently widowed, and inwardly grieving white physician named Minas Nolan. In many regards, Branwyn incorporates the qualities found in other domesticating women in Mosley's work. Like EttaMae or Bonnie Shay, Branwyn combines strength, compassion, and sexuality; also like them she is the foundation for all of the central characters' sense of home.[5] Seeing Branwyn's maternal love in her efforts to keep Tommy alive in the hospital, Nolan, too, falls for this warm, loyal figure and moves her into his own stately Beverly Hills house. She assumes the calming role of mother for Eric, who is the same age as Tommy but twice his size and who is described early on as an untamed "force of nature" (22). Her presence regenerates Minas and creates the homey comfort and security essential for two young boys. Her unanticipated death when the boys are six years old precipitates Tommy's unwilling departure from this privileged white home and separation from the white brother to whom he feels bonded.

As in the case of Easy and Mouse in the Easy Rawlins series or Paris and Fearless in the Fearless Jones novels, *Fortunate Son* uses binary male characters to develop its plot and themes, though here one is black and one white. The novel evolves through an alternation of scenes drawn from the life of Eric the "golden boy" and that of trouble-prone Tommy, who acquires the ironic nickname "Lucky" on his first day of school. After Branwyn's untimely death, Tommy's biological father, Elton Trueblood, a proud black man full of anger and paranoia, but also good (if also somewhat belated) paternal intentions, takes him from the world of white privilege and plunges him into the violent world of Compton. Elton's home is fraught with difficulties for Tommy, perhaps the most notable being the physical absence of both his beloved "brother" Eric and deceased mother. Resentful of the white doctor's influence over his son, Elton wants to bring Tommy up to be a man, but he is ill equipped for this undertaking as his own concept of manhood is grossly attenuated, limited largely to violence and sexual performance. Elton's improvised and often cursory attempts at making a home for Tommy include a domesticating figure in Elton's occasional live-in woman May. She dotes on Tommy and serves briefly as a surrogate mother, caressing him, protecting him from his father, and providing home cooking. However, May cannot escape addiction to drugs and repeated infidelity; consequently, Tommy witnesses her relationship with Elton only in the alternating contexts of sexual passion or violent abuse, never in any form that can account for, much less accommodate, his needs as a child. Neither Elton nor May is in a position to notice (or perhaps care) when Tommy stops attending school after a series of humiliating and unsettling experiences in his first grade classes.

The physically fragile, introspective boy ultimately moves through a dark, threatening world that he only dimly comprehends, withdrawing as much as he can into isolated safe spaces between the injurious situations that are his seemingly inevitable lot. He suffers numerous wounds—some minor, some life threatening—over the course of several years and winds up being sentenced to prison for a crime he did not commit. Meanwhile, Eric (without whose name Tommy later points out, one cannot spell America [285]) can seemingly do no wrong, and is on the path to success in sports, education, and sex. But while he cannot fail by the putative standards of happiness or good fortune, he finds his life sterile, empty, without the emotional bonds so essential to a sense of home. He misses both Tommy, who listened and "explained things" to him, and Branwyn, the surrogate mother who took the place of the mother who died during the process of his own birth. Both boys find solace in memories and dreams of Branwyn. She is a sustaining presence, even if she appears only in dreams and reveries. Not even death separates Tommy from Branwyn as he learns on the night after her funeral that he could kneel down and "bond with the floor . . . [and] be joined with everything, and then he would know where his mother was and they could talk again" (42).

Despite all these seemingly insurmountable barriers to the development of any meaningful notions of belonging, Tommy exemplifies Mosley's belief in African Americans' talent for survival and improvising homelike spaces. After having decided to stop attending school, Tommy takes up daily residence in an abandoned and garbage-strewn alley, which he describes as "his paradise" and "the only stable respite his childhood would know" (116). Shielded by his isolation from most of the violence of Compton, he is at peace living in his "alley valley" and communing primarily with an escaped parrot called No Man and a dead girl named Alicia, a victim of random violence whose abandoned corpse he discovers and inters. He also finds a measure of solace and acceptance with Monique, the teenaged sister of his friend Bruno. Monique defends Tommy against local bullies, shelters him in Elton and May's absence, and even provides him with his first sexual experience on his twelfth birthday. Tommy in return becomes a makeshift head-of-household by providing Monique and her illegitimate child with money earned by running drugs for a local drug dealer. Although none of the improvised homes Tommy finds himself in are close to ideal or even particularly stable, they are all marked by genuine, if not always successful, attempts at human kindness amid dreadful circumstances. The lasting value of such gestures is accentuated later in the book, while Tommy is living on the streets with all his possessions in a shopping cart. Despite (or perhaps because of) his difficult situation, Tommy keeps a ledger of kind deeds done to him: "He penned these events as well as he could into a bound book he'd found behind a stationery store. Every now and then he'd copy the acts of kindness onto a new leaf in the book and admire his penmanship and the benevolence of his fellow man" (202–3).

In the end, both boys are reunited though a series of contrived plot incidents. But it is theme, not plot that motivates this novel. Indeed, Tommy, the son seemingly neglected by the entire world, accidentally saves not only Eric's physical life (he takes a bullet intended for Eric) but also his spiritual life, as Tommy's return provides a connection to the lost Branwyn. Such transcendent bliss is not exclusively Eric's, though; the novel ends with Tommy in a hospital recovering from a grievous injury that he suffered in the course of saving Eric yet again. Verging on death, he feels comforted by the phantasmagorical appearance of Branwyn that dissipates, yet ultimately reveals his whole horrible life and gives it a special redemptive pattern: "Thomas came awake suddenly. In the corner of the room stood his mother. . . . As he watched her the color slowly drained away from her image. She turned gray and then slowly transparent, like glass. When she was almost completely clear, her form began to sparkle from the inside. The cloud of iridescent light then drifted toward the window, out through the glass, and away into the dark sky. The lights kept moving until they covered the nighttime horizon, becoming stars" (313). At first he feels bereft, as if "his body had been cut from his soul" (313), but looking out into the sky, Branwyn's presence in the stars both comforts him and fills him "with wonder" and "grace" (313) as he comes to understand that he, like his mother who is written in the sky, has a special fate, that his life has redemptive meaning for others, despite his painful past. Not only is he reunited with his white brother, Eric, but Tommy, the derided son, finally has a place in the world, a home. Although this may be cold comfort for his wrecked body, it provides unmistakable solace for his soul, a situation akin to the postmortem vindication afforded to characters such as Chill Bent, Frendon Blythe, Neil Hawthorne, and "Bits" Arnold in *Futureland*.

If Tommy's ultimate reward seems somewhat ambiguous, consider the lot of Cordell Carmel, the protagonist of *Killing Johnny Fry*. In the opening pages of the novel, Cordell accidentally discovers his longtime girlfriend Joelle in the midst of vigorous and adventurous sex with a white man named Johnny Fry. He sneaks away from her apartment before being noticed by the lovers and wanders the streets in a state of bewilderment, especially at the bright red condom Johnny was wearing. Joelle's apparent betrayal unleashes a torrent of sexual energy within the normally staid Cordell, the first manifestation of which is his purchase of a pornographic film entitled *The Myth of Sisypha* (presumably the "sexistential" counterpart to Albert Camus' *The Myth of Sisyphus*) at an adult bookstore on the way home from his unwanted discovery. This purchase is the first step in what becomes a Rabelaisian journey of sexual indulgence that fundamentally challenges everything Cordell believes about himself and perhaps human nature in general.

Cordell returns home and begins watching the DVD, which consists of a series of scenes involving an African American woman named Sisypha and her white husband Mel, who are initially described as so mundane that "the effect was that you felt that the cameras were spying on actual people just living their lives" (*Killing* 16). At first, Cordell identifies so closely with the couple that he wonders whether he mistakenly received a tamer version of the film: "Maybe there were R-rated versions of their triple-X-rated movies . . . but the story was still interesting to me. It was a lot like my story with Joelle. She always said that she loved me, that she was satisfied with our situation" (16). This sense of identification quickly becomes ironic and painful as Sisypha cheats on Mel with a lusty young workman (in a parody of a classic porn cliché) and then forces Mel to watch when he discovers them: "My breath was coming fast, and when I looked into Mel's pleading eyes, I wanted to cry along with him. After all, wasn't I in the same position as he? Forced to see my lover groaning and writhing in the embrace of another man? . . . I was Mel. Impotent, restrained, submissive" (19). By the time Sisypha has violently dominated and sodomized Mel, Cordell has seen enough. He considers breaking the disc, but goes to bed instead, only to be awakened hours later by an intense fit of vomiting that seems as much the result of his revulsion at what he has been watching as of the cognac he has been drinking. When Joelle calls immediately thereafter, Cordell refrains from expressing his knowledge of her betrayal and instead surprises her by talking dirty to her, which clearly arouses her desire for their planned meeting the next evening.

The three words Cordell uses to compare himself to Mel—impotent, restrained, submissive—describe his life quite accurately, and not just in relation to Joelle. Despite having been together for eight years—Cordell has had two prior marriages of brief duration—his insistence that they "might as well have been married" seems somewhat dubious given the nature of their relationship. They apparently only see one another on weekends because neither feels that a "material commitment" is necessary beyond a pledge to remain monogamous. Joelle categorizes their relationship as "[s]eparate lives that are lived together" (3–4) but, as her secretive dalliance with Johnny Fry demonstrates, this outwardly stable-seeming arrangement has not, despite her assertions to Cordell, left her "satisfied with [their] situation" either sexually or emotionally. Cordell's blissful ignorance in regard to this dissatisfaction seems to stem as much from a lack of curiosity as a lifelong habit of repressing his desires, especially sexual ones. When he openly expresses his sexual longing for her in the wake of watching *The Myth of Sisypha*, Joelle notes that he hadn't "talked like that for . . . ever" (47). The "home" he has created with Joelle is not only not truly his—he emphasizes her ownership of the apartment in which their weekends together are spent when he says that he "loved staying at Joelle's place" (5)—nor particularly authentic, as it is predicated on an emotional distance that results from dishonesty and sublimation of desire.

The orgiastic and occasionally priapic encounters that follow include Cordell having sex with multiple partners including not only Joelle, but also his upstairs neighbor, a young photographer whose work Cordell is promoting, a young woman he meets on the subway, and even a stranger at a sex club to which he is taken by Sisypha herself. Many of these encounters reproduce (sometimes parodically[6]) both what Cordell witnessed between Johnny Fry and Joelle and between Sisypha and Mel on the DVD. Cordell's sudden insatiability (and the assertiveness he needs in order to realize the sexual liaisons he had previously only fantasized about) exemplifies Carl Jung's psychological concept of enantiodromia, in which the unconscious mind generates values and self-conceptions that are in diametrical opposition to damagingly extreme ones in an effort to restore balance in the psyche.[7] Cordell's profligacy, especially his sex with Joelle, does not create any greater comfort than his relatively repressed earlier condition did, but it does bring him into a greater understanding of how sexuality, especially sexuality proscribed as deviant or dangerous, can be used as a coping mechanism to mask old psychological injuries. Both Joelle and Sasha, his upstairs neighbor, have been involved in incestuous relationships described as partly coerced and partly voluntary, and

Cordell's sexual partners repeatedly echo this taboo with such exhortations as "Fuck me, Daddy!" (132).

By the end of the book, Cordell comes to realize that although he can sympathize with this pain and even forgive the behaviors it seems to cause, he cannot fully share in it, especially while his own pain is unresolved. Although Sasha dies and his relationship with Joelle comes to and end, Cordell has four women in his life in varying capacities who collectively represent the potential for an authentic expression of his identity. Even as he engages in his sexual adventures, Cordell has a series of telephone conversations with a help-line worker named Cynthia, who gives him the opportunity to work through the confusion and self-loathing he feels at his increasing desire for Joelle in the wake of not only of her initial infidelity, but also her continuing denials thereof. Cynthia encourages Cordell not to bury his pain within himself (as has been his habit) or displace it (as many of those he comes into contact have done), but rather to give voice to it. She does so in words that echo existential sentiments that Mosley himself has expressed in his nonfiction, especially in *Life Out of Context*: "You are the one in pain. You are the man in need of trust and love. I feel for the pain you brought to me when I first heard your voice tonight. . . . I'm not going to betray you. Your pain was the onset of the despair that we experience when we are marooned in life" (*Killing* 126). Though her attentions by themselves are not sufficient to heal Cordell, Cynthia plays much the same reassuring role that the memory of Branwyn did for Tommy in *Fortunate Son* in terms of articulating an antidote to seemingly endless suffering.

It is through Cynthia that Cordell meets Sisypha (whose real name is Brenda), who takes him through New York on a night of sexual escapades—first to a sort of sexual Olympics and then to a sex club—that push Cordell's understanding of his desires well past their limits. Importantly, Brenda/Sisypha herself never satisfies these desires, but in the process of shepherding Cordell though this scene, she helps him reveal a long-repressed self: "This was the person I always wanted to be. When my father slapped me or humiliated me or told me where I could go and how long I could be there even when I was sixteen—I wanted to be that man. When teachers refused to believe that I was smart and when the police stopped me for walking in neighborhoods where I had white friends. I wanted to stand up to my father and every racist and bully I'd ever known, but I'd never had the courage until that night" (222). The range of influences—from personal to social to societal—that Cordell cites in the course of this epiphany suggests the extent to which he has repressed his own frustrations and pain and Mosley uses the vivid language and metaphor of sexual release to symbolize the necessity of emotional/spiritual release in all of these spheres if one is to achieve genuine empowerment, rather than the illusory contentment of Cordell and Joelle's earlier relationship. Sisypha/Brenda tells Cordell "after all these years of looking, you are my brother and I am your sister. And we will look after each other" (241).

His relationship with the photographer Lucy Carmichael is not only a sexual one, but also involves redefining his professional identity. Instead of being a free-lance translator for tech companies, Cordell decides to act as Lucy's agent and helps her publicize her photographs of displaced persons in Darfur. When he first sees these photographs he is more interested in Lucy's amatory charms: "It was, of course, awful what was happening in Darfur. Children were dying from being deprived of the most basic necessities. They were being displaced, slaughtered, enslaved, raped. But what got my heart going was the expectation of Lucy Carmichael's moist peck at the corner of my mouth" (2). By the end of the book, he has gotten considerably more than a "moist peck" from Lucy, but he has also gotten Lucy's photos into a highly regarded gallery while simultaneously insuring that some of the proceeds from the sale of her photos go directly to help the children depicted therein.[8] He recognizes that this act of philanthropy initially arose in part out of his "selfish and cynical" desire to bed Lucy, but asserts that he "can change" with his newfound awareness (240).

Finally, Monica, a young African American single mother, represents the most unambiguously positive female presence in his life. Seeking a better life for herself and for her daughter through education, Monica initially seems drawn to Cordell for his ability to help her achieve her professional goals. Nevertheless, once they become sexually involved, Monica represents a sense of connection that Cordell explicitly associates (during oral sex, no less) with the comfort of a place of love and positive family ties: "You know what you taste like? . . . You taste like home. . . . You taste like my dreams in the back room I shared with my brother. You taste like all the love I ever wanted" (256). The racial and cultural element that Monica brings (i.e., her familiarly African American dialect marks her literally and figuratively as a "home-girl") to Cordell's pantheon of females completes the influences that Mosley seems to suggest will collectively help steer Cordell away from the unhealthy mindset represented by Joelle and Johnny Fry. Not only does Cordell give up his quest for revenge against Johnny (who ends up precipitating his own death in one final act of malevolent disregard toward Cordell) but he tells the reader at the end of the book that he now deletes her phone messages "as soon as [he hears] her voice" (280). Like *Fortunate Son*, the novel ends with a qualified expression of hope for a better future for its protagonist: "I try to tell myself that there's always time for redemption and that sometimes even the worst decisions turn out to be just fine" (280).

Like *Fortunate Son* and *Killing Johnny Fry*, *Blonde Faith* presents a lost soul on a twisting road to redemption. Mosley dedicates the tenth (and possibly concluding) episode of the Easy Rawlins saga, to August Wilson. By doing so, Mosley explicitly aligns himself with an artistic agenda set to capture the evolving African American social consciousness of place in the American homeland. While Wilson's ten-play cycle of African American experience covers each decade of the twentieth century, Mosley's ten-novel cycle moves Easy from the return to peacetime normalcy after World War II up to a socially stressed 1967. In *Blonde Faith*, Easy's search for two lost fathers (both of whom are also versions of the "badman"/"bad nigger" archetypes[9]) in the persons of his friend Mouse Alexander and a disaffected "ex-Green Beret" (264) named Christmas Black is woven into a narrative with unsettling echoes of the 1965 Watts riots and America's destructive, morally ambiguous role in Vietnam. At EttaMae's request, Easy seeks Mouse to exonerate him of the murder of Pericles Tarr, a father of twelve to whom Mouse is actually giving assistance in escaping a horrible home life. Easy seeks Christmas Black because he has left Easter Dawn, his adopted Vietnamese daughter and a survivor of his own murderous actions in the service of America, at Easy's house for safekeeping. Christmas is being pursued by a murderous ring of drug dealers composed of Vietnam War veterans posing as military officers. As in *The Man in My Basement*, Mosley connects America's racial tensions and disruption of the African American home with America's increasingly imperialistic role in the world. Hunting for Christmas Black, Easy encounters the deadly drug traffickers that link homeland crime to international crime and American domestic racial tension to a colonial racism that corrupts the homeland.

Set against this social background of an America that has "lost its way" (46) and within the mystery narrative is Easy's dissolving sense of home precipitated by his expulsion of Bonnie Shay, his longtime female companion and surrogate mother for his adopted children. The loss has shattered him; he is now "uneasy," "lost in my own home, my own skin" (20), obsessed with self-loathing and death. One of Easy's characteristic literary allusions illuminates his problems: LeRoi Jones's *The System of Dante's Hell* (1965) sets Easy's own loss of and quest for home in a double context.[10] First, the allusion frames Easy's personal problem as a lost soul in midlife, akin to Dante's fictionalized self lost in a morally ambiguous dark wood, needing a luminous female guide to find his way home. Additionally, the allusion links Easy's struggle to redeem himself with his larger identity problem, his double consciousness. Like the fictionalized Jones trekking through the gray ambiguities of America as inferno—a version of McKay's "cultured hell"—Easy seeks to resolve the tensions of his own African American double consciousness (Jones's, of course, transformed into black cultural nationalist Amiri Baraka). For Easy, Jones's lyric novel is "a difficult tome," but he responds emotionally to it because "the author's tone made me think about freedom" (198). Jones's identity quest reflects the tension Easy experienced earlier about himself: "I remembered what it was to be a man living in the cracks: a slave, nigger, jigaboo, coon, spade, spear-chucker, darky, boy . . . always a target . . . but . . . I was an American citizen too; a citizen who had to watch his step . . . distrust the police and the government, public opinion, and even the history taught in schools" (163).

Blonde Faith might be read as Easy's liberation from the tension of double consciousness and the traditional American Dream that fueled his move west to Los Angeles after World War II in an attempt to create a new self and a new home free of the poverty and pain of his rural Texas and Louisiana past. In *Blonde Faith*, the Dream has gone bad, festered, and exploded, because America has lost its soul; conquest and greed rather than compassion now seem to rule Easy's homeland. Within the narrative, Christmas Black and Faith Laneer represent the schizophrenia of the Unites States in 1967, a place where the civil rights gains and the Watts riots have created an atmosphere of paranoia for blacks and whites (though the novel is also speckled with positive racial relationships). Furthermore, the nature of the military action in Vietnam has revealed the dark, corrupting side of a war fought ostensibly to preserve freedom and democracy. Serving in Vietnam, former major Christmas Black, a man from a family of patriots and military heroes, discovers that his own slaughter of peasants dishonored the ideals of America and dishonored him. On the other hand, the Faith Laneer, "a vivacious Hollywood blonde" (139), is the embodiment of America's great humanitarian impulse, as demonstrated by the orphanage she ran for the child victims of violence in Vietnam. As Easy notes after her death: "Faith Laneer had been a heroine. . . . She stood up for children and weak men and for what was right" (257). She redeemed Christmas Black by persuading him to adopt Easter Dawn, a child of peasants he had killed; but she is also the novel's central victim, murdered brutally by the drug-runners who selfishly exploited the resources of Vietnam while nominally serving their country.

Both Christmas and Easy have brief but life-affirming affairs with Faith. For both, blonde Faith signifies on their blind faith in America's redemptive potential. Although he is "a government-trained killer, one of the best of his kind in the world" (40) and "a killer on a par with Mouse" (21), Christmas Black salvages a modicum of his humanity through his relationship with Faith and by accepting her suggestion to adopt Easter Dawn. Easy's affair with Faith soothes the pain of losing Bonnie. Moreover, Faith represents all the allure of a black male formulation of the American Dream in stereotypically sexualized terms signifying autonomy and power. After making love to her, Easy reflects: "As we stood there kissing under the silver moon, I felt a howl in my soul. There I was, a black man kissing the epitome of northern European beauty, with a gun in one pocket and a short fuse in the other. There was no sex in the world better than that" (170). At several levels, Faith represents the archetypal domesticating feminine principle for Easy—loving mother, sexual lover, and beloved motherland. Maternal care marks his love scene with Faith as she undresses him, guides him to the shower, washes him with a soft sponge, and offers to powder him after drying him off (168). Later, reflecting on her brutal murder by the corrupt Vietnam veterans, Easy's loneliness echoes the old spiritual lyric, "Sometimes I feel like a motherless child . . . a long ways from home," as he recalls the death of his own mother and his impotence at his "failure to protect her" and comments longingly: "I wanted my mother" (260).

With Faith dead, Easy seems to have abandoned hope in fulfilling his American Dream in traditional terms of home: wife, family, house. Instead, to free himself from what is now a dead weight, Easy intensifies his search for Mouse and Christmas Black to seek their devastating power in revenge against Faith's murderers. In the process, however, he makes several tentative gestures toward preserving the ideal of home and satisfying his own longing for a loving woman. Freeing Easy from the shackles of the dead Dream starts with abandoning his first Los Angeles house, lovingly described in *Devil in a Blue Dress* as his proud, partial achievement of the American Dream. In *Blonde Faith*, Easy detaches himself from this narrow, materialistic image of the Dream. In an act of generosity that sadly recognizes the racial polarization of American society in 1967 while also valorizing diversity, Easy gives the house to his Mexican friend Primo who had sheltered various members of Easy's "family" (notably Jesus) in difficult times. In the wake of the Watts riots, Primo's own family feels threatened by African American kids. To create the possibility for a better family life—a home for Primo's kin—Easy lets go of the property that "he couldn't bear to let go" (174). He gives the house to Primo, allowing his family to move to East LA, "where the Mexicans live" (178) to shelter his family from the violence of a racially atomizing homeland.

In addition, Easy exonerates Mouse not only by finding Pericles Tarr alive but also by completing Mouse's task in ensuring the security of Tarr's home, albeit in a way that is typically (for Easy) ambiguous in terms of conventional morals. He delivers the thirty thousand dollars that Mouse and Pericles had stolen in a payroll robbery to Mrs. Tarr even as he lets Pericles abandon his sprawling family in pursuit of the beautiful but venal Pretty Smart. Finally, Easy creates a "blutopian" home to ensure the safety of his own adopted rainbow coalition of a family: the Hispanic Jesus; his black woman Benita, their biracial child, the black and white Feather; and now also the Asian Easter Dawn. To shield them from the murdering drug traffickers, he puts them in the care of Jewelle, a brilliant, rich, and powerful professional black woman who has the means to protect them. There is a male presence, too, adding to Easy's unconventional family home security system: Jackson Blue, the cowardly black genius, capable and successful in the white world of corporate, technologically driven business. Later, to complete the male layer of security, Easy positions Christmas Black, the trained killer, "[s]ix foot four with the shoulders of a giant" (263), as surrogate father/protector. The house that encompasses this diverse family of the emerging American majority is a parodic image of the American Dream, a "California Dream house" (286), signifying both its attraction and potential as well as its unreality: a gated mansion in the Hollywood Hills that Easy refers to as "Buckingham Palace" (290), where the children swim and frolic in the sun.

Once Easy has discharged his responsibilities to family, he is free to move literally and figuratively into blackness, his "negative freedom . . . my liberation"

(165), and into the pantheon of heroic badmen, a sort of home above and beyond the transient world of historical America. *Blonde Faith* ends with the inevitable revenge and justice by alternative means as it resonates with the power of blackness through Easy's manipulation of the LAPD and his own death. Easy finds Mouse and, ever the trickster, he manipulates Mouse's cultural significance as a "bad nigger" to destroy his (and American society's) enemies. Mouse's absence proves more potent than his actual presence.[11] Easy knows that the LAPD is driven, especially in the wake of the Watts riots, to erase Mouse and all the social chaos that he and blackness in America represent. Easy also knows that the drug dealers are eager to destroy Christmas Black because of his knowledge of their operation. Consequently, Easy uses the badman figures to undermine both the alleged agents of justice and the known corrupters of justice. First, feigning belief that he is helping the government find Christmas Black, Easy tells the drug dealers that the ex-Green Beret will be present in an abandoned building at a given time knowing that they plan an ambush. Under the assumed identity of a man cuckolded by Mouse, Easy lures the police to the same building at the same time telling them that Mouse will be there. In the end, the police riddle the building with bullets and causing it to burn down, in the process destroying the real criminals. Thus, Mouse goes free, as he is actually innocent of any crime (this time), the drug dealers receive harsh justice, and Easy (and Christmas and perhaps America itself) get revenge for the murder of Faith Laneer.

Blonde Faith concludes the series with its hero free and Easy. Easy cuts himself loose from his former responsibilities and from the middle-class American Dream. He has made peace with Bonnie and her decision to marry her African Prince. He has had a renewing sexual affair with Tourmaline Goss, a beautiful and intelligent black college woman.[12] Like Pericles Tarr, he has provided for his family's security and then abandoned them. The concluding scene depicts Easy in terms resonant with blues imagery. He becomes a blues man, a transcendent vector of pain and survival, as he revels in remembered pain and the speed of his car, cruising in the midnight darkness beside the black void of the vast Pacific on the coastal highway. Assuming some of his old joys, he has a bottle of cognac between his legs and smokes a cigarette, vices he had long ago given up as he accumulated family responsibilities. Recklessly passing a loitering eighteen-wheeler, Easy's car veers off the road, literally flying into the void. His narrative voice records the pain of the crash, but also the exhilaration of leaving this earth. Airborne, he reminds one of Milkman Dead as he too flies into the void grasping his alter ego, the murderous Guitar, at the end of Morrison's *Song of Solomon*. While the literary analogue seems relevant, so too is the old vernacular tale of the black man who illegally entered heaven and seized the moment to soar before he was ejected;[13] like that folk figure, when Easy is flying, he is a flying fool. As he searches for "the image I needed to see before I died," Easy still seeks a sense of home located in lost women: "I was grasping for Bonnie, Faith, and my mother. But none of them was around for my last seconds" (308). Rather than an earthly home and a caring female presence, Easy smiles as "the world went black" (308) and he transcends death and the detective noir genre, entering, still talking, legend and lore and becoming another rich black resource in African American literary tradition.

To conclude our exploration of Mosley's fictive world, we briefly return to the question framing this epilogue—Whither Walter? There seems to be no literary-critical GPS to fix Mosley's position for good; he is an artist in seemingly perpetual motion through his fictionalized America. Of one thing, however, we feel sure: he is already and always on his way home. Having concluded the highly acclaimed Easy Rawlins series, his recent work suggests that he is in an experimental period that finds him exploring well-known genres with mild undertones of both parody and pastiche. This period is tonally a dark one if we consider the "sexistentialist" bent of *Killing Johnny Fry* and *Diablerie*. Nevertheless, *Fortunate Son, Blonde Faith* and *Tempest Tales* also remind us that Mosley can still "blue" this dark world to treat death and disillusionment with transcending irony by mining the African American vernacular and literary tradition, exploiting its resources rhetorically as tools of resistance and survival.

Notes

1. Kelly Connelly, Laura Quinn, and Lisa Thompson discuss *Cinnamon Kiss*; Jerrilyn McGregory discusses *Fear of the Dark*; and Juan Elices discusses *The Wave*. Rather than duplicating here the work they have already done, we would direct you to those essays for critical analysis of these works within Mosley's larger body of work.

2. Not only has he returned to the respective fictional worlds of Easy Rawlins and Fearless Jones, but Mosley has hinted that a third Socrates Fortlow book is also in the works.

3. Dibbuk's surname in *Diablerie* also clearly evokes the Jewish folkloric figure of the *dybbuk*, a malevolent (or at least mischievous) spirit who has escaped from Gehenna to wreak havoc on Earth, much as Dibbuk's former life comes back to haunt him. Mosley has always been fond of using localized mythic metaphorical associations of this sort (cf. Jerrilyn McGregory's discussion of the mythic resonance in the names of Tristan "Fearless" Jones and Paris Minton), but *Tempest Tales* marks the first instance of such a metaphor being totalized throughout an entire text.

4. See Daniel Stein's essay for a delineation of the blutopian mode in Mosley's work.

5. See Lisa Thompson's essay in this volume for more on the symbolism related to female characters in Mosley's work.

6. See Laura Quinn's essay for more on Mosley's complex and often noncomic use of parody.

7. See C. G. Jung, *Aspects of the Masculine* (Princeton, NJ: Princeton UP, 1989), especially chapter 7, for a full discussion of enantiodromia.

8. The essays by Francesca Sautman and Keith Hughes in this volume discuss the geopolitical implications of Mosley's work in ways that are conversant with this seemingly innocuous (or perhaps even incongruous) detail in *Killing Johnny Fry*.

9. For more on these archetypes, see the essays by Kelly Connelly, Albert Turner, and Terrence Tucker.

10. Mosley's allusions to Dante and Jones/Baraka suggest the kind of "black Atlantic" interpretation that Keith Hughes's essay provides for *Always Outnumbered, Always Outgunned.*

11. Laura Quinn explores this phenomenon in several of the earlier Easy Rawlins novels in her article.

12. Easy's relationship with Tourmaline seems to be part of a pattern in which Mosley's heroes find a restorative emotional and sexual bond with an intellectual black woman. In *Fortunate Son,* Tommy is befriended during one of his brushes with the law by Clea Frank, "a language major [at NYU who] wanted to work at the UN" (246). Clea first offers him friendship, then sex, and finally a declaration of love just prior to the final apparition of Branwyn's spirit that leaves him feeling that "maybe things might be okay" after all (310). As mentioned above, one of the women that makes up the composite female presence that portends Cordell's renewal in *Killing Johnny Fry* is Monica Wells, a student at City College of New York who takes an active role not only in her own education but in that of her young daughter: "I want my girl to know everyone's history . . . [b]ecause she needs to know where we came from—all of us" (177).

13. In this regard, the resolution of Easy's story seems to be a noncomic foretaste of the character of Tempest Landry from *Tempest Tales.*

Works Cited

Aldridge, Alexandra. *The Scientific World View in Dystopia*. Ann Arbor, Michigan: UMI Research Press, 1984.

Allen-Taylor, J. Douglas. "Obscured by 'Blue Light.'" Review of *Blue Light*, by Walter Mosley. *Metroactive* (February 25, 1999). http://www.metroactive.com/papers/ metro/02.25.99/cover/lit-mosley-9908.html (accessed December 10, 2007).

Atwater, Deborah F., and Sandra L. Herndon. "The Use of Public Space as Cultural Communicator: How Museums Reconstruct and Reconnect Cultural Memory." In *Understanding African-American Rhetoric: Classic Origins to Contemporary Innovations*, edited by Ronald L. Jackson II and Elaine B. Richardson, 69–82. New York: Routledge, 2003.

Baehr, Peter. "Identifying the Unprecedented: Hannah Arendt, Totalitarianism, and the Critique of Sociology." *American Sociological Review* 67, no. 6 (2002): 804–31.

Bakhtin, Mikhail Mikhailovich. *The Dialogic Imagination: Four Essays*. Trans. Michael Holmquist. Austin: University of Texas Press, 1981.

Baldwin, James. "The American Dream and the American Negro." In *Collected Essays*, edited by Toni Morrison, 714–19. New York: Library of America, 1998.

———. *The Fire Next Time*. New York: Vintage International, 1993.

———. "Going to Meet the Man." In *Going to Meet the Man: Stories*, 227–49. New York: Vintage International, 1995.

Bell, Derrick. "Property Rights in Whiteness: Their Legal Legacy, Their Economic Costs." In *Critical Race Theory: The Cutting Edge*, edited by Richard Delgado, 75–83. Philadelphia: Temple University Press, 1995.

Berger, Roger A. "'The Black Dick': Race, Sexuality, and Discourse in the L.A. Novels of Walter Mosley." *African American Review* 31, no. 2 (1997): 281–95.

Bergevin, Gerald W. "'Traveling Here Below': John Edgar Wideman's *The Island: Martinique* and the Strategy of Melancholy." In *Critical Essays on John Edgar Wideman*, edited by Bonnie TuSmith and Keith E. Byerman, 71–92. Knoxville, TN: The University of Tennessee Press, 2006.

Bernstein, Richard. "Books of the Times: Dark Streets, Stolen Goods, and a Hard-Bitten Dame." Review of *Fearless Jones*, by Walter Mosley. *New York Times*, July 2, 2001.

Beauchamp, Gorman. "Technology in the Dystopian Novel." *Modern Fiction Studies* 32, no. 1 (1986): 53–64.

Blake, Susan L. "Ritual and Rationalization: Black Folklore in the Works of Ralph Ellison." *PMLA* 94, no.1 (1979): 121–36.

Bongmba, Elias Kifron. *African Witchcraft and Otherness: A Philosophical and Theological Critique of Intersubjective Relations.* Albany: State University of New York Press, 2001.

Booker, M. Keith. *The Dystopian Impulse in Modern Literature: Fiction as Social Criticism.* Westport, CT: Greenwood, 1994.

———. *Dystopian Literature: A Theory and Research Guide.* Westport, CT: Greenwood, 1994.

Brickhouse, Thomas C., and Nicholas D. Smith. *Plato's Socrates.* New York and Oxford: Oxford University Press, 1994.

Brown, Charles N. "Walter Mosley: A Seat at the Table." Interview. *Locus* 49, no. 6 (2001): 6–7, 75–76.

Bryant, Jerry H. *"Born in a Mighty Bad Land": The Violent Man in African American Folklore and Fiction.* Bloomington: Indiana University Press, 2003.

Bunyan, Scott. "No Order from Chaos: The Absence of Chandler's Extra-Legal Space in the Detective Fiction of Chester Himes and Walter Mosley." *Studies in the Novel* 35, no. 3 (2003): 339–65.

Butler, Johnella. "African American Literature and Realist Theory: Seeking the 'true-true'." In *Identity Politics Reconsidered,* edited by Linda Martín Alcoff, Michael Hames-García, Satya Mohanty, and Paula M. Moya, 171–92. New York: Palgrave, 2006.

Canadé Sautman, Francesca. "The Race for Globalization: Modernity, Resistance and the Unspeakable in Three African Francophone Texts." *French and Francophone/Yale French Studies* 103 (2003): 106–22.

Canon, Peter, and Jeff Zaleski. Review of *Fearless Jones,* by Walter Mosley. *Publishers Weekly,* May 28, 2001.

———. Review of *Fear Itself,* by Walter Mosley. *Publishers Weekly,* June 16, 2003.

Chandler, Marilyn R. *Dwelling in the Text: Houses in American Fiction.* Los Angeles: University of California Press, 1991.

Chandler, Raymond. *Farewell My Lovely.* New York: Vintage Books, 1992.

———. *The Simple Art of Murder.* New York: Vintage Books, 1988.

Charters, Samuel. *Robert Johnson.* New York: Oak Publications, 1972.

Chaudhuri, Una. *Staging Place: The Geography of Modern Drama.* Ann Arbor: University of Michigan Press, 1995.

Chua, Amy. *World on Fire: How Exporting Free Market Democracy Breeds Ethnic Hatred and Global Instability.* New York: Doubleday, 2003.

Clark, Clifford Edward, Jr. *The American Family Home, 1890–1960.* Chapel Hill: University of North Carolina Press, 1986.

Crooks, Robert. "From the Far Side of the Urban Frontier: The Detective Fiction of Chester Himes and Walter Mosley." *College Literature* 22, no. 3 (1995): 68–91.

Crowther, Bruce. *Film Noir: Reflections in a Dark Mirror.* London: Virgin, 1990.

Daeninckx, Didier. *Meurtres pour mémoire.* Paris: Gallimard, 1984.

Dance, Daryl. *Shuckin' and Jivin': Folklore from Contemporary Black Americans.* Bloomington: Indiana University Press, 1978.

Davis Jr., Ben. "The African American Science Fiction Character in Literature, Television and Film." *SFFWorld.com*. http://www.sffworld.com/authors/d/davis_ben/articles/africansfi.html (accessed December 10, 2007).

Delgado, Richard, ed. *Critical Race Theory: The Cutting Edge*. Philadelphia: Temple University Press, 1995.

Dick, Philip K. *Do Androids Dream of Electric Sheep?* New York: Doubleday and Company, 1968.

Dickos, Andrew. *Street With No Name: A History of the Classic American Film Noir*. Louisville: University of Kentucky Press, 2002.

Dillon, Nikki. "Live from Dystopia." Review of *Futureland*, by Walter Mosley. *New York Times Book Review*, November 25, 2001.

Douglas, Mary. *Purity and Danger: An Analysis of Concepts of Pollution and Taboo*. Baltimore: Penguin, 1970.

Douglass, Frederick. *Narrative of the Life of Frederick Douglass, An American Slave, Written by Himself*. Edited by John W. Blassingame, John R. McKivigan, and Peter P. Hinks. New Haven CT: Yale University Press, 2001.

Du Bois, W. E. B. *The Souls of Black Folk*. In *Writings*, 357–547. New York: Library of America, 1986.

Du Plessis, Max. "Historical Injustice and International Law: An Exploratory Discussion of Reparation for Slavery." *Human Rights Quarterly* 25, no. 3 (2003): 624–59.

Early, Gerald. *The Culture of Bruising: Essays on Prizefighting, Literature, and Modern American Culture*. Hopewell, NJ: Ecco Press, 1994.

Ellison, Ralph. "The Art of Fiction: An Interview." In *The Collected Essays of Ralph Ellison*, edited by John F. Callahan, 210–24. New York: The Modern Library, 1995.

———. "Brave Words for a Startling Occasion." In *The Collected Essays of Ralph Ellison*, edited by John F. Callahan, 151–54. New York: The Modern Library, 1995.

———. "Change the Joke and Slip the Yoke." In *The Collected Essays of Ralph Ellison*, edited by John F. Callahan, 100–112. New York: The Modern Library, 1995.

———. "The Charlie Christian Story." In *The Collected Essays of Ralph Ellison*, edited by John F. Callahan, 266–72. New York: The Modern Library, 1995.

———. *The Collected Essays of Ralph Ellison*. Edited by John F. Callahan. New York: The Modern Library, 1995.

———. Introduction. *Invisible Man*. New York: Random House, 1994. vii–xxiii.

———. "Introduction [to *Shadow and Act*]." In *The Collected Essays of Ralph Ellison*, edited by John F. Callahan, 49–60. New York: The Modern Library, 1995.

———. *Invisible Man*. New York: Random House, 1952.

———. *Juneteenth*. New York: Vintage, 2000.

———. "Richard Wright's Blues." In *The Collected Essays of Ralph Ellison*, edited by John F. Callahan, 128–44. New York: The Modern Library, 1995.

Emerson, Ralph Waldo. *Essays and Lectures*. New York: The Library of America, 1983.

Ewert, Jeanne C. "'A Thousand Other Mysteries': Metaphysical Detection, Ontological Quests." In *Detecting Texts: The Metaphysical Detective Story from Poe to Postmodernism*, edited by Patricia Merivale and Susan Elizabeth Sweeney, 179–98. Philadelphia: University of Pennsylvania Press, 1999.

Fabre, Geneviève, and Robert O'Meally. Introduction to *History and Memory in African-American Culture*, edited by Geneviève Fabre and Robert O'Meally, 3–17. New York: Oxford University Press, 1994.

Fine, David M. *Imagining Los Angeles: A City in Fiction*. Reno: University of Nevada Press, 2004.

Fitzsimmons, Lorna. "'Hellhound on My Trail': *Crossroads* and the Racist Ravishment." *European Journal of American Culture* 20, no. 3 (2002): 164–82.

Fleming, Michael. "HBO's 'Little' deal; Wright, Def in cabler's 'Scarlet' Tale." *Variety.com*. http://www.variety.com/article/VR1117944857.html (accessed December 10, 2007).

Fleming, Robert E. "Ellison's Black Archetypes: The Founder, Bledsoe, Ras, and Rinehart." *CLA Journal* 32, no. 4 (1989): 426–32.

Ford, Elisabeth A. "Miscounts, Loopholes, and Flashbacks: Strategic Evasion in Walter Mosley's Detective Fiction." *Callaloo* 28, no. 4 (2005): 1074–90.

Forter, Greg. *Murdering Masculinities: Fantasies of Gender and Violence in the American Crime Novel*. New York: New York University Press, 2000.

Foucault, Michel. *Discipline and Punish: The Birth of the Prison*. Trans. Alan Sheridan. New York: Vintage Books, 1995.

Fraser, Nancy. "Rethinking the Public Sphere: A Contribution to the Critique of Actually Existing Democracy." In *Habermas and the Public Sphere*, edited by Craig Calhoun, 109–42. Cambridge, MA: MIT Press, 1992.

Frazier, E. Franklin. *Black Bourgeoisie*. Glencoe, IL: Free Press, 1957.

Gaines, Kevin K. *Uplifting the Race: Black Leadership, Politics, and Culture in the Twentieth Century*. Chapel Hill: University of North Carolina Press, 1996.

Galtseva, Renata, and Irina Rodnyanskaya. "The Obstacle: The Human Being, or the Twentieth Century in the Mirror of Dystopia." *The South Atlantic Quarterly* 90, no. 2 (1991): 293–322.

Gates, Henry Louis, Jr. *The Signifying Monkey: A Theory of African-American Literary Criticism*. New York: Oxford University Press. 1988.

Genovese, Eugene. *Roll, Jordan, Roll: The World the Slaves Made*. New York: Vintage Press, 1972.

Gibson, William. *Neuromancer*. New York: Ace, 1984.

Giddins, Gary. Review of *RL's Dream*, by Walter Mosley. *New York Times Book Review*, August 13, 1995.

Gilroy, Paul. *The Black Atlantic: Modernity and Double Consciousness*. Cambridge, MA: Harvard University Press, 1993.

Glissant, Edouard. "La Barque ouverte." In *Poétique de la Relation. Poétique III*. Paris: Gallimard, 1990: 17–21.

Goodheart, Eugene. *Culture and the Radical Conscience*. Cambridge, MA: Harvard University Press, 1973.

Gosselin, Adrienne Johnson, ed. *Muticultural Detective Fiction: Murder from the "Other" Side*. New York: Garland, 1999.

Goya, Francisco. [*Duel with Cudgels*]. Museo del Prado, Madrid.

Graff, Keir. Review of *Fear Itself*, by Walter Mosley. *Booklist*, May 15, 2003.

Graham, Lawrence Otis. *Our Kind of People: Inside America's Black Upper Class*. New York: Harper Perennial, 2000.

Works Cited

Grant, Nathan. *Masculinist Impulse: Toomer, Hurston, Black Writing, and Modernity.* Columbia: University of Missouri Press, 2004.

Gray, W. Russel. "Hard-Boiled Black Easy: Genre Conventions in *A Red Death.*" *African American Review* 38, no. 3 (2004): 489–98.

Griffin, Farah Jasmine. *"Who Set You Flowin'?": The African-American Migration Narrative.* New York: Oxford University Press, 1995.

Grossman, Lev. Review of *Fear Itself,* by Walter Mosley. *Time,* August 11, 2003.

Gruesser, John Cullen. "An Un-Easy Relationship: Walter Mosley's Signifyin(g) Detective and the Black Community." In *Muticultural Detective Fiction: Murder from the "Other" Side,* edited by Adrienne Johnson Gosselin, 235–55. New York: Garland, 1999.

Guralnick, Peter. *Searching for Robert Johnson.* New York: Dutton, 1989.

Gussow, Adam. *Seems Like Murder Here: Southern Violence and the Blues Tradition.* Chicago: University of Chicago Press, 2002.

Habermas, Jürgen. "The Public Sphere." *New German Critique* 3 (1974): 49–52.

———. *The Structural Transformation of the Public Sphere: An Inquiry Into a Category of Bourgeois Society.* Trans. Thomas Burger. Cambridge: MIT Press, 1989.

Hahn, Robert C. "PW Talks with Walter Mosley." Interview. *Publishers Weekly,* May 28, 2001, 54.

Hareven, Tamara K. "The Home and Family in Historical Perspective." In *Home: A Place in the World,* edited by Arien Mack, 227–59. New York: New York University Press, 1993.

Harris, Cheryl I. "Whiteness as Property." In *Critical Race Theory: The Key Writings that Formed the Movement,* edited by Kimberlé Crenshaw, Neil Gotanda, Gary Peller, and Kendall Thomas, 276–91. New York: New Press, 1995.

Harris, Trudier. *Saints, Sinners, Saviors: Strong Black Women in African American Literature.* New York: Palgrave, 2001.

Hickman, Miranda. "Introduction: The Complex History of A 'Simple Art.'" *Studies in the Novel* 35, no. 3 (2003): 285–304.

Hill-Collins, Patricia. *Black Feminist Thought: Knowledge, Consciousness, and the Politics of Empowerment.* New York: Routledge, 2000.

Hill, Logan. "Free Radical." *New York* (September 26, 2005). http://nymag.com/nymetro/arts/books/14455/ (accessed December 10, 2007).

Hobson, Janell. *Venus in the Dark: Blackness and Beauty in Popular Culture.* New York: Routledge, 2005.

Hogue, W. Lawrence. *The African American Male, Writing, and Difference.* Albany: State University of New York Press, 2003.

Hollander, John. "It All Depends." In *Home: A Place in the World,* edited by Arien Mack, 27–45. New York: New York University Press, 1993.

hooks, bell. *Feminist Theory from Margin to Center.* Boston: South End Press, 1984.

Hoppenstand, Gary. "Murder and Other Hazardous Occupations: Taboo and Detective Fiction." In *Forbidden Fruits: Taboos and Tabooism in Culture,* edited by Ray Browne, 83–96. Bowling Green, OH. Bowling Green State University Press, 1984.

Horsley, Lee. *Twentieth-Century Crime Fiction.* New York: Oxford, 2005.

Hutcheon, Linda. *The Politics of Postmodernism.* London: Routledge, 1989.

Hyde, Lewis. *Trickster Makes This World: Mischief, Myth, and Art.* New York: Farrar, Strauss, and Giroux, 1998.

Ishay, Micheline R. *History of Human Rights from Ancient Times to the Globalization Era.* Berkeley: University of California Press, 2004.

Johnson, Alex. "Damsels in distress: If you're missing, it helps to be young, white and female." MSNBC.com. http://www.msnbc.msn.com/id/5325808 (accessed December 10, 2007).

Johnson, Charles. Preface to *Juneteenth*, by Ralph Ellison, xv–xviii. New York: Vintage, 2000.

Johnson, Robert. "Cross Road Blues." *The Complete Recordings.* Sony, 1990. CK 46222.

———. "Kind Hearted Woman Blues." *The Complete Recordings.* Sony, 1990. CK 46222.

———. "Me and the Devil Blues." *The Complete Recordings.* Sony, 1990. CK 46222.

Jones, LeRoi [Amiri Baraka]. *Blues People: Negro Music in White America.* New York: Quill/William Morrow, 1999.

———. *Home: Social Essays.* New York: William Morrow and Co., 1966.

Kelley, Robin D. G. *Race Rebels: Culture, Politics, and the Black Working Class.* New York: Free Press, 1996.

Kennedy, Liam. "Black *Noir*: Race and Urban Space in Walter Mosley's Detective Fiction." In *Diversity and Detective Fiction*, edited by Kathleen Gregory Klein, 224–39. Bowling Green, OH: Bowling Green State University Popular Press, 1999.

Kilgore, De Witt Douglas. *Astrofuturism: Science, Race, and Visions of Utopia in Space.* Philadelphia: University of Pennsylvania Press, 2003.

King, Nicole. " 'You Think Like You White': Questioning Race and Racial Community through the Lens of Middle-Class Desire(s)." *Novel: A Forum on Fiction* 35, nos. 2–3 (2002): 211–30.

Kochman, Thomas. *Black and White Styles in Conflict.* Chicago: University of Chicago Press, 1981.

Kumar, Krishan. *Utopia and Anti-Utopia in Modern Times.* Oxford: Blackwell, 1987.

Lane, James B. "Underground Man to Manhood: Ralph Ellison's *Invisible Man*." *Negro American Literature Forum* 7, no. 2 (1973): 64–72.

Lawson, Bill, and Frank M. Kirkland, eds. *Frederick Douglass: A Critical Reader.* Malden, MA and Oxford: Blackwell, 1998.

Lemann, Nicholas. *The Promised Land: The Great Black Migration and How It Changed America.* New York: Knopf, 1991.

Lester, Julius. Review of *RL's Dream*, by Walter Mosley. *The Washington Post*, August 20, 1995.

Levecq, Christine. "Blues Poetics and Blues Politics in Walter Mosley's *RL's Dream*." *African American Review* 38, no. 2 (2004): 239–56.

Levine, Lawrence W. *Black Culture and Black Consciousness: Afro-American Folk Thought From Slavery to Freedom.* Oxford: Oxford University Press, 1977.

Lindsay, Tony. Review of *Fearless Jones*, by Walter Mosley. *Black Issues Book Review* 3 (2001): 28.

Lipsitz, George. *The Possessive Investment in Whiteness: How White People Profit from Identity Politics.* Philadelphia: Temple University Press, 1998.

Lock, Graham. *Blutopia: Visions of the Future and Revisions of the Past in the Work of Sun Ra, Duke Ellington, and Anthony Braxton.* Durham: Duke University Press, 1999.

Lock, Helen. "Invisible Detection: The Case of Walter Mosley." *MELUS* 26, no. 1 (2001): 77–89.

Lomax, Sara M. "Double Agent Easy Rawlins: The Development of a Cultural Detective." *American Visions* 7, no. 2 (1992): 32–34.

López, Ian F. Haney. "The Social Construction of Race." In *Critical Race Theory: The Cutting Edge*, edited by Richard Delgado, 191–203. Philadelphia: Temple University Press, 1995.

———. "White by Law." In *Critical Race Theory: The Cutting Edge*, edited by Richard Delgado, 542–50. Philadelphia: Temple University Press, 1995.

Lowney, John. "Langston Hughes and the 'Nonsense' of Bebop." *American Literature* 72, no. 2 (2000): 357–85.

MacDonald, Janice. "Parody and Detective Fiction." In *Theory and Practice of Classic Detective Fiction*, edited by Jerome Delamarter and Ruth Prigozy, 61–73. Westport, CT: Greenwood Press, 1997.

Mack, Arien, ed. *Home: A Place in the World*. New York: New York University Press, 1993.

Mamdani, Mahmood. *When Victims Become Killers. Colonialism, Nativism, and the Genocide in Rwanda*. Princeton, NJ: Princeton University Press, 2001.

Marks, Stephen P. "From the 'Single Confused Page' to the 'Decalogue for Six Billion Persons': The Roots of the Universal Declaration of Human Rights in the French Revolution." *Human Rights Quarterly* 20, no. 3 (1998): 459–514.

Mason, Theodore O., Jr. "Walter Mosley's Easy Rawlins: The Detective and Afro-American Fiction." *The Kenyon Review* 14, no. 4 (1992): 173–83.

McIntosh, Roderick. "Just Say Shame." In *Plundering Africa's Past*, edited by Peter R. Schmidt and Roderick J. McIntosh, 45–62. Bloomington: Indiana University Press, 1996.

Memmott, Mark. "Spotlight Skips Cases of Missing Minorities." *USA Today.com*. http://www.usatoday.com/news/nation/2005-06-15-missing-minorities_x.htm (accessed December 10, 2007).

Merivale, Patricia, and Susan Elizabeth Sweeney, eds. *Detecting Texts: The Metaphysical Detective Story from Poe to Postmodernism*. Philadelphia: University of Pennsylvania Press, 1999.

Mills, Charles W. *The Racial Contract*. Ithaca, NY: Cornell University Press, 1997.

Mohanty, Satya. "The Epistemic Status of Cultural Identity: On *Beloved* and the Postcolonial Condition." In *Reclaiming Identity: Realist Theory and the Predicament of Postmodernism*, edited by Paula M. Moya and Michael R. Hames-García, 29–66. Berkeley: University of California Press, 2000.

Morrison, Toni. "City Limits, Village Values: Concepts of the Neighborhood in Black Fiction." In *Literature and the Urban Experience: Essays on the City and Literature*, edited by Michael C. Jaye and Ann Chalmers Watts, 35–43. New Brunswick, NJ: Rutgers University Press, 1981.

———. "The Site of Memory." In *The Norton Anthology of African American Literature* (2nd ed.), edited by Henry Louis Gates, Jr. and Nellie McKay, 2290–99. New York: Norton, 2004.

Morson, Gary Saul. *The Boundaries of Genre: Dostoevsky's* Diary of a Writer *and the Traditions of Literary Utopia*. Evanston, IL: Northwestern University Press, 1981.

Mosley, Walter. *Always Outnumbered, Always Outgunned*. New York: W. W. Norton, 1998.

———. *Bad Boy Brawly Brown*. Boston: Little, Brown and Company, 2002.

———. *Black Betty*. New York: W. W. Norton, 1994.

———. "The Black Dick." In *Critical Fictions: The Politics of Imaginative Writing*, edited by Philomena Mariani, 131–33. Seattle: Bay Press, 1991.

———. "The Black Man: Hero." In *Speak My Name: Black Men on Masculinity and the American Dream*, edited by Don Belton, 234–40. Boston: Beacon, 1995.

———. "Black to the Future." In *Dark Matter. A Century of Speculative Fiction from the African Diaspora*, edited by Sheree R. Thomas, 405–7. New York: Aspect, 2000.

———. *Blonde Faith*. New York: Little, Brown and Company, 2007.

———. *Blue Light*. Boston: Little, Brown and Company, 1998.

———. *Cinnamon Kiss*. New York: Little, Brown and Company, 2005.

———. *Devil in a Blue Dress*. New York: W. W. Norton, 1990.

———. *Diablerie*. New York: Bloomsbury USA, 2008.

———. *Fear of the Dark*. New York: Little, Brown and Company, 2006.

———. *Fear Itself*. Boston: Little, Brown and Company, 2003.

———. *Fearless Jones*. Boston: Little, Brown and Company, 2001.

———. *47*. New York: Little, Brown and Company, 2005.

———. *Fortunate Son*. New York: Little, Brown and Company, 2006.

———. *Futureland: Nine Stories of an Imminent Future*. New York: Warner Books, 2001.

———. *Gone Fishin'*. New York: Pocket Star, 1997.

———. Interview by Samuel Coale. In *The Mystery of Mysteries: Cultural Differences and Designs*, by Samuel Coale, 200–210. Bowling Green, OH: Bowling Green University Popular Press, 1999.

———. *Killing Johnny Fry: A Sexistential Novel*. New York: Bloomsbury USA, 2007.

———. *Life Out of Context, Which Includes a Proposal for the Non-violent Takeover of the House of Representatives*. New York: Nation Books, 2006.

———. *Little Scarlet*. New York: Little, Brown and Company, 2004.

———. *A Little Yellow Dog*. New York: Pocket Books, 1996.

———. *The Man in My Basement*. Boston: Little, Brown and Company, 2004.

———. *A Red Death*. New York: Pocket Books, 1991.

———. *RL's Dream*. New York: Norton, 1995.

———. *Six Easy Pieces*. New York: Atria, 2003.

———. *Tempest Tales*. Baltimore: Black Classic, 2008.

———. *This Year You Write Your Novel*. New York: Little, Brown and Company, 2007.

———. *Walkin' the Dog*. Boston: Little, Brown and Company, 1999.

———. *The Wave*. New York: Warner Books, 2006.

———. *What Next: A Memoir toward World Peace*. Baltimore: Black Classic, 2003.

———. *White Butterfly*. New York: Pocket Books, 1992.

———. *Workin' on the Chain Gang: Shaking Off the Dead Hand of History*. New York: Ballantine, 2000.

Moynihan, Daniel Patrick. *The Negro Family: The Case for National Action*. Washington, D.C.: Office of Policy Planning and Research, United States Department of Labor, 1965. http://www.dol.gov/oasam/programs/history/moynchapter4.html (accessed June 28, 2007).

Mudge, Alden. "New crime fiction with a twist from noir master Walter Mosley." Interview. *BookPage*. http://www.bookpage.com/0106bp/walter_mosley.html (accessed December 10, 2007).

Muller, Priscilla E. *Goya's 'Black' Paintings: Truth and Reason in Light and Liberty*. New York: Hispanic Society of America, 1984.

Murray, Albert. *Stomping the Blues*. New York: Da Capo, 2000.

Nash, William R. " 'Maybe I killed my own blood': Doppelgangers and The Death of Double Consciousness in Walter Mosley's *A Little Yellow Dog*." In *Multicultural Detective Fiction: Murder from the "Other" Side*, edited by Adrienne Johnson Gosselin, 303–24. New York: Garland, 1999.

Neighbors, Jim. "Plunging (outside of) History: Naming and Self-Possession in *Invisible Man.*" *African American Review* 36, no. 2 (2002): 227–42.

Nora, Pierre. "Between History and Memory: *Les Lieux des Mémoire.*" Trans. Marc Roudebush. In *History and Memory in African-American Culture,* edited by Geneviève Fabre and Robert O'Meally, 284–300. New York: Oxford University Press, 1994.

Nyman, Jopi. *Men Alone: Masculinity, Individualism, and Hard-Boiled Fiction.* Atlanta: Editions Rodopi, 1997.

Oakley, Giles. *The Devil's Music: A History of the Blues.* 2nd updated ed. New York: Da Capo, 1997.

O'Meally, Robert G. " 'Game to the Heart': Sterling Brown and the Badman." *Callaloo* 14/15 (1982): 43–54.

Okorafor, Nnedi. "Walter Mosley Looks Ahead in *Futureland.*" *Africana.* http://archive .blackvoices.com/articles/daily/index_20011126.asp (accessed June 28, 2007).

Orwell, George. *Nineteen Eighty-Four.* London: Longman, 1992.

Panek, LeRoy. *New Hard-Boiled Writers, 1970s–1990s.* Bowling Green, OH: Bowling Green State University Popular Press, 2000.

Panek, Leroy Lad. *Probable Cause: Crime Fiction in America.* Bowling Green, OH: Bowling Green State University Popular Press, 1990.

Patterson, Orlando. "Slavery, Alienation, and the Female Discovery of Personal Freedom." In *Home: A Place in the World,* edited by Arien Mack, 159–87. New York: New York University Press, 1993.

Pearson, Barry Lee, and Bill McCulloch. *Robert Johnson: Lost and Found.* Urbana: University of Illinois Press, 2003.

Pepper, Andrew. "Black Crime Fiction." In *The Cambridge Companion to Crime Fiction,* edited by Martin Priestman, 209–26. Cambridge: Cambridge University Press, 2003.

Pepper, Andrew. *The Contemporary American Crime Novel.* Chicago: Fitzroy Dearborn, 2000.

Pérez, Hugo. "Walter Mosley Talks Technology, Race and His Return Trip into *Futureland.*" Interview. *Science Fiction Weekly.* http://www.scifi.com/sfw/issue237/interview.html (accessed December 10, 2007).

Pithouse, Richard. "Frantz Fanon and the Persistence of Humanism." Council for Research in Values and Philosophy homepage. http://www.crvp.org/book/Series02/II-7/ chapter_i.htm (accessed December 10, 2007).

Plato. *Gorgias.* Trans. Robin Waterfield. Oxford and New York: Oxford University Press, 1994.

Pogge, Thomas. "Human Rights and Human Responsibilities." In *Global Justice and Transnational Politics,* edited by Pablo De Greiff and Ciaran Cronin, 151–95. Cambridge, MA: MIT Press, 2002.

Potter, Russell. *Spectacular Vernaculars: Hip-Hop and the Politics of Postmodernity.* Albany: State University of New York Press, 1995.

Prince, Valerie Sweeney. *Burnin' Down the House: Home in African American Literature.* New York: Columbia University Press, 2005.

Reddy, Maureen. *Traces, Codes, and Clues: Reading Race in Crime Fiction.* New Brunswick, NJ: Rutgers University Press, 2003.

Roberts, Adam. *Science Fiction.* New York: Routledge, 2006.

Roberts, John W. *From Trickster to Badman: The Black Folk Hero in Slavery and Freedom.* Philadelphia: University of Pennsylvania Press, 1989.

Robinson, Randall. *The Debt: What America Owes to Blacks*. New York: Dutton/Penguin, 2000.

Rodriguez, Ralph. *Brown Gumshoe: Detective Fiction and the Search for Chicano/a Identity*. Austin: University of Texas Press, 2005.

Rogers, Michael. Review of *Fear Itself*, by Walter Mosley. *Library Journal*, June 15, 2003.

Rybczynski, Witold. *Home: A Short History of an Idea*. New York: Viking, 1986.

Rykwert, Joseph. "House and Home." In *Home: A Place in the World*, edited by Arien Mack, 47–58. New York: New York University Press, 1993.

Rzepka, Charles J. "'I'm in the Business Too': Gothic Chivalry, Private Eyes, and Proxy Sex and Violence in Chandler's *The Big Sleep*," *Modern Fiction Studies*, 46, no. 3 (2000): 695–724.

Saunders, Charles R. "Why Blacks Should Read (and Write) Science Fiction?" In *Dark Matter: A Century of Speculative Fiction from the African Diaspora*, edited by Sheree R. Thomas, 398–404. New York: Aspect, 2000.

Scaggs, John. *Crime Fiction: New Critical Idiom*. New York: Routledge, 2005.

Schafer, William J. "Irony from Underground—Satiric Elements in *Invisible Man*." In *Twentieth Century Interpretations of* Invisible Man*: A Collection of Critical Essays*, edited by John M. Reilly, 39–47. Upper Saddle River, NJ: Prentice Hall, 1970.

Schmidt, Peter. "The Human Right to a Cultural Heritage." In *Plundering Africa's Past*, edited by Peter R. Schmidt and Roderick J. McIntosh, 18–28. Bloomington: Indiana University Press, 1996.

Schmidt, Peter R., and Roderick J. McIntosh, eds. *Plundering Africa's Past*. Bloomington: Indiana University Press, 1996.

Schwartz, Richard. *Nice and Noir: Contemporary American Crime Fiction*. Columbia: University of Missouri Press, 2002.

Schroeder, Patricia R. *Robert Johnson, Mythmaking, and Contemporary American Culture*. Urbana: University of Illinois Press, 2004.

"SciFi.com Chat Transcript: Walter Mosley, November 27, 2001." *SciFi.com*. http://www.scifi.com/transcripts/2001/mosley_chat.html (accessed December 10, 2007).

Scragg, John. *Crime Fiction: New Critical Idiom*. New York: Routledge, 2005.

Scruggs, Charles. *Sweet Home: Invisible Cities in the Afro-American Novel*. Baltimore: The Johns Hopkins University Press, 1993.

Shapiro, Michael J. "Blues & Politics." *Theory & Event* 4, no. 4 (2000): n. pag.

Sidran, Ben. *Black Talk*. Edinburgh: Payback, 1981.

Skinner, Robert E. *Two Guns From Harlem: The Detective Fiction of Chester Himes*. Bowling Green, OH: Bowling Green State University Popular Press, 1989.

Smith, David L. "Walter Mosley's *Blue Light*: (Double Consciousness)^{squared}." *Extrapolation* 42, no. 1 (2001): 7–26.

Smith, Valerie. *Not Just Race, Not Just Gender*. New York: Routledge, 1998.

Soitos, Stephen F. *The Blues Detective: A Study of African American Detective Fiction*. Amherst: The University of Massachusetts Press, 1996.

Staples, Robert. *The Urban Plantation: Racism and Colonialism in the Post Civil Rights Era*. Oakland, CA: Black Scholar, 1987.

Stein, Thomas Michael. "The Ethnic Vision in Walter Mosley's Crime Fiction." *Amerikastudien/American Studies* 39 (1994): 197–212.

Works Cited

Suvin, Darko. "On Gibson and Cyberpunk SF." *Foundation* 46 (1989): 40–51.

Taylor, Christopher C. *Sacrifice as Terror: The Rwandan Genocide of 1994*. Oxford, NY: Berg, 1999.

Thomas, H. Nigel. *From Folklore to Fiction: A Study of Folk Heroes and Rituals in the Black American Novel*. New York: Greenwood, 1988.

Thomas, Sheree R., ed. *Dark Matter: A Century of Speculative Fiction from the African Diaspora*. New York: Warner Books, 2000.

———. "Introduction: Looking for the Invisible." Introduction to *Dark Matter: A Century of Speculative Fiction from the African Diaspora*, edited by Sheree R. Thomas, ix–xiv. New York: Warner Books, 2000.

Thoms, Peter. *Detection and Its Designs: Narrative and Power in Nineteenth-Century Detective Fiction*. Athens: Ohio University Press, 1998.

Titon, Jeff Todd. *Early Downhome Blues: A Musical and Cultural Analysis*. 2nd ed. Chapel Hill: University of North Carolina Press, 1994.

Waberi, Abdourahman A. *Moisson de crânes. Textes pour le Rwanda*. Paris: Le Serpent à Plumes, 2000.

Wald, Elijah. *Escaping the Delta: Robert Johnson and the Invention of the Blues*. New York: Amistad/HarperCollins, 2004.

Wallace, Michelle. *Black Macho and the Myth of the Superwoman*. New York: Verso, 1990.

Warner, Michael. *Publics and Counterpublics*. New York: Zone Books, 2005.

Watts, Jeffery Gafio. *Heroism and the Black Intellectual: Ralph Ellison, Politics, and Afro-American Intellectual Life*. Chapel Hill: The University of North Carolina Press, 1994.

Weinstein, Arnold. *Nobody's Home: Speech, Self, and Place in American Fiction from Hawthorne to DeLillo*. New York: Oxford University Press, 1993.

Werner, Craig Hansen. *Playing the Changes: From Afro-Modernism to the Jazz Impulse*. Urbana: University of Illinois Press, 1994.

Wesley, Marilyn C. "Power and Knowledge in Walter Mosley's Devil in a Blue Dress." *African American Review* 35, no. 1 (2001): 103–16.

West, Cornel. "Black Strivings in a Twilight Civilization." In *The Cornel West Reader*. New York: Basic Civitas Books, 1999.

———. "The New Cultural Politics of Difference." In *Out There: Marginalization and Contemporary Cultures*, edited by Russell Ferguson, Martha Gever, Trinh T. Minh-Ha, and Cornel West, 19–36. New York: The New Museum of Contemporary Art and Massachusetts Institute of Technology, 1990.

Wilson, Charles E., Jr. *Walter Mosley: A Critical Companion*. Westport, CT: Greenwood, 2003.

Woods, Clyde. *Development Arrested: The Blues and Plantation Power in the Mississippi Delta*. London: Verso, 1998.

Wright, Richard. *Black Boy*. New York: Vintage, 2000.

Yarborough, Richard. "Race, Violence, and Manhood: The Masculine Ideal in Frederick Douglass's *The Heroic Slave*." In *Frederick Douglass: New Literary and Historical Essays*, edited by Eric Sundquist, 166–83. Cambridge: Cambridge University Press, 1990.

Young, Mary. "Walter Mosley, Detective Fiction and Black Culture." *Journal of Popular Culture* 32, no. 1 (1998): 141–51.

Youngquist, Paul. "The Space Machine: Baraka and Science Fiction." *African American Review* 37, nos. 2–3 (2003): 333–43.

Contributors

Owen E. Brady is associate professor of humanities and coordinator of the American Studies Program at Clarkson University in Potsdam, New York, where he teaches drama, African American literature, Japanese culture and society, and an interdisciplinary seminar on the theme of home. His research interests include African American literature, American drama, and performance criticism. He has published a range of articles on Wright, Ward, Wilder, Auden, Baraka, Rabe, and Shakespeare. His interest in Mosley began with two gifts from his wife, Barbara, an avid mystery reader: *Devil in a Blue Dress* and *Always Outnumbered, Always Outgunned.* And, all quite naturally, those gifts led to this book.

Kelly C. Connelly is a Ph.D. candidate and adjunct professor in the English Department at Temple University in Philadelphia, Pennsylvania. She is also an attorney for the federal government. She is currently completing her dissertation on the origins of the dissolution of certainty and identity associated with the postmodern detective novel.

Juan F. Elices teaches eighteenth- and nineteenth-century English literature and postcolonial literature in English in the Departamento de Filología Moderna of the Colegio Menor San José Caracciolos at La Universidad de Alcalá in Spain. His research interests center on contemporary British and postcolonial literature, especially on those aspects related to satiric theory and dystopia. His publications include *The Satiric Worlds of William Boy: A Case-Study* (Bern: Peter Lang, 2006), *Historical and Theoretical Approaches to English Satire* (Munich: LINCOM Europa, 2004) and "The Satiric and Dystopic Legacy of George Orwell in Robert Harris's *Fatherland*" in *The Road from George Orwell: His Achievement and Legacy* (Bern: Peter Lang, 2001). He is now working on alternative and speculative fiction in the African American context.

Keith Hughes lectures in American literature at the University of Edinburgh in the UK. His main research and teaching interests lie in the fields of African American literature and "the black Atlantic." His works-in-progress include: comparative readings of African American and Scottish literature up to the contemporary period; Frederick Douglass's mid-nineteenth-century tour of the British Isles; Richard Wright and Africa. Theoretical interests include the ongoing development of ideas of "the black Atlantic," for which he believes Mosley is a key writer.

Derek C. Maus is associate professor of English at the State University of New York College at Potsdam. His Ph.D. from the University of North Carolina indicates that he specializes in contemporary Russian and American literature, but he frequently forgets this fact and publishes on subjects such as devil imagery in Gogol and Hawthorne; Schopenhauer's notion of the *gesamtkunstwerk* in the paintings of Pavel Filonov and Andrey Bely's novel *Petersburg;* the Harlem Renaissance; and paternalistic violence in colonial South Africa. He has edited seven collections of essays for high school and college-level readers on topics including postmodernism, Russian history, and the Cold War, and is currently completing a book-length comparative study of American and Russian subversive satires during the Cold War.

Jerrilyn McGregory is an associate professor of folklore in the Department of English at Florida State University. She is the author of *Wiregrass Country,* a regional folklife study of the South. Besides this ethnographic study, she has conducted fieldwork in Jamaica, Bermuda, and the Bahamas. She also has presented papers in the U.S., Canada, and Europe. Her essays and literary criticism have appeared in a variety of books and journals, including a special edition of *FEMSPEC,* focused on African American women's speculative fiction. She is currently working on publications related to African American folklore, African diaspora studies, and onomastics. Her interest in Mosley derives from her abiding interest in folklore and literary theory and his ability to immerse protagonists in African American folk culture without essentializing.

Laura Quinn is professor of African American literature and coordinator of the Black Studies Program at Allegheny College in Meadville, Pennsylvania. Her overlapping research interests are in the intersection of politics and literary form and black fiction in the early Cold War period. Her interest in Mosley is grounded in the author's supple appropriations of popular formulaic genres and the distinctive political/historical bent of his fictions.

Francesca Canadé Sautman is professor of French and women's studies at Hunter College and the Graduate Center of the City University of New York, executive officer of the Ph.D. program in French, and director of the Henri Peyre French Institute at the Graduate Center. An early modernist, who also works in Francophone studies and cultural studies, she has authored *La Religion du Quotidien: Rites et croyances populaires de la fin du Moyen Age* (1995), co-edited

Same-Sex Love and Desire Among Women in the Middle Ages (2001), and *Telling Tales: Medieval Narratives and the Folk Tradition* (1998), as well as published many articles on folk culture, women's culture and history, marginality, gender, and queer sexualities. She is an area editor for the *Encyclopedia of Sex and Gender* (2007). She has also published on the representation of race in American film. As an assiduous and passionate reader of Walter Mosley since his very first novels, admiring in him at once the consummate artist and one of our most profound thinkers on the meanings and impact of race in modern U.S. society, she is delighted and honored to be part of this much overdue volume on his work.

Daniel Stein teaches in the American studies program at Georg-August-University in Göttingen, Germany, where he is about to finish his dissertation on Louis Armstrong's autobiographical writings and music. He has published several articles on American literature (on Lee Smith, Toni Morrison, jazz autobiography) and music (jazz, blues, country) in international journals (*European Journal of American Culture, Genre, Amerikastudien/American Studies, Interdisciplinary Humanities*) and essay collections. He is currently co-editing a volume of essays with Frank Kelleter, to be published in 2008 (*American Studies as Media Studies*). His interest in Walter Mosley goes back to the moment when he pulled *Devil in a Blue Dress* from his father's bookshelf and began reading.

Lisa B. Thompson is an assistant professor of English at the University at Albany, State University of New York. Her research and teaching interests include African American literature and culture, literary theory, contemporary drama, and film. Thompson is currently completing a book that explores representations of black middle-class sexuality. Also a playwright, she is the author of "Single Black Female."

Terrence Tucker received his B.A. from Louisiana State University and his Ph.D. in 2006 from the University of Kentucky and is currently an assistant professor at the University of Arkansas. His general topics of interest are twentieth-century American literature and drama, African American literature, and popular culture. He is especially interested in post–Civil Rights African American literature and black popular culture. His love of Walter Mosley began long before Bill Clinton's and is shared by his mother who steals all of his books. In addition to his interest in Walter Mosley, he examines post-1970s black writers such as August Wilson, Ernest Gaines, and Toni Morrison. His dissertation, currently being revised into a book manuscript, is entitled "Furiously Funny: Comic Rage in Late 20th Century African-American Literature," and gives historical elaboration of this significant form of cultural expression. It contains work on artists from George Schuyler to Richard Pryor. His work, which explores race and pedagogy, appears in *Pedagogy*.

Albert U. Turner, Jr. is an assistant professor of English at Morehouse College. His teaching interests include nineteenth- and twentieth-century African American and American literature with a specific focus on the *bildungsroman*, the neo-slave narrative, crime fiction, the literature of war, and the intersections of imaginative writing and philosophy. His research interests include the outlaw figure in African American culture, slavery and memory in American culture, public sphere and counterpublic sphere discourses, and Bakhtinian novelistic theory. His interest in Walter Mosley stems from an appreciation of "Mosley's interrogation of American categories of identity, collective history, and social justice" as well as "the matchless enjoyment that comes from reading Mosley's insightful, artful prose."

Index

www.ingramcontent.com/pod-product-compliance
Lightning Source LLC
Chambersburg PA
CBHW020656030726
47498CB00002B/529